OLD ADAM,
NEW EVES

OLD ADAM, NEW EVES

by

Richard Grunberger

VISION PRESS · LONDON

Vision Press Ltd.
c/o Vine House Distribution
Waldenbury, North Common
Chailey, E. Sussex BN8 4DR

ISBN 0 85478 317 2

British Library Cataloguing-in-Publication Data
A catalogue record for this book
is available from the British Library

To L.G.—my Eve

Printed and bound in Great Britain by
Billing & Sons, Worcester.
Typeset by Galleon Photosetting,
Ipswich, Suffolk.
MCMXCI

Contents

CONTENTS

Introduction:

From the French to the Sexual Revolution

L OOKING back, from the vantage point of the 1990s, on the century's diverse conflicts it is not all that easy to identify the most significant one. Was it either of the two World Wars? The Cold War? The North-South confrontation? The West's collision with Islam? Or was (is) it the battle of the sexes?

The first five of these half dozen conflicts were large-scale and ranged across vast—even if geographically, or conceptually, clearly defined—areas. In contrast, the war of the sexes (unless politicized) involves one-to-one combat and can break out over any issue.

It is said of the poor that they are always with us. The same holds good of the war of the sexes, which, like a sporting fixture, can have three possible outcomes: win, lose or draw. Since draws do not make for interesting copy this book focuses on win or lose situations—or, to put it another way, on women as victims or victors.

However, before getting down to specific cases, we need to put the topic in context, and this context, like so much of the modern world, was engendered by the French Revolution.

1989 witnessed the bicentenary of the outbreak of the French Revolution. The exact import of that revolution is still a matter for debate, but it can be said that the upheaval of 1789 (and after) triggered both horizontal and vertical shifts in the French social landscape. The stratification of society along class lines was so drastically changed as to rule out a return to the virtual caste system of the *Ancien Régime*. Along the vertical plane—that is in male-female relations—there was also change, but here the shifts amounted to portents of the future rather than accomplished facts.

Fifteen years after the Storming of the Bastille the Code Napoleon, which was designed to consolidate the achievements of the Revolution, defined the interrelationship between men and women in the following terms: 'Woman is given to man in order to have children; she therefore belongs to him as the fruit tree belongs to the gardener.' The Code practically set at nought the work of the pioneers who tried to give *Liberté, Egalité et Fraternité* a universal significance—such as the Marquis de Condorcet, who wrote *An Essay on the Admission of Women to Citizenship*, the playwright Olympe de Gonges, who drew up *The Declaration of the Rights of Women*, and the political hostess Madame Roland, whose *crie-de-coeur*, 'Oh Liberty, what crimes are committed in thy name', uttered at the foot of the guillotine, had become a catchphrase.

As a hostess presiding over the salon of the Girondin faction in the French Revolution Madame Roland had been a force in the land; in England political hostesses of the Whig persuasion, such as Lady Holland and Lady Oxford, were exercising similar influence under less hectic and sanguinary circumstances. However, the influence exerted by those women was strictly predicated upon their possession of husbands with titles, wealth or political leverage. One (English) woman with none of these advantages—and not even a husband for long—was Mary Wollstonecraft, author of *The Vindication of the Rights of Women* and founder of feminism in these islands. In turn governess and publisher's assistant, Mary left Britain in 1792, the year in which the *Vindication* appeared, for France—a destination to which other advanced spirits such as William Wordsworth and 'Citizen' Tom Paine had preceded her. In France she lived with a man she called her husband and had a child. After the 'marriage' split up, she attempted suicide by drowning but was rescued. She returned to England where she frequented radical circles, meeting William Blake and William Godwin, the first exponent of Anarchism in these isles. Godwin and Mary were attracted to each other. She became pregnant and married Godwin, only to die a week after bearing him a daughter, also named Mary.

As the joint offspring of the founders of English Feminism and of English Anarchism, Mary Godwin could be said to have been predestined to pioneering status. It was a rôle she fully lived up to both in her public persona and her private one. In the public domain the most important fact about Mary was that she wrote, while still only 18, the horror novel *Frankenstein*, which made her arguably the most widely read woman author ever. Her personal life bore similar traces of the extraordinary. She not only eloped with Percy B. Shelley and bore him a son while he was still another woman's husband; after marrying the poet she declared herself ready—in accordance with Shelley's espousal of free love—to become his best friend's mistress. In her assertion of personal freedom untrammelled by social conventions Mary was eventually trumped by her stepsister Claire, whose triangular relationship with Shelley and Lord Byron merits a psychological investigation beyond the scope of this foreword. Suffice it to say that for Byron—who admired Napoleon *inter alia* because the latter would, when receiving females in his tent, say '*déshabillez vous*' without glancing up from his battle plans—Claire provided no more than 'cockfodder'. At any rate, Godwin's daughters only occupied centre stage for the briefest period of time. Hereafter England saw no surge of comparable free female spirits for close on half a century, and when these finally appeared—in the shape of George Eliot and Annie Besant (see Chapter X)—they were considerably more straitlaced.

They ordered such things better in France. There two libido-oriented literary lionesses prowled around in succession in the public arena. The first was Madame de Staël, pivot of a renowned Parisian salon in between spells of exile, author of the influential study *De l'Allemagne*, and a divorcee notorious for her affair with fellow writer Benjamin Constant. The second was George Sand, the scandal-encumbered free-living novelist. Something of a Socialist, Sand also used her work—particularly the bestseller *Indiana*—to protest social conventions that bound a wife to her husband against her will. Since she conducted her life according to the same rebellious code, she, not surprisingly, attracted scurrilous gossip and censure. It was alleged that she had betrayed de Musset and, more damningly, that she had destroyed Frédéric Chopin. Both charges were based, at best, on half-truths. Concerning Chopin: what Sand actually did was to transpose her love for him, in response to his deteriorating health, from amorousness to maternal concern—which he misconstrued as sexual rejection.

In a distorted mirror image of this transformation Jean-Paul Sartre, in the next century, turned himself into the father of one of his mistresses by formally adopting her as his daughter (see Chapter II). Sartre's initial action in choosing as sexual partner someone young enough to be his daughter illustrated a widespread syndrome among middle-aged men: that of bedding their juniors as a means of holding advancing age—and its corollary, death—at bay. At 45 Charles Dickens, whose *Christmas Carol* was a paean to family life, relegated Mrs. Dickens to the periphery of his life the better to pursue his amour with the young actress Ellen Ternan. Pablo Picasso contrived a sort of mathematical spoonerism at the age of 72 by taking a 27-year-old mistress. The painter, who once famously asked Louis Aragon 'How can you always go on loving the same woman? She's going to grow old like everybody else!', also rather enjoyed setting present and past inamoratas at each others' throats; even so, he lacked the chilling indifference Auguste Rodin displayed towards discarded mistresses such as the reclusive Gwen John and the pitifully demented Camille Claudel.[1]

These diverse dramatic variations on the theme of human love are all subsumed under the heading of *la vie bohème*, and it is therefore fitting that both Giacomo Puccini, composer of *La Bohème* (see Chapter IV), and Jaroslav Hašek, creator of *The Good Soldier Švejk* and most *bohémien* of Bohemians (see Chapter III) figure in our book.

Puccini's Tosca sings '*Vissi d'arte*'; 'living for art' has also often served creative men as a rationalization for their cavalier treatment of women. Gustave Flaubert intimated to Louise Colet[2] that she was less important to him than *Madame Bovary*; leaving his wife encumbered with a brood of children,

---

1. Camille Claudel: Rodin's mistress and model, sister of the renowned French writer Paul Claudel.
2. Louise Colet (1810–76): French poet and novelist who presided over a Parisian literary salon.

Gauguin set off to paint in Tahiti; Rainer Maria Rilke (see Chapter III) believed that the parties to any partnership, including marriage, were obliged to guard each others' solitude.

But there was more to this issue than the alleged incompatibility of creative males and domesticity-craving females. Such gender-stereotyping breaks down when we consider the case of the great Colette. Her first husband, the *soi-disant* author Henri Gauthier-Villars (aka 'Willy'), kept his young wife as a domestic literary serf busily writing her schoolgirl memoirs which he passed off, and marketed profitably, as products of his own fertile pen. Other husbands of gifted women have gone to the equally unpalatable extreme of stifling their partners' creative impulses lest they compete with their own. Gustav Mahler thought Alma better occupied transcribing his scores than nursing her own ambitions to compose. Scott Fitzgerald felt threatened by Zelda's attempts at authorship, and André Malraux told his wife Clara that one writer in the family was enough. But attention also needs to be drawn to men of quite different disposition who, far from exploiting, excluding or victimizing women, were prepared to become victims for their sake. George Gissing, for instance, married an alcohol-addicted prostitute in order to reclaim her—but as a toiler in Grub Street himself he, far from raising his wife from the gutter, let her pull him down into it. An identical act of personal philanthropy was undertaken by Moses Hess, a wealthy German-Jewish proto-Communist and sometime colleague of Karl Marx (see Chapter I).

The prostitute Hess married to redeem her was a Gentile, or Aryan in Nazi-speak. A century later Joseph Goebbels ordered the Aryan actor Joachim Gottschalk to divorce his Jewish wife Ruth, whom the former dubbed a *chonte* (the Yiddish word for prostitute). Refusing to desert his wife Gottschalk committed suicide with Ruth the night before her scheduled deportation.

Nazi Fascism tapped the same roots of power-seeking and sadism as male chauvinism. Goebbels was the best-known philanderer in the Third Reich, and Mussolini enjoyed an analogous reputation in Italy. Their stance was copied by many intellectuals who followed in their wake—exemplified by Martin Heidegger's extra-marital liaison with his pupil Hannah Arendt,[3] Gabriele D'Annunzio's[4] humiliation of Eleanora Duse,[5] and Ezra Pound's bigamous life style. Interestingly enough many figures from the Pantheon of the Left were driven by the identical impulse of priapic self-gratification. This applied both to the Founding Fathers (see Chapter I) and to a motley of Left culture heroes: Bertrand Russell, Pablo Picasso, Bertolt Brecht (see Chapter VII) and the above-mentioned Jean-Paul Sartre. In addition, where the Marxist Left rules female powerlessness differs only in degree, but not in kind, from the feminine condition under fascist dictatorships. Within those two disparate and yet not totally dissimilar systems of totalitarian control two women have nonetheless managed to get their hands on the levers of power; they are Jiang Qing, alias Madame Mao (see Chapter I), and Evita Perón (see Chapter IX).

In fact, contrary to feminist mythology, political or politicized women have not shown themselves to be markedly more humane than men in their choice of means for achieving stated ends. This goes beyond the propensity of individual women leaders—such as Madame Mao, Eva Perón, Imelda Marcos or Madame Thieu (who dubbed the self-immolation of Buddhist monks in Saigon a 'barbecue')—for evil; it was an overwhelmingly female audience of nurses and Blitzmädchen who cheered Hitler to the echo in 1940 when after some relatively small-scale R.A.F. raids he 'promised' to raze Britain's cities to the ground. But all this in no way invalidates the premise that Nazism inhabited a mental universe shared by those who for whatever reason—maniacal religiosity, horror of sex, philosophical or aesthetic aberration—advocated the murder of women. *Murder, Hope of Women*, the title of Oskar Kokoschka's only play, may have been an Expressionist conceit, but it reflected a strand in *fin de siècle* thinking. At the time, the attribution of evil to the daughters of Eve, which suffuses Pauline Christianity and helped instigate the

3. Hannah Arendt (1906–75): American policial scientist of German-Jewish birth (*The Origins of Totalitarianism, Eichmann in Jerusalem*).
4. Gabriele D'Annunzio (1863–1938): Italian poet, novelist, dramatist and political adventurer (*The Triumph of Death*).
5. Eleanora Duse (1858–1924): Italian actress, famous interpreter of Ibsen's heroines.

medieval witch-hunts, became a fashionable literary theme. The Pole Stanislas Przybyszewski explored it in *Satan's Brood*, the Viennese Otto Weininger gave it intellectual cachet in his philosophical tome *Sex and Character*, and the German Frank Wedekind part-based his masterpiece *Lulu* on the Jack the Ripper legend. (The potency of that legend over a period of a hundred years has recently been demonstrated by the huge public interest in Peter Sutcliffe, the Yorkshire Ripper.)

Thus sexual politics in their most extreme form cost lives— just as do 'normal' politics. The fact that the various Rippers made prostitutes their quarry is causally connected with the age-old depiction of woman—whether she be Eve, Potiphar's wife or Salome—as the embodiment of carnality who will, unless resisted, drag man into the mire. Where sex, dirty by definition, is purveyed for filthy lucre, its purveyors, i.e. prostitutes, invite divine retribution. Therefore, according to the demented logic of a Peter Sutcliffe, killers of prostitutes are cleansing the world of evil.

By coincidence two remarkable women featured in this book (both, happily, still alive) have been involved with prostitution—the one in the abstract, through her art, and the other experientially. Jane Fonda's *Klute*, which earned her an Oscar (see Chapter VII), was the most mature attempt ever to get inside the mind of a prostitute on film. Maya Angelou's experiences as a teenage brothel madam and, subsequently, as a hooker for the pimp she loved (see Chapter X) form part of her widely read autobiography. The fact that she felt no need to bowdlerize her account encourages, at the very least, moderate optimism. So indeed does her present position at the point of intersection between feminism, black rights and the arts. She is an apparently predestined victim metamorphosed into a victor.

I

Revolutionary Wives

Jenny Marx

ON a slight rise of ground in London's Highgate Cemetery stands a 12-foot high black marble slab, crowned by a monitory, leonine head. It is the tomb of Karl Marx. All year round flowers deck the foot of the slab, the inscription on which reads: 'The philosophers have tried to understand the world—it is our task to change it.'

One way in which Marx's executors have changed the world is demonstrated on the spot. The contents of the Marx grave represent a radical departure from customary burial arrangements, ringing the changes on the received meaning of a skeleton in the cupboard. Under the marble slab at Highgate lies a mouldering *ménage à trois*: husband (Karl), wife (Jenny) and mistress (Lenchen Demuth) conjoined in eternal sleep. The last mentioned, her name duly incised on the old tombstone, was the housekeeper-cum-family confidante whom Karl slept with and got pregnant during Jenny's absence. Such misconduct notwithstanding, Karl and Jenny acted out a true romance in their lives. In so doing they very much conformed to the *Zeitgeist*—unless they obeyed astrological influences—since their births coincided with the heyday of German Romanticism. The subsequent lovers' romantic entanglement started practically in the nursery where the children of Ludwig von Westphalen, first Councillor of Trier, and those of his near neighbour, Justizrat Heinrich Marx, were playmates.

The two families had no natural affinity: the von Westphalens descended from the Prussian nobility and the Marxes from Jewish rabbis. However, Ludwig von Westphalen was a Liberal with a bent for philosophy, while Heinrich Marx had converted to Christianity (so as to acquire, *pace* Heine,[1] his entrance ticket to European culture). Though Karl Marx was four years younger than Jenny von Westphalen, their childhood friendship matured into teenage infatuation, and the romance endured even when Jenny 'came out' and had men twice Karl's age pay court to her at carnival balls and parties. Later when he went up to University at Berlin, she visited him in the capital, losing her virginity in the process; subsequently she struggled to keep remorse at bay. They prepared to marry after the newly graduated Marx had launched out into freelance journalism (thus defying his father who wanted him to practise law). Preparatory to the wedding Jenny inserted a clause into the marriage contract stipulating that each partner should pay the debts he had incurred—an instance of rare foresight which, given the misery indebtedness was to cause her throughout the marriage, had a certain ironic poignancy. At first she took the difficulties inherent in marriage to an impecunious radical journalist in her stride. Trouble with the German authorities soon made them move to Paris where the Marxes entered the febrile dissension-ridden world of political emigrés. Initially they shared a communal household with some German fellow exiles, but the experiment was shortlived. Certain notions well in advance of communal living, such as free love and the 'communisation' of women, were also being bandied about in the radical circles in which the Marxes moved, and these elicited her vehement disapproval. Although married to a revolutionary, she refused to have any truck whatever with Bohemianism. When Georg Herwegh, a German radical poet (and chronic womanizer), made advances to her she put him firmly in his place.

Another exiled poet of their acquaintance with a rackety life-style was the afore-mentioned Heinrich Heine, whose wife appalled Marx. (Madame Heine, whom the poet dubbed his 'domestic Vesuvius', was an earthy creature without any inkling of her husband's gifts, and of such naïveté that once, puzzled by the strange sound of Heine and his amanuensis

---

1. Heinrich Heine (1797–1856): renowned German Romantic poet and satirist of Jewish origin (*The Book of Songs*).

chanting Hebrew psalms, she believed their tongue-in-cheek explanation that they were singing German folksongs.) An even more exotic couple encountered among the politico-literary avant garde were the radical newspaper publisher Moses Hess and the street-walker he had taken for a wife, expressly to wean her away from prostitution.

In due course Karl Marx was expelled from Paris, as previously from Cologne, for subversion. He moved the household, which now included the first of the six children they would ultimately have, to Brussels. In the Belgian capital they led a penurious existence; Jenny, facing her second pregnancy, complained of living in a 'pauper colony'. In this hour of need her mother, Baroness von Westphalen, sent her a 25-year-old servant, Lenchen Demuth, from Trier as a helpmeet and Lenchen soon became the family's in-dispensible maid-of-all-work enabling Jenny to act intermit-tently as Marx's amanuensis. Someone else equally impor-tant for their future who now entered into the Marxes' lives was Karl's subsequent collaborator (and financial sup-port system) Friederick Engels. The bachelor son of a textile manufacturer, Engels kept a mistress—an impropriety which appalled Jenny, comrade-in-arms of the gravedigger of bour-geois society. The wife of the leader of the world proletariat, moreover, condemned the poor mill-girl involved in the liaison far more severely than the propertied Engels. Others felt differently. At a social gathering of the Brussels branch of the German Workers Union the organizer tried to effect an introduction between the married and unmarried pairs. His account reads:

> A fair distance separated both couples. When I approached Marx he gave me to understand by a glance and meaningful smile that his wife strictly refused to make the acquaintance of that—lady. Concerning questions of honour and morals the noble lady was intransigent. . . . This intermezzo increased my high regard for Mrs. Marx. By bringing his mistress to this group of mostly working class people Engels risked the reproach often made that the sons of rich manufacturers use the young girls of the people for their pleasure.

Brussels, too, proved only a temporary stopping-place. The 1848 Revolution, whose outbreak prompted Marx and Engels to write *The Communist Manifesto*, found them both in their native Germany. The subsequent defeat of the revolution led to yet another change of domicile. The Marxes took up residence in England, the only country from which they were never to be expelled, and one ideally suited for the study of industrial capitalism. (In addition Engels lived in the textile city of Manchester, just several hours' train ride distant.) Upon arrival in London Jenny, hopeful of making an entry into polite society, had visiting cards printed on which she described herself as 'Mrs. Karl Marx, née Baroness Jenny von Westphalen'. The fact that the hoped-for invitations to fashionable 'at homes' failed to materialize was—as things turned out—to be the least of her worries. In London she saw money problems increase almost in parallel to the growth of her family. Having been chased out of country after country on the continent by the police, they now had unpaid landlords and tradesmen hound them from one lodging to the next. When they took up residence in Dean Street, Soho, their accommodation was so squalid that even the Prussian plain-clothes agent sent to spy on them seemed moved to pity:

> There is not one piece of good, solid furniture in the entire flat. Everything is broken, tattered and torn, and in the greatest disorder, with finger-thick dust everywhere. A large, old fashioned table, covered with waxcloth, stands in the middle of the drawing-room, on it lie manuscripts, books, newspapers, then the childrens' toys, bits and pieces of womens' sewing things, as well as a few teacups with broken rims, dirty spoons, knives, forks, candlesticks, inkpot, glasses, Dutch clay pipes, tobacco ash, in a word all kinds of trash, and everything on one table; a junk dealer would be ashamed of it.
>
> When you enter the Marx flat your sight is dimmed by coal and tobacco smoke so that you grope around at first as if you were in a cave, until your eyes get used to the fumes and, as in a fog, you gradually notice a few objects. Everything is dirty, everything covered with dust; it is dangerous to sit down. Here is a chair with only three legs, there the children play kitchen on another chair that happens to be whole; true, it is offered to the visitor, but the childrens' kitchen is not removed; if you sit on it you risk a pair of trousers.

Actually, in describing the toddlers at play, the police spy painted a somewhat idealized picture; frequently serious, even fatal, illness among the children compounded Jenny's other problems. Cumulatively these worries affected her looks to such an extent that when she visited Marx's rich uncle in Holland to solicit funds he quite failed to recognize her.

Jenny had set out on the Dutch trip in the early stages of pregnancy and was surprised on her return to see Lenchen beginning to show symptoms of the same condition. During the following year the Marxes' Soho attic, totally bereft of such amenities as a bath, a lavatory or running water, briefly resembled a nursing home—with Jenny delivering a child in March and Lenchen another in June. Marx, who in the preceding months had derived wry amusement from the sight of two protuberant ladies squeezing past each other in a confined space, was the father in each case. However, to still Jenny's well-founded suspicion he ascribed paternity of Lenchen's child to the 'philanderer' Engels—to which end he also arranged for the lad to be baptised Friederick. Marx had previously informed Engels of this rôle assigned to him in the affair. The latter had consented to accept nominal paternity for the sake of the cause which proof of Marx's infidelity would discredit—but on condition that he be spared any involvement in the boy's fate. (Subsequently Engels would quip that *The Communist Manifesto* was not the only product of his and Marx's collaborative efforts.) As for Lenchen Demuth, she had precious little reason for making quips. Since raising the child under Marx's roof would provide ammunition for his detractors, she could either leave with little Friederick or stay on without him. Lenchen decided on the latter course and handed Friederick over to foster parents, an artisan couple in Hackney. The severance must have caused her a great deal of pain since, as the Marx girls attested, Lenchen loved children; at her death forty years later she left her entire modest fortune to the son she had not seen since his birth.

It is a moot point which of Marx's two women—the maid or the mistress—suffered greater unhappiness. Jenny, after all, endured persecution by debt-collectors and bailiffs, marital infidelity, illness, and most shatteringly the death of half her children; in addition her seventh (and last) pregnancy ended in a stillbirth.

Death also struck at the Engels' household, carrying off Friederick's mistress, Mary Burns. When the Marxes heard the news, they reacted with a coolness which surprised and hurt Engels. Karl's letter contained brief condolences as, so to speak, a preamble to the sender's financial problems; as for Jenny she would not overcome her aversion to 'kept women' sufficiently even to put pen to paper. In this, she at least proved herself a woman of principle since silence in face of a benefactor's loss did little to alleviate her squalid circumstances.

Life *chez* Marx, though, was not by any means all unrelieved gloom. For one thing Jenny relished the aura of political excitement her husband generated; for another, the couple maintained, irrespective of material circumstances, close sociable relations with a number of fellow exiles. In the middle '60s the horizon suddenly brightened when they received two far from insubstantial legacies. The money not only relieved the Marxes of growing financial anxiety, but enabled them to indulge in the bourgeois life-style dear to Karl's as well as to Jenny's heart. (Actually their attitude to this windfall was aristocratic rather than bourgeois: instead of eking out their newfound moderate wealth over several years they spent it all in two.) Their ramshackle house at Haverstock Hill which had seen so much misery now incongruously became a venue for parties—and even the occasional ball at which a frock-coated Karl, monocle dangling from a ribbon, and Jenny in a new ball dress greeted the guests while hired musicians played and liveried servants handed round food and drink. All too soon, though, hard times returned. Sundry creditors—coalmen, butchers, bakers, doctors—came knocking at the door, family heirlooms had to be pawned again, and Jenny's mood darkened as she let her thoughts dwell obsessively on the four children she had lost. Even though Marx admitted that she had ample reason for melancholy, her near incessant lamentations were a source of excruciating annoyance to him.

He was now the head of the First International, in close touch with revolutionaries in various European countries. As a result of these contacts the two eldest Marx girls made the acquaintance of the young Frenchmen they were later to marry. Jenny, worn down by half a lifetime spent in chill penury, viewed her daughters' emotional involvements with considerable misgivings, warning of 'anxieties and vexations that are the lot of all political women'. One special anxiety of hers—finance—was partly allayed when in the late 1860s Engels settled a small pension on Marx. But if their personal economic situation showed a marginal improvement, politically one setback followed on another. The nascent German labour movement took a reformist path, the First International fell apart and the Paris Commune went down to bloody defeat; in addition, the publication of *Das Kapital*, after seventeen years' laborious research, met with widespread indifference.

These reverses failed to deflect Marx from his chosen path, even though his body—as if in response to years of stress—erupted in boils and carbuncles. Buoying him up in adversity was faith in his own predictions of the inevitable capitalist collapse, the slow but discernible growth of his influence, and the unstinting support of a handful of disciples, chief among them his daughters. He paid tribute to the last-mentioned in a letter to Engels:

> My wife has been in a hysterical state for years—understandable from the circumstances, but for that reason not more pleasant—and is torturing the children with her lamentations, crankiness and ill-humour, although no children could bear it in a more jolly way.

Marx's favourite among the children was the youngest daughter Eleanor, better known by her nickname Tussie. Tussie came close to being a prodigy in intellect (she translated an account of the Paris Commune into English at the age of 17), political commitment and love of the arts, especially theatre. Marx unwittingly blighted her life by prohibiting her engagement to a (much older) French journalist she had set her heart on, which had the long-term effect of driving Tussie into the unspeakable Dr. Aveling, her—albeit indirect—murderer.

Jenny, though fortunately spared any foreknowledge of Tussie's ultimate end, spent her declining years in inspissated melancholy. By the late 1870s her emotional debility was compounded by worrying physical symptoms. This was no flight into illness such as she had often had recourse to in the past when life seemed too hard to bear; her disease, at first misdiagnosed as dyspepsia, turned out to be cancer of the liver. As, pain-wracked, she fought her last fight, her thoughts alternated between conjuration of the bright Socialist dawn-to-come and regret over a life from which want and worry had cumulatively driven all joy.

Marx knew *au fond du coeur* that he had imposed an insupportable burden on the woman who had loved and sustained him almost since their nursery days. This becomes clear from the letter he wrote to his would-be son-in-law in an attempt to save his middle daughter from a 'political marriage':

> You know that I have devoted my entire fortune to the revolutionary struggle. I do not regret it. On the contrary, I would do the same if I had to start my life again. But I would not marry. As far as it lies in my power, I shall protect my daughter from the cliffs upon which her mother's life was wrecked.

Marx's belated realization that revolutionaries should abstain from marriage out of consideration for their intended wives carried little weight with his successors. Lenin had a wife and, some would have us believe, a mistress. Stalin married twice; Trotsky copied his deadly rival in this—and philandered. Mao Tse-Tung contracted four marriages, three of his own free will. Among those who implemented Marx's political vision, only Fidel Castro and Ho-Chi-Minh (apparently) heeded his personal advice and stayed unmarried.

Krupskaya

Lenin's marriage to Krupskaya was characterized by mutual devotion, shared hardships in the underground and exile, and shared triumphs—none greater than in 1917. When in 1923, effectively removed from power by an incapacitating stroke, Lenin came to draw up his political testament, he warned the Politburo members against Stalin for, among other reasons, the rudeness he had shown to Krupskaya. After Lenin's death Stalin suppressed the testament, but the apotheosis of the dead leader, which he helped instigate in order to legitimize his own rule, prevented him from attacking Lenin's widow directly. Instead, he undermined her position by various stratagems, one being the officially licensed publication of a story entitled *A Great Love*. The authoress Alexandra Kollontai,[2] a Communist feminist with plentiful experience of sex partners professing equality and practising male dominance, had also been an intra-Party opponent of Lenin's lurch into dictatorship. Her *roman à clef A Great Love* depicted Lenin as a less than faithful husband to Krupskaya. It was based on the historical fact that the couple had for some time shared their Kremlin apartment with Inessa Armand, a Party activist of Russo-French background. Inessa had worked immensely hard as head of the Communist Party's Womens' Bureau in the aftermath of the Revolution. Debilitated by strenuous activity under grim conditions, she had left Moscow in 1920 to recuperate in the South, had contracted cholera and died. It was a common assumption among the Bolshevik inner circle that Lenin felt strongly attracted to Inessa, and Alexandra Kollontai had expected him to break down at her funeral. He had, in fact, maintained his composure—which proved nothing either way. At any rate, Kollontai felt justified in writing a tale of an eternal triangle from which informed readers could infer what had happened between Lenin, Krupskaya and Inessa Armand.

Although it served Stalin's immediate purpose to sanction publication of the story, he soon divested himself of Madame Kollontai's uncomfortable presence by dispatching her abroad as a diplomat (a form of external exile).

Alleluyova Stalin

Stalin's relationship with women is fortunately better documented than Lenin's. His first wife, Ekaterina Svanidze, whom he married in the 1900s, shared Georgian nationality but little else except youth with him. She was an Orthodox believer, a *hausfrau* and a doting wife. When Stalin was away on underground missions for the Party, she would spend

---

2. Alexandra Kollontai (1872–1952): Russian revolutionary and feminist, first woman to serve as an accredited minister to a foreign country.

long hours in prayer that he might turn away from ideas displeasing to God. The arrival of a son, Yakov, provided her with someone more amenable to dote on, but she died when the lad was still in his infancy.

In mid 1918, during the lull between Revolution and Civil War, the widower, now a member of the new governing élite, married for the second time. The bride, Nadya Alleluya, daughter of an Old Bolshevik was twenty-two years his junior and romantically overawed by the erstwhile underground courier and veteran escaper from Siberia (exploits which accounted for his soubriquet 'man of steel'). Her youthful romantic notions received a brutal jolt, however, when newly-wed, she accompanied her husband to Tsaritsyn, a strategic town bloodily contested between the Red and White armies. After experiencing the full horrors of internecine warfare, Nadia returned with her husband to the Kremlin where he occupied a succession of senior posts and she worked in Lenin's secretariat. In the post-Civil War years Nadia bore Stalin a son, Vasily, and a daughter, Svetlana. Family relationships soon showed a bizarre dichotomy, with Stalin, by now virtual dictator of the country, indulging the girl and harassing the boy. The domestic situation became even more fraught when, on grandfather Svanidze's insistence, Yakov joined the household and Stalin made him the butt of his sadistic ill-humour, whereupon Nadia, herself only a few years older than her stepson, felt moved to protect him. Eventually Yakov, maltreated beyond endurance, made a suicide attempt that failed—hearing of which Stalin sneered, 'He can't even shoot straight.'

Simultaneously elsewhere in the country straight shooting was being practised on a massive scale. The collectivization of agriculture had prompted peasant resistance which was being crushed with military force. As architect of this gigantic transformation costing millions of lives Stalin was under heavy pressure which he abreacted by ill-tempered behaviour at home. Even his rare displays of geniality might generate domestic friction, however, since Nadia had an obsession about the evils of drink, whereas he would, in typical Georgian fashion, offer the children wine at meals.

Nadia was actually not overly interested in the children,

preferring to have nannies look after them. Young and lacking in self-confidence, she took lessons in French, music and literature to help her, now 'first lady' of the U.S.S.R., perform adequately on official occasions. She shrank from the over-exposure that went with her exalted position, avoiding travel by car if it made her conspicuous. In 1932, at a time when Stalin's drive against the recalcitrant peasantry was reaching its gory climax and famine gripped the Ukraine, Nadia enrolled at a textile design college. The prospect of attending the course seemed to raise her spirits. However, talking to fellow students she received confirmation of what her brother and sister-in-law had already hinted at, namely that millions were suffering hardship, even death, as a result of her husband's policies. These intimations of country-wide misery combined with Nadia's marital unhappiness to plunge her into a black depression. At a Kremlin reception on the fifteenth anniversary of the Revolution, when Stalin turned to her, the committed teetotaller, with the brusque command 'Hey you, have a drink', she jumped up, screamed 'Don't you dare speak to me like that!' and ran from the room. Polina Molotov went after her into the freezing Kremlin grounds, but could not talk Nadia, who declared herself sick of everything, even the children, out of her dejection. Later that night, in the privacy of her bedroom she turned a gun on herself; unlike her stepson she shot straight. The news stunned Stalin. His first reaction was defensive. Did it really matter so much, he demanded of his entourage, that overburdened with work as he was, he could not go to the theatre with her whenever she asked. Soon, though, he interpreted her death as a betrayal of himself. He stayed away from the funeral, refused to visit her grave, and moved into a new apartment at the Kremlin. He constructed a private demonology in which blame for his wife's suicide was variously ascribed to her relatives, to Polina Molotov, and to Michael Arlen's decadent novel *The Green Hat* which had allegedly—to use modern parlance—'blown her mind'.

Thereafter the dictator lived in paranoid isolation, the only person with whom he maintained a relatively normal relationship being his daughter. When Svetlana in turn had a seven-months' baby, he sent her the most human message he was capable of: 'Take care of your daughter. The state needs people—even those born prematurely.' But since he disapproved of all the men of her choice, the Red Czar's detachment from people other than toadies became almost complete.

The private life of his arch-adversary Trotsky followed an entirely different path. Exiled to Mexico, where threats from Stalin's myrmidons forced him into a virtual state of siege, Trotsky nonetheless remained gregarious to the end. His need for close human contact even spilled over into the sexual sphere. With his cause defeated, his supporters—even outside Russia—shadowed by the K.G.B., and his wife distraught, the elderly exile had an amour with Frida Kahlo, wife of the painter Diego Rivera. What lent special poignancy to their affair was the fact that Rivera had, through his influence with President Cardenas, enabled Trotsky (whom everyone else denied asylum) to come to Mexico in the first place. Nor was the affair conducted with particular discretion. At the hearings of the Dewey Commission—an unofficial tribunal adjudicating on the truth of Stalin's accusations—Frida Kahlo, in vivid Indian costume and Tarascan jewellery, sat close to Trotsky flaunting looks that contrasted markedly with the careworn appearance of his wife Natalie. The similarly jauntily attired Diego Rivera, himself a prodigious womanizer, seemed not to care, but Natalie Trotsky did. To soothe her feelings Trotsky made reiterated protestations that Frida meant little to him. One letter to that effect he sent ended in: 'How I love you my eternal one, my faithful one, my love, my victim.' The last phrase indicates that Trotsky, like Marx before him, had sufficient self-knowledge to realize that in choosing a woman as his marriage partner he had condemned her to a lifetime of privation and grief.

Jiang Qing

As for Mao Tse-Tung, he warrants attention not only on account of his four marriages, but because he was the only Marxist founding father with a wife who took the reins into her own hands. In keeping with the mores of a peasant society, Mao's first marriage was arranged by his father.

Though only 15 at the time, the future revolutionary was already self-willed enough to defy convention by refusing to consummate the marriage. (The shame this caused the bride was such that the villagers kept the name of her clan secret ever after.) Mao's second bride, and first real wife, had more elevated antecedents. Yang Kai Hui was a professor's daughter, as well as a fellow Communist; they met in the early 1920s while working at Peking University Library. At that time Chiang Kai-Shek collaborated with the Communists. His *volte face* from collaboration to extermination in the late '20s started the heroic period of Chinese Communism, when party members became dead men, and women, on leave. The couple had to separate; soon after Mao's wife was captured by Chiang's men, tortured and executed.

Mao next married Ho Tzu Chen, a Party cadre, in Kiangsi province, a Red island in the surrounding Nationalist sea. Ho bore him two children, who had to be left with local peasants when the Communists set out on the long march to escape Chiang's encirclement; the children were never seen again. The Long March ended in Yenan, where a little later Mao's third marriage also ended. The great helmsman and author of the dictum 'Woman carries half of heaven upon her shoulders' divorced Ho Tzu Chen—Party cadre, veteran of the Long March and bereaved mother—for a reason that had little to do with ideology, and a lot with libido: he was lusting after a younger woman.

Jiang Qing had had a chequered career. A twice-divorced actress trained in Shanghai, she had left that town when the Japanese occupied it and first made her way to the Nationalist Capital Chungking. Failing to obtain work there, she had gone North to Communist-held Yenan. There she became a member of a propaganda team that toured the countryside with plays for the peasantry, and met Mao. Their marriage, which aroused criticism among Mao's colleagues, went ahead on the understanding that Jiang would stay out of public life. This she did for over two decades, only emerging in the mid '60s as a cultural commissar who with puritanical relentlessness aligned first opera, and eventually all art forms, to the Communist party line. While privately indulging her taste for silks and Western films she banned dresses, make-up, hairdos and anything that smacked of Western influence. Lovers holding hands in public were pilloried, unmarried mothers sent to the countryside or labour camps. In the Cultural Revolution, which she and three other prominent zealots—'The Gang of Four'—unleashed, the rich heritage of Chinese opera was whittled down to eight ideologically sound works; temples were vandalized and statues destroyed; education virtually ground to a halt. The country endured a whole decade of turmoil and self-inflicted privations; finally in 1976 a groundswell of popular discontent combined with pressure by Party pragmatists to put an end to the witches' sabbath. The term is not inappropriate for after Mao's death in the same year, when Jiang Qing was arrested and faced trial, she appeared to the relieved populace as a witch—thus reinforcing an age-old anti-female stereotype in the Chinese national subconscious.

Mao, his once towering reputation retrospectively diminished by association with Jiang Qing's excesses, would, it appears, have done well to heed Marx's warning, issued for the dialectically opposite reason, that revolutionaries should not marry.

II

Women Writers

Vera Brittain

VERA Brittain was endowed with many gifts, none more outstanding than her capacity for self-resurrection. She twice underwent rebirth from the death-like state of having nothing left to live for. This gift was not bestowed on her by ineluctable destiny; on the contrary, whenever fate impinged on Vera's life, other than in the material circumstances of her birth, it was to disastrous effect: her lover and her brother fell in the Great War, her best friend died young and, less traumatically, Mr. Brittain committed suicide. Fortune only favoured her when she willed it to do so, and she summoned up sufficient reserves of will-power on several occasions from her teens onwards to reconstruct a life grown stale or unendurable. Her youth in Edwardian Buxton, Derbyshire, had been wrapped in a cocoon of soft comfort and stiff convention from which she craved escape. Having attended a superior boarding-school till 18, she was subsequently expected to busy herself with minor domestic chores, piano exercises, tennis and flower arrangements while awaiting the arrival of Mr. Right. Vera's escape route led to Oxford; denied financial support by her father, a paper manufacturer, she knuckled down to preparing herself for the exams single-handed and, aged 20, gained an exhibition to Somerville College. (Mr. Brittain's refusal of support, incidentally, arose not from parsimony but from a rooted conviction that a female was as much out of place in academe as, *pace* Samuel Johnson, a dog in the pulpit.)

The Brittain household tended in general towards philistinism; it contained no more than a dozen books, and some of those on paper-making(!) On the other hand, Vera's mother was an accomplished amateur pianist, and her public school-educated brother Edward studied the violin. The last-mentioned played an important part, by accident as well as by design, in crystallizing Vera's ideas during her formative years. The fact that Edward was, so to speak, predestined to go on from public school to Oxford fired her ambition to do likewise, as well as making her aware of sex discrimination; through Edward, too, she met his school chum Roland Leighton, who was to be the one great love of her life. When she was 21, a concatenation of circumstances produced the intertwining of three separate strands—the outbreak of the Great War, commencement of university studies and the burgeoning love affair with Roland Leighton—in Vera's life. Summer 1914 saw Armageddon welcomed all over England; in the Brittain household, both Vera and her mother pressed Edward to volunteer, as Roland, and practically all other public school graduates, were doing. Vera's introduction to Roland's family took place during her first vacation from Oxford in the winter of 1914, by which time the country was sobering up from its earlier it-will-all-be-over-by-Christmas mood. Mrs. Leighton was unlike anyone she had ever encountered before, a woman who earned her, and the family's, keep by churning out romantic fiction for novels and newspaper serials. Despite the faint aura of raffishness exuded by this lady, the young lovers had to conduct their courtship with utmost propriety: they dared not meet unchaperoned, and hesitated to announce their engagement because Roland lacked the means with which to support a wife. Mr. Brittain, a depressive whose habitual pessimistic predictions began to sound like hard-edged realism in war time, bluntly warned Vera off an engagement to young Leighton, who was bound to get killed, sooner or later. Not that she needed reminding specially of those harsh realities. After a year at Oxford, she had volunteered to become a V.A.D. (nursing auxiliary), and by Christmas 1915 she was working twelve-hour shifts at Camberwell hospital attending to severely wounded men sent back from France. It was then, while awaiting Roland to come on leave, when they would make their engagement official, that she heard of his death in action. The blow shattered Vera, whose mourning took the form of ferreting out, from brother officers, every last single detail of Roland's death, and of composing reams of poetry in memory of their love.

A change of scenery was urgently required, so early in 1916 she went, undeterred by the danger of torpedoes, to Malta, where she did the same work as at Camberwell. Mid-1916 found Vera at Etaples, at a hospital a mere forty miles behind the front line. The war having now reached its bloodiest phase, with 60,000 British soldiers killed on one day alone, the ward in which she worked resembled a charnel-house. In the same year her brother Edward was wounded in action, earning the Military Cross, and required lengthy hospitalization in England. Amid this holocaust of young lives Vera conceived the quixotic idea of marrying a former schoolmate of Roland's and Edward's who had been blinded in battle. He, alas, died of his injuries before she could implement her plan. The following year Edward, his health restored, was posted to the Italian front in anticipation of a major Austrian offensive. Filial duty meanwhile obliged Vera to exchange nursing wounded soldiers for playing nursemaid to her hypochondriac mother and prematurely retired, melancholic father. The Brittains lived in London by this time—and it was there that news reached them of Edward's death in action. Vera's response to this second shattering blow in her young life differed markedly from the way she had reacted to Roland's death. This time her grief fuelled neither poetic effusion nor detailed interrogations of witnesses to the tragic event; instead, she subsided into a low-level depression—a condition that was to characterize her emotional state throughout much of her subsequent life.

With the return of peace Vera went back to Oxford to resume her interrupted studies, deciding, probably under the impact of the War, to read History instead of, as previously, English. At Somerville College she met a somewhat younger student with a record of voluntary war service: Yorkshire-born Winifred Holtby, whose Viking looks contrasted markedly with her own darker and more petite appearance. The two became such firm friends that after graduation, determined to earn an independent living through writing and lecturing, they moved to London and set up house together. Since Winifred was the daughter of a retired gentleman farmer, both had a fall-back position if their bid for female freedom suffused with a dash of bohemianism failed—which, in fact, it did not. That it succeeded was mainly due to the two blue stockings' talent and determination, but it also owed something to the plentiful availability—in those pre-central heating, pre-domestic gadgetry days—of cheap domestic labour; as the two with incremental literary success moved to increasingly spacious lodgings, staff attending to their domestic needs grew steadily in numbers. At first, though, finance presented something of a problem and the main source of income was teaching and lecturing (the latter largely on behalf of the League of Nations, which cause elicited both Vera's and Winifred's enthusiastic support). As time went on journalism and novel-writing occupied them more and more, with Winifred forging ahead of Vera in both spheres.

Even so, Vera brought out a first novel in 1923, paying for the publication herself. Entitled *The Dark Tide*, it showed, like some of her subsequent work, traces of the overblown prose style of Mrs. Leighton. The critical reaction was tepid; the *Saturday Review* for instance commented, 'One day Vera Brittain may write a good book.' The muted fanfares attending her literary début failed to dent Vera's determination to press on with novel-writing. While busy at work on her second *oeuvre*, she received a 'fan letter' from a reader by the name of George Catlin. Catlin, an Oxford-educated politics lecturer about to take up an academic post in the U.S.A., wrote to say that he had seen Vera at Somerville debates some years before; now, to reciprocate the pleasure she had given him in *The Dark Tide*, he offered to send her a recently published monograph of his own. Her affirmative reply started an exchange of letters that continued throughout Catlin's academic stint in America, culminating in a virtual offer of marriage before the correspondents had ever met. When they finally did meet, it needed only a few days for them to agree on arrangements for their eventual marriage. During the year-long engagement Catlin went back to Cornell University to teach, while Vera spent some time attending the annual League of Nations Convention at Geneva (on which she also reported).

The marriage, in 1925, was celebrated according to the Roman rite, Catlin having, like Roland Leighton, converted to Catholicism in the army. Winifred Holtby, finding herself suddenly bereft of her close companion of many years, went off to spend six months in Africa—an extended stay which, apart from its value as therapy, afforded her an insight into that country's race problems, invaluable to a crusading journalist. (Therapy should not be taken to imply that there were any lesbian undertones in the close friendship between Vera and Winifred; the latter had since her late teens nurtured an intense unreciprocated affection for Harry Pearson, a Yorkshire acquaintance.)

Vera, meanwhile, was trying—and failing—to fit into the rôle of a faculty wife at Cornell in Upstate New York. She found university society male-orientated and exclusive, and resented being looked upon as the wife of 'brilliant young' Professor Catlin, instead of a person in her own right. (To demonstrate how highly she valued her status as an individual woman, she had insisted on retaining her maiden name after marriage.) Now, after less than a year's stay, she took the characteristically drastic step of leaving America, to which her husband's livelihood tied him, to return to London where she and Winifred, just back from South Africa, reconstituted their joint household. Catlin, who had during their epistolary courtship agreed that neither of them should let family considerations interfere with their work, proved true to his word and concurred with Vera's suggestion that they place their marriage on a 'part-time' basis; consequently, over the next few years he spent term-time in the States and his vacations with Vera and Winifred in London. The resultant *menage à trois* caused considerable consternation among their Chelsea neighbours; the latter were equally bewildered by the succession of black visitors (consequence of Winifred's South African trip) to Glebe House.

Despite its novel, not to say bizarre, aspects the Catlins' part-time marriage worked—outward proof of its success being the birth of a son, John, in 1927 and a daughter, Shirley, in 1930. That the marriage bond proved so durable owed more to the husband than the wife; Catlin not only submitted to long stints of solitary discomfort without complaint, but made little demur when Vera's advocacy of pacifism placed obstacles in the path of his obtaining political preferment in Britain. His periodical absences in America had not helped his political career prospects either, until the crisis of 1931 (which, uniquely in Britain's peace-time history, bought a coalition government to power) opened two windows of opportunity for him. One could have led on to a parliamentary career: he contested Brentford and Chiswick for Labour in the 1931 General Election, but, despite Vera's and Winifred's enthusiastic support, failed to overturn the Tory majority. The other was journalistic: in the ongoing political realignment exemplified by the formation of a coalition government and the rise of Mosley's New Party, George Catlin was asked to edit a new journal, *The Realist*, for which Lord Melchett provided financial backing. Contributors to the journal included H. G. Wells, J. B. S. Haldane,[1] Julian Huxley and Harold Laski,[2] whose attendance at the Catlins' dinner parties turned Glebe House into one of the meeting-places of London's intellectual society. (It was at one such gathering that Rebecca West met her husband Henry Andrews.) However, *The Realist* only printed a few issues before Lord Melchett, his personal fortune squeezed by the Depression, withdrew his subsidy. Catlin took the blow with good grace, saying he preferred action to words (though, except for fighting one more election, his 'action' thereafter consisted mainly of fact-finding visits to Nazi Germany, Soviet Russia and Spain).

Vera was meanwhile engaged in the most important effort of her writing career, extruding *The Testament of Youth* through her pores of memory. The work was important, not only because its publication in 1933 turned Vera Brittain into a household name, but because in detailing her personal journey from peacetime Buxton through manifold war-time traumas—the deaths of Roland and Edward and her nursing at Camberwell, Malta and Etaples—to post-war Oxford, she

---

1. J. B. S. Haldane (1892–1964): noted geneticist, academic and popularizer of science with left-wing leanings (*The Causes of Evolution*).
2. Harold Laski (1893–1950): political scientist and member of Labour Party executive (*Reflections on the Revolution of our Time*).

performed a needful act of exorcism. It may not be out of place, though, to add that Vera could only summon up the intense concentration that went into this three-year effort, thanks to the presence of five servants at Glebe House, as well as to Winifred Holtby's unfailing readiness to play surrogate mother to toddler John and baby Shirley. Not that Winifred had a great deal of time to spare. Though domestically less stretched, she was professionally busier and, till 1933, more successful than Vera. Having been made a director of *Time and Tide* (Lady Rhondda's radical weekly with a feminist bias) in the mid-'20s, she had nonetheless continued to put out generally well-received novels. When she collapsed after her exertions in the 1931 Election campaign, her doctors first of all diagnosed overwork, and later high blood pressure. After lengthy spells in nursing homes and country cottages produced little amelioration, it was found that she had Bright's disease (a progressive and ultimately fatal condition). However, she spared her friends, even the closest, the knowledge that she only had a few years to live, and Vera, immersed in the composition of *Testament*, apparently never sought to find out.

In 1932, while Winifred was 'resting' in the country, Vera invited her Yorkshire friend Phyllis Bentley—newly famous for *Inheritance*, a 'trouble-oop-at-mill' epic—to stay at Glebe House. The two women quickly became fast friends, though inwardly each harboured complementary feelings of envy towards the other: Vera, the host, envied her guest's best-seller status, while Phyllis, a provincial spinster, envied her host's possession of a husband and children. When Winifred returned, she found that Vera had all but transformed Phyllis from frump to fashion plate and was guiding her round London's literary cocktail circuit. Even so, there were under-currents of friction between host and guest; after one tiff between them had ended with Phyllis walking out in tears, Winifred snapped at Vera, 'You've been the most important person in too many people's lives, you bitch!' Shortly after-wards the publication of *The Testament of Youth* made Vera important in infinitely more people's lives—namely, whole cohorts of female readers who felt that her book constituted a tribute to the war-time sacrifices of women worthy to stand alongside Erich Remarque's or Robert Graves's tribute to the suffering of men.

There was one person, however, in whose young life Vera did not become the most important person he would have wanted her to be: her son. In his childhood, John Catlin recalls the object of his fiercest jealousy was neither father George nor sister Shirley, but his mother's typewriter—adding that his happiest moments at Glebe House were spent in Winifred's company. Such happiness was not vouchsafed him for long. In 1935, aged only 38, Winifred finally succumbed to Bright's disease. Her untimely death was made more poignant by the presence of Harry Pearson who, summoned to the clinic by Vera, agreed to go through a death-bed marriage ceremony with Winifred. Out of earshot of the ceremony, meanwhile, the dying woman's closest friends, Lady Rhondda and Vera, enacted another macabre scene by accusing each other of the exploitation of Winifred—the one for the benefit of her paper, and the other for the benefit of her family.

There was only formal truth in Lady Rhondda's charge, for Winifred had delighted in playing surrogate mother to John and Shirley. But, whatever the exact credit and debit balance of their relationship, for Vera the loss of her companion of fifteen years' standing was a blow hardly less shattering than Roland Leighton's death two decades earlier. 'Winifred's dying', she wrote in her diary, 'took away with her that second life she initiated for me after the war. Can I make a third? Can I, once more begin again? Are books and children enough for living?' This diary entry is remarkable on a number of counts: for its elevation of friend above family, assumed equivalence of children with books, and omission of husband. The semi-detached nature of Vera's marriage had never been more obvious than just then. A few months earlier she had had a brief, but intense, love affair with George Brett, her American publisher and a married man; now the lack of Catlin's affection for her was demonstrated when he left her the morning after Winifred's death to attend the Labour Party Conference at Brighton. Admittedly the deliberations at Brighton warranted his undivided attention in the run-up to the General Election, and he had been adopted, with discreet help from Ellen Wilkinson,[3] as Labour candidate for Sunderland. Alas, the outcome was hardly different from that at Brentford and Chiswick four years earlier.

Vera meanwhile was purposefully engaged on a more rewarding enterprise: seeing the MS of Winifred's last novel through to publication. When *South Riding* appeared it was, paradoxically, a greater success than any of its predecessors and soon received the ultimate accolade of being turned into a film (with Edna Best and Ralph Richardson in the lead parts). That chore completed, Vera embarked on a final act of homage to Winifred: the composition of *The Testament of Friendship*, which took her three years.

At around the time of the start of her new literary labours the Catlins took up residence in Cheyne Walk, a most desirable address. This move, made possible by Vera's inheritance of her father's estate, after the latter's suicide, and her royalty income from *The Testament of Youth* earned them the nickname 'Dorchester Socialists' in Labour Party circles. This witticism coined by Herbert Morrison, however, alienated Vera far less than Morrison's and Bevin's deposition of Labour leader George Lansbury on account of his pacifism. Labour's switch to national self-defence was one reaction to the gathering international crisis; another, and diametrically opposite one, was the formation of the Peace Pledge Union by the Reverend Dick Sheppard. The P.P.U., which enrolled 100,000 members within two years, found its most valuable recruit in Vera Brittain; others, like Aldous Huxley or Benjamin Britten, may have been equally, or more, prominent, but she was easily the most active in the cause of pacifism.

By coincidence the year 1939 that wrote *finis* to all pacifist illusions also saw Vera end her labour of love in memory of Winifred. When published *The Testament of Friendship* was however perceived as falling short of the standard set in the previous *Testament*; mired in Edwardian literary clichés it was

---

3. Ellen Wilkinson (1891–1947): English Labour politician and M.P. involved in the Jarrow Crusade.

adjudged closer to hagiography than biography.

At the outbreak of war Vera decided to stay in Britain while sending the children to stay with friends in the U.S.A. The Ministry of Information wanted to harness her talents as a communicator to the war effort—but she started putting out a fortnightly pacifist newsletter to subscribers. Despite this she remained unmolested by the authorities. At the height of the war, alongside producing the fortnightly *Letters to Peacelovers,* she sat on a tribunal screening conscientious objectors and worked for the Childrens' Overseas Reception Board arranging evacuation to Commonwealth countries. In addition she wrote *England's Hour,* a documentary book for which she gathered material by accompanying air-raid wardens on tours of duty, visited reception centres for bombed-out families, and toured the most heavily blitzed parts of London.

Such close engagement with the reality of war did not, however, give her an insight into the nature of the conflict. Advocating peace by negotiation with Hitler she perforce had to find the guilty men closer to home. She agreed with her husband that those most to blame were:

> (a) Communists and near-Communists like Gollancz and Laski, who urged hatred of Germany on us in the name of Soviet Russia; (b) foolish pugilistic Liberals who wanted us to guarantee small powers all over Europe without knowing whether we could; (c) Francophiles like Vansittart and Duff Cooper who tied us to France and over-estimated France's military strength.

Occasionally the couple's flight from reality plunged from the merely ludicrous to the downright macabre. The entry in Vera Brittain's diary of 20 December 1942 read:

> All the papers are so full of horrors of the Nazi behaviour to the Jews in Poland, and all of them get more and more fantastic. George has a theory that all this material about atrocities being so widely publicised just now is a method of making people subdued over Christmas and therefore discouraged from spending much money.

Other of her diary entries, in contrast—such as those deploring the saturation bombing of German cities—make far less

contentious reading today. Be that as it may, Vera's frequently aberrant interpretations of war-time events remained
private at the time. What the British public learnt was that
her name appeared on the Gestapo's 'hit list' of 2,000 Britons
to be liquidated after the invasion—and this enhanced her
reputation considerably.

In the immediate post-war years she lapsed into prolonged inertia. Subsequently her interest switched from public engagement to personal salvation and she began a biography of John Bunyan, with whom she strongly identified. In
1957 she published an autobiography entitled *The Testament
of Experience*. Soon afterwards she joined C.N.D., the third
of the peace movements to elicit her fervent support in the
course of a war-encumbered lifetime.

Vera Brittain died in 1970.

Simone de Beauvoir

The fact that the French minted the word bourgeois was
entirely appropriate. This is not merely a matter of euphony;
one would be hard put to think of another society which
could have given rise to that term with all its diverse implications, positive as well as negative. No one generated
a more quintessentially bourgeois ambience than the (still
largely provincial) French middle classes of the *fin de siècle*.
Anyone who, curious about that ambience—an amalgam of
dark furniture, gleaming napery and musty servants' quarters—wants to steep himself in it, is well advised to read
Memoirs of a Dutiful Daughter, Simone de Beauvoir's account
of her upbringing.

Simone was born in Edwardian Paris into a family some
members of which still lived in Limoges (where she spent
long summer holidays). She grew up in a cocoon of stability,
moderate comfort and culture, though her precocious vision
also picked up, quite early on, evidence of caste consciousness and sexual prudery. The father whom she, already dabbling in authorship as a schoolgirl, initially admired for his
literary erudition and sceptical mind later revealed himself
as unsympathetic and indolent; insensitive to his daughter's adolescent insecurity, he was a patriarch within the

household and a xenophobe beyond it. The mother, a pious Catholic, transmitted her internalized sexual repression to the daughter. So as not to see her own naked body Simone was made to change underwear without uncovering herself; she had her books and correspondence censored, and her questions on 'delicate' topics left unanswered. Even so she could count herself fortunate in comparison with other girls of similar background. Her best friend, Zaza, was being groomed for an arranged marriage by parents who made her learn how to prepare elaborate meals in preference to studying school subjects.

Her own younger sister, Helene, to whom scholarly success came less easily than to herself, made a desperate bid for paternal approbation by learning to recite the names of all Napoleon's marshals by rote; it availed her nothing. When Simone excelled at exams the father praised her in terms typical of a country whose women only received the vote after the Second World War: 'Simone has a man's brain; she thinks like a man: she is a man.' In the mid-1920s the parents decided to foster this 'mannishness' to an extent that would subsequently enable Simone to earn her own living. The reason for such a drastic departure from the bourgeois norm of preparing a girl for the estate of matrimony was financial stringency: although Monsieur de Beauvoir had married into a wealthy family, as a moderately remunerated legal secretary he could not provide his daughter with an adequate dowry.

She was therefore not merely allowed, but encouraged, to go on to university, though her father vetoed philosophy as a subject of study. She read History and Classics instead, but won the post-graduation battle; rather than entering the Civil Service she opted for a career in teaching, a profession de Beauvoir *père* thought overrun with radicals. Aiming to become a *lycée* teacher she had to undergo a difficult exam, the postgraduate *agrégation*. It was in the course of preparing for the *agrégation* that she met Jean-Paul Sartre. In Sartre she encountered the soul-mate she had yearned for throughout her troubled, and often solitary, adolescence. Somewhat older, he instantly assumed the position of Simone's mentor by saying, 'From now on I'll take you under my wing.'

Astonishingly the feminist-minded young woman did not reject Sartre's masculine tutelage; in fact she welcomed it. (In later yeas she explained that she could not have deferred to a man she knew to be her intellectual equal—but in Sartre she detected a superior intellect.) How superior emerged when he came first country-wide in the *agrégation* exams; not that she did badly either, becoming the youngest woman ever, at 21, to have competed successfully in that gruelling test.

Intellectual closeness engendered intimacy in personal relations. Although each was drawn to the other, Simone readily consented to Sartre's proposal—couched in the vocabulary of Existentialist philosophy—that they should enter into an open (non-) marriage. 'What we have is an *essential* love, but it would be good if we both experienced *contingent* love affairs as well.' Sartre even adumbrated a contractual basis for their *affaire*—suggesting they sign a two-year lease, separate for a further two to three years, then live together again, and so forth. Separation was, in any case, forced upon them by circumstances when they obtained teaching posts at opposite ends of the country, he at Rouen and she in Marseilles. When she took up her appointment in the Mediterranean port, Simone, who had left home for the first time in her student days only to move into her grandmother's house, experienced a sense of liberation:

> When, armed with my teacher's certificate, I stood at the top of that flight of steps, I turned dizzy with sheer delight; it seemed to me that far from enduring my destiny I had deliberately chosen it.

Choice of one's own destiny is part of the Existentialist emphasis on the individual; while teaching at Marseilles Simone deepened her sense of selfhood by undertaking long solitary hikes into the surrounding countryside. She also continued to dabble in the solitary art of writing, but none of her efforts reached completion. Lack of faith in her literary accomplishment inhibited her; so did the awareness that Sartre, simultaneously essaying authorship, had devised a philosophical matrix in which to root his writing, whereas hers seemed to float in a vacuum.

After a while she moved to another *lycée* at Rouen. This enabled her to see Sartre, who was teaching at nearby Le Havre, much more often and to spend most weekends at Paris. Sartre had meanwhile made the acquaintance of Olga Kosakiewicz, a wilful and precocious teenager of White Russian extraction on whom he subsequently modelled Ivich in *Roads to Freedom*. Olga unsettled and attracted Sartre—a state of affairs which Simone was to describe with exemplary candour: 'He let himself go at risk to his emotional stability and experienced feelings of frenzy, alarm and ecstasy such as he had never known with me.' Though Simone found herself caught up in a classic 'eternal triangle' situation, she reacted with the forbearance enjoined upon her by Sartre's contract differentiating between essential and contingent love. She also felt attracted herself to Olga on account of her impulsive nature and Rimbaud-like personality. The triangular tension was resolved when Sartre and Simone adopted Olga as a representative of youth—a first step in the creation of Sartre's 'wider family'—and Olga married. (Her husband, too, joined the 'family'.) At the same time Sartre commenced a contingent affair with Olga's younger sister, while still maintaining his essential amorous–cum–intellectual partnership with Simone.

The Kosakiewicz affairs demonstrated the imbalance of the bargains Sartre had struck with her. Although in theory their contract gave both partners equal scope for pursuing extra-marital liaisons, in practice he was the only one who did. There can be little doubt that in so doing he inflicted suffering on Simone, who at one stage had to resort to the drug orthodene to assuage the hurt. Early on, though, while caught up in the toils of the Olga *affaire*, Simone sought sublimation in creativity. She began to gestate a novel about a *ménage à trois*—eventually published as *L'invitée*—whose three protagonists were transpositions of Sartre, herself and the invited guest Olga. The plot replicated their situation exactly. In the novel Pierre (Sartre), sensing Françoise's (Simone's) distress, offers to break with Xavière (Olga). Such chivalry makes it even more difficult for Françoise to object, for she has in turn been given freedom in love. However, such freedom is more abstract than real, since it leaves out of account

Pierre's greater power in the world—a man's world. After a severe psychomatic illness, Françoise resolves her problem by killing Xavière. Vicariously murdering Olga probably helped Simone sluice the toxins of jealousy out of her own psyche. Although she had to wait several years before *L'invitée* appeared in print, the act of writing and actually—unlike some earlier efforts—completing the novel must have somewhat alleviated the stress she was under.

In the meantime Sartre had managed to place his foot on the first rung of the ladder of fame by publishing *La Nausée*. Long imbued with authorial ambitions, he regarded the acclaim that greeted this pioneering existential novel as no more than his due, and continued, oblivious of the darkening political horizon, to pursue the pleasures of the intellect, of sexual promiscuity and of foreign travel.

On the outbreak of war he was called to the colours and life suddenly turned deadly serious. The French collapse in 1940 left him, and a million other *poilus*, PoWs in German hands. Then, after some months behind barbed wire, he was released and returned to Nazi-occupied Paris. From there, *incredibile dictu*, he and Simone de Beauvoir set off on a bicycle tour of unoccupied France. That the two of them were both interested in, and capable of, undertaking such a jaunt in the middle of a relentless war indicates how adroitly the Nazi authorities and their Vichy collaborators fostered the illusion that French life was continuing normally, despite—or even because of—defeat and occupation. For the same reason they encouraged manifestations of a busy cultural life, with new plays staged, exhibitions mounted, and books published. In 1943, by which time war-time shortages had long forced an habitual restaurant user (and hotel guest) like Simone to do her own cooking, she had the satisfaction of seeing *L'invitée* appear in print. In the same year Sartre gained further fame with the première of *Les Mouches* (*The Flies*). This did not indicate any degree of collaboration with the Occupation authorities on their part. On the contrary, Simone lost her teaching post, and Sartre founded a resistance group, which she also joined. The *Socialisme et Liberté* group was small, and actually not very effective, since it restricted itself to collecting and disseminating intelligence about the Occupation régime.

At one point even this activity became risky and the group disbanded; thereafter Sartre concentrated on devising an ideology appropriate to post-war conditions in France. At the same time both engaged in intense literary activity—Simone published a second book in 1944—and intellectually bracing debates with the likes of Albert Camus and Raymond Queneau.[4]

1945 was a creative *annus mirabilis* for the pair of them. Sartre scored a hat trick launching the novel sequence *Roads to Freedom*, a philosophical tome *Being and Nothingness*, and the play *Huis Clos*; Simone had a double: her third novel *The Blood of Others* and a rather undistinguished first play. And, as if that were not enough, they founded, jointly with Merleau-Ponty,[5] the left-wing journal *Les Temps Modernes*.

Sartre now enjoyed, alongside celebrity status, sufficient income to permit Simone to concentrate entirely on writing. But though generous with money and—equally valuable—counsel, he was, as ever, averse to giving Simone his individual attention. In fact, by this time he had worked out a pattern of scheduled promiscuity enabling him to see, and sleep with, three or four women per week. In 1947, when Simone was away on an American lecture tour, he asked her to delay her return lest she cramp his style in pursuit of a new *affaire*. In response Simone took, for the first time in their eighteen-year-long relationship, a lover of her own. This was Chicago-bred Nelson Algren, author of *The Man with the Golden Arm*. At one point Algren even proposed marriage, but, since neither could really have adapted to life in the other's country, the *affaire* simply went on inconclusively for several years. Halfway through that period Simone stood poised, thanks to the publication of *The Second Sex*, on the verge of international recognition. Although she subsequently wrote a Goncourt Prize novel and a highly regarded four-volume autobiography, *Le Deuxième Sexe* proved her most widely-read and influential work. It was the book that

---

4. Raymond Queneau (1903–76): French author, journalist and scholar influenced by Surrealism (*Zazie dans le métro*).
5. Maurice Merleau-Ponty (1908–61): French philosopher, academic and journalist (*The Structure of Behaviour*).

compellingly posed the women's question afresh during the trough between the peaks of 1920s' Suffragism and 1960s' Feminism. The main thrust of *The Second Sex* went along the following lines: women's fate is invented not inherited, housework is unrewarded drudgery, marriage servitude and maternity not a saccharine experience, but constricting, often painful and sometimes downright fatal.

It seems clear that the leitmotifs of *The Second Sex*, however closely argued, derive in part from Simone's own experience and subjective perceptions. The outright rejection of marriage, an institution that turns spontaneous feelings into compulsory rights and duties, reflected her so-called contract with Sartre, but it also denoted—and this is where she laid herself open to criticism—a uniquely well-educated and fulfilled woman's pride in her successful career. The derogation of housework likewise bespeaks the career woman's ability to pay others for the provision of domestic comforts. However, in the disparagement of maternity an aberrant notion deeply rooted in Simone's psyche revealed itself. It was the concept that the foetus constituted some sort of parasite eating into the independence of a woman. The language employed to project a negative image of 'value-free' physiological processes was extraordinarily loaded. 'Wherever life is in the making—germination, fermentation—it arouses disgust. . . . the slimy embryo begins the cycle that is completed in the putrefaction of death.'

The book had huge sales, but also aroused furious censure. Margaret Mead considered it deeply anti-feminist. 'By denigrating maternity', she wrote, 'the author constructs a picture in which the only way a woman can be a full human being is to be as much like a man as possible.' By contrast, Albert Camus complained that Simone had made the French male look ridiculous, while François Mauriac,[6] who took exception to the book's sexual explicitness, told a journalist on the staff of *Les Temps Modernes*, 'The vagina of your employer holds no secrets for me.' The French Communists also reacted disapprovingly. For them expatiating on the problematical

---

ó. François Mauriac (1885–1970): French Catholic novelist, essayist and journalist, winner of Nobel Prize for Literature (*A Woman of the Pharisees*).

female condition was a diversion from the main task—of bringing about Socialism—the advent of which would solve all problems *tout court.*

By dialectical inversion, the problems the advent of Socialism-in-One-Country posed for a group of Parisian intellectual luminaries provided Simone with the subject of her next book, *The Mandarins.* In it she showed thinly disguised personal acquaintances—Sartre, Albert Camus and Arthur Koestler, etc.—interacting abrasively with one another while debating inflammatory post-war issues such as the existence of concentration camps in the Soviet Union. The novel won its author France's most prestigious literary award, the Prix Goncourt. The period between the conception of *The Mandarins* and the award of the prize was far from happy for Simone. The gradual atrophy of the *affaire* with Algren left her depressed over the apparent end of an active sex life at 43. (Sartre, a priapic activist recalling a chess grand master forever playing 'simuls', had already stopped frequenting her bed some time earlier.) Then, in 1952, she imagined that she had cancer, and although that particular fear proved groundless, she would never thereafter be entirely free of premonitions of dying. She nonetheless began to climb out of the pit, re-energized by the inception of a new love affair. The man involved was young—just 27—a Jewish ex-*résistant,* *Temps Modernes* journalist, and member of Sartre's 'family' by the name of Claude Lanzmann. Simone's relationship with Lanzmann, subsequently the director of *Shoa,* lasted for seven years.

In 1954 France lost the decisive Battle of Dien-Bien-Phu, a debâcle that forced her to withdraw from Indo-China after many years fighting. As a critic of colonialism Simone welcomed that defeat, which did not endear her to majority opinion in the country. Sartre was meanwhile embroiled in more complicated controversies arising out of his ambivalent attitude to Communism. Although critical of detailed aspects of Soviet policy, such as the suppression of the 1956 Hungarian Uprising, he basically sided with Moscow in the Cold War against the West. The contradictions inherent in his stance had the bizarre result that he now banned performances of his own play *Les Mains Sales* (about a reversal of the

46

Communist Party line) lest it be construed as anti-Soviet. In the late 1950s developments closer to home preoccupied and disturbed Sartre and de Beauvoir. Both opposed the French colonial war in Algeria from the outset, thus courting patriotic death threats, and were appalled by the political fallout from the war, viz. de Gaulle's accession to power. But the end of the decade also brought countervailing positive developments: the enthusiastic reception, by critics and public alike, of *Memoirs of a Dutiful Daughter*, the joy derived from a joint trip to newly Castroite Cuba, and the excitement of visits to the Soviet Union during Khrushchev's thaw.

In 1964 Sartre was offered the Nobel Prize for Literature, and proceeded—astonishingly—to turn it down. There were those who applauded the gesture as conforming with his proclaimed anti-bourgeois principles, while others merely found it perverse. In the following year he took an action far more deserving of the epithet perverse: he formally adopted a part-time mistress of several years standing, the Algerian Jewess Arlette Elkaim, as his daughter. The adoption represented a fusing of a number of Sartre's main compulsions: an Oedipal urge to dethrone the fathers—expressed both in the writings and through bonding young disciples as his 'family'—the itch to *épater le bourgeois*, and the wish to demonstrate solidarity with the Third World. (By the symbolic act of choosing a Jewess as heir Sartre may also have expressed remorse at the insufficient help he had given Hitler's chief victims during the war.)

The adoption elicited no protest from Simone, but she exacted her own type of revenge by reducing the rival-turned-daughter to non-person status through the omission of any reference to her from her own autobiography. By the mid-'60s she had become the widely respected First Lady of the European Left. It was a position she had earned twice over: both through her work, and by her courage in publicizing revelations about the French torture of Algerian women prisoners in the teeth of threats to fire-bomb her apartment. Together with Sartre she attended International Peace Conferences and participated in Bertrand Russell's Tribunal on American War Crimes in Vietnam. 1967 saw them visit the crisis-prone Middle East (where, with an eye to symmetry, they had Arlette as companion on the outward journey and Claude Lanzmann on the return trip).

1968 switched the focus of their attention from abroad to the *événements* at Paris, during which Sartre adopted a considerably higher profile in support of the students than Simone, who felt ill at ease at public gatherings. The collapse of the Student Revolt pushed them both further to the Left. At the time several ultra-Left sheets were in trouble with the authorities for appearing under a collective imprint—a stratagem designed to sidestep the law which held a single editor liable for a paper's contents. Sartre and Simone assumed the token editorship of two rather scurrilous Maoist newspapers and defied officialdom to arrest them, but the powers that be had the nous to deny them the hoped-for aureole of martyrdom by taking no action. From this near-brush with the law Simone moved onto another public demonstration of equally doubtful legality but rather greater consequence. In the early '70s, a time of feminist mobilization in France, she signed the Manifesto of the 343 women who made public admission of having undergone illegal abortions. The campaign to decriminalize abortion eventually succeeded; French feminists also stole a march on their British sisters by having a special Ministry for the Feminine Condition set up.

With advancing age—the subject of another influential book of hers—Simone's own feminine condition also altered appreciably. The *affaire* with Lanzmann now a dim memory, her existence was interwoven with that of Sylvie Le Bon. Her junior by an entire generation, Sylvie had almost replicated Simone's own life from university studies to *lycée* teaching, first at Rouen and then in Paris. Simone claimed never to have regretted her own childlessness, because she found the relationship mothers she knew had with their children, especially daughters, dreadful. Now she and her surrogate daughter saw each other daily, and went on joint holidays, during which they, of course, always spent an allotted span of time with Sartre. Sylvie, said *'la grande Sartreuse'*, gave her a feeling of being reincarnated and free of the burden of her own age.

Age and illness were, meanwhile, taking their toll of Sartre. He was inexorably losing his sight and had to be moved about in a wheelchair; worst of all, the medication taken to counter-act high blood pressure made him lose control over his bodily functions. These various problems were compounded by some of Sartre's mistresses (whom he still saw on a rota basis) smuggling alcohol and cigarettes into the sick room at his bidding. Although Simone had received numerous slights from Sartre, some of which, such as marriage proposals to other women and the designation of Arlette Elkaim as his heir, amounted to downright acts of betrayal, she carried out her nauseous nursing duties with uncomplaining dedication. Hospitalized, Sartre slipped into a coma in mid-April 1980. Just before losing consciousness he gripped Simone's wrist and mumbled with eyes closed, 'I love you very much, my dear Beaver'—his life-long nickname for her. After he had died she stayed overnight with the body and actually tried to lie down next to it under the sheet. Warned by a nurse of possible gangrene infection, she lay down on top of the sheet and slept.

Sartre's funeral cortège was followed by a 30,000-strong crowd. Simone, her sister Helene and Sylvie Le Bon, rode together with the officially next-of-kin Arlette Elkaim inside the hearse. At the cemetery Simone only got out of the hearse after the coffin had been lowered into the ground, and sat beside the open grave for ten minutes. It is futile to surmise what she thought and felt at the irrevocable end of a love relationship of fifty-one years' standing. Was it sorrow pure and simple—or was her sense of bereavement suffused with bitterness? She would have had sufficient reason: Sartre having died intestate, everything of his—including a literary estate of inestimable value—had passed into Arlette's keep-ing. This meant that Simone could not even publish Sartre's letters to herself without Arlette's permission. When this was refused she, nonetheless, brought out two volumes of his letters showing how ardently he had declared his love to her during the first sixteen years of their relationship. Their pub-lication goaded Arlette into attacking her in the press, and an undignified quarrel between the two women—unthinkable during Sartre's lifetime—ensued.

Simone also published *Le Cérémonie des adieux*, her own farewell to Sartre, writing in the preface: 'Here is the first of my books—no doubt the only one—that you will not have read before it was printed.' Simone de Beauvoir died in 1986, rich in years and honours. Since then her reputation as a seminal figure of the feminist awakening has undergone drastic revision. When Deirdre Bair published her biography in 1990, the *Daily Telegraph*, a paper not normally given to rhetorical flourishes, carried a review of the book entitled *De Beauvoir the doormat*.

III

Writers' Wives

Sonia Tolstoy

NO one was ever more aptly described as a legend in his own lifetime than Count Leo Tolstoy. The crowds that poured onto the streets of Europe's capitals at the news of his death in 1910 enacted what was probably the largest spontaneous tribute ever paid to any man. The bizarre circumstances of his death—as a senile runaway at an obscure Russian railway station overrun by reporters and newsreel cameramen—focused world attention, but the main trigger for the massive display of public grief was the veneration in which pre-war Europe's thinking classes held the sage of Yasnaya Polyana, a much-photographed bearded figure in peasant blouse and home-made bark shoes. Contemporary newsreels show women forming a large percentage of the mourners. One wonders, though, if closer acquaintance with Tolstoy would have left them equally grief-stricken at his decease—for a close reading of his life, especially as partner in a marriage, shows him to have been a deeply flawed apostle of enlightenment.

Aged respectively 34 and 18 at the time of the wedding Tolstoy and his wife Sonya (née Behr) had spent nearly half a century in what both concurred in regarding as the indissoluble state of matrimony. Though concurring in this they agreed on little else; in consequence their marriage eventually resembled a gladiatorial contest. The epithet is apt for several reasons: they fought each other to the point of exhaustion, and their clash provided, especially in later years, a veritable public spectacle. Also gladiators used nets as weapons and Tolstoy for much of his married life saw himself as wriggling inside a net, entrapped by his own sexuality. The co-existence within one and the same person of powerful libidinous impulses—Tolstoy remained sexually active till well into his sixties—and a yearning for monk-like celibacy placed an obvious strain on relations with his wife. Despite her increasingly desperate entreaties, he would not be swayed from his theologically derived conviction that indulgence in sex without procreative intent diminished man to a rutting animal. For Sonya the result of her husband's adherence to Church doctrine were thirteen pregnancies extending over an entire quarter of a century. Then in an access of spirituality that coincided with his wife's thirteenth delivery Tolstoy began to incubate the story that was to be his *gran rifiuto* of fornication, 'The Kreutzer Sonata'.

Contradiction was in fact a recurrent motif in Tolstoy's life. The latter-day social reformer had in his dissolute bachelor days at Yasnaya Polyana fathered an illegitimate son on his peasant mistress, subsequently employing them both as servants like any others on the estate. He denounced property, but had availed himself of the opportunity of acquiring Bashkir land cheaply near Samara. He preached the Christian virtues, which include tolerance, but was intolerant of dissenting views within the family. Apropos of family—a subject closer than any other to Sonya's heart—Tolstoy, whose fiction painted an idyllic picture of family life among the Russian nobility, in his own life increasingly distanced himself from his wife and children (other than those who inclined to Tolstoyanism). Of course, none of this distracts from his greatness as an artist—an artist who, moreover, once wrote with disarming candour: 'The poet skims off the best of his life and puts it in his work; that is why his work is beautiful and his life bad.'

But to return to family matters, which were to dominate and all but destroy the Tolstoy marriage: Dr. Behr was physician to the Tsar's palace staff and occupied, together with his wife, three daughters and some servants, a service flat inside the Kremlin complex. The presence of three high-spirited teenage girls in the over-furnished apartment generated an atmosphere of insouciant sociability. (The coltish charm of the youngest so captivated the future author of *War and Peace* that he modelled Natasha on her.) What Tolstoy looked for *chez* Behr was diversion and, probably, respite from violent swings of mood between excess and introspection characteristic of his bachelor state. What he found, fortuitously, was a wife in the shape of the attractive middle daughter, Sonya.

At 18 Sonya was just over half Tolstoy's age when they married. Just before the wedding he had, in a characteristic display of candour, given her his diary to read. A conventional upbringing had ill-prepared her for its revelations about 'darling Lyovochka's' past profligacy and debauch (not to mention the attendant mental and emotional somersaults). The shock realization that her idolized husband-to-be—aristocrat, soldier and writer—was a veritable Jekyll and Hyde figure drained Sonya's wedding day of all joy. As for the wedding night, Tolstoy's brutally precipitate consummation of the marriage in the jolting dormeuse taking them to Yasnaya Polyana did little to soothe her wrought-up feelings. Once arrived on the estate the town-bred young bride made a determined and largely successful effort to adapt to a rural existence, even if Tolstoy's absences on tours of inspection or hunting trips often left her quite lonely.

At the end of nine months came the joy of childbirth, overshadowed at once by marital disagreement. Although suckling the babe caused Sonya intense pain, her husband, with Rousseau as his chief mentor, insisted that she persevere with it. 'Why', he expostulated heatedly, 'must a common girl perform what Countess Tolstoy considers beyond her strength?' When Sonya, backed by Dr. Behr, who berated his son-in-law (by post) for insensitivity and ridiculed his ambition to turn himself into a *muzhik*, engaged a wet-nurse from among the village women, the latter refused to set foot inside the nursery. Not long after he chose the eve of their wedding anniversary to announce his intention to enlist in the Russian forces which were engaged in putting down insurrection in Poland. Sonya took his motive to be not so much the Crimean War veteran's martial ardour as an ex-bachelor's revulsion from domesticity, and although Tolstoy changed his mind on the morrow, the hurt rankled. It was not many months before another event supervened to threaten Sonya's emotional balance more gravely than any of the foregoing. One morning the house was permeated with the smell of strong lye soap and dirty water. A broad dark-skinned peasant woman with muscular shoulders and large breasts was on her hands and knees. A child played in the open doorway. . . . An instinctive realization that the woman was Tolstoy's ex-mistress and the toddler their bastard child pierced Sonya's mind like a knife. For the young, traditionally brought up, and frequently lonely wife the encounter with the flesh-and-blood witnesses to her husband's unspeakable past was truly traumatizing—and he compounded the trauma by refusing to shield her from the sight of them in future. For all that Sonya still felt sufficient affection for Lyovochka to want to act as his helpmeet. Barely 20 she assumed the burden of administering the estate to enable Tolstoy to devote himself to his favourite pursuits, which ranged from organizing the village school through philosophical studies and meditation to literary composition. It was the last-mentioned that she most wanted him to pursue, and for which she would make quite extraordinary sacrifices. She copied out the manuscript of *War and Peace* an incredible seven times; it has said that transcribing Tolstoy's scribbled MSS gave her more pleasure than anything else, including—though she loved him—his embraces.

Although both possessed strong libidos their divergent attitudes to conjugal relations created severe strains in the marriage. Tolstoy, the would-be-ascetic plagued by carnal desire, deplored, while enjoying, his weakness of the flesh and, in a characteristically male reflex as ancient as the Eve archetype and as modern as Schopenhauer, projected his sexual guilt on to Sonya. He also without consulting his wife designated her months of gestation and lactation a close season—although he was not above breaching his own taboo. (Once his insistence on coitus within a month of Sonya's delivery—her ninth(!)—brought on a haemorrhage and the midwife had to 'discipline' him.) The close season for a nursing mother, according to Tolstoy, also applied to her going into society. His worst offence against her as an autonomous human being stemmed, of course, from what he considered his irrefragable right to deposit semen in her womb for as long as desire stirred his loins. The seemingly endless sequence of pregnancies that ensued, with their attendant discomforts intensified by Tolstoy's various taboos, forced Sonya's life into a narrowly circumscribed pattern. To escape the constriction of this sort of existence she cajoled her country-squire husband to let the family spend part of the year in Moscow. As befitted a protagonist of Rousseau's natural man, Tolstoy viewed the town as matrix of a corrupt social organism; he nonetheless consented to the move and himself took up residence in the metropolis for brief spells. While there he characteristically insisted that Sonya and the children accompany him on tours of slum districts and charity hospitals. Once after his return to the estate the marriage partners' letters crossed each other; hers described a ball at the gubernatorial mansion of Prince Dolgorukov, while his told of hand-making a pair of shoes for an old woman servant.

But the social freedom Sonya had secured for herself through the alternation between Yasnaya Polyana and Moscow in no way eased her servitude on the sexual treadmill. Attempts to persuade her husband to practise the withdrawal form of birth control met with an appalled refusal; the notion of indulging in coitus, the divinely ordained means of perpetuating life, purely for pleasure, revolted him. When Sonya became pregnant for the nth time she asked the midwife at Tula (the district town) to abort her, but the latter, fearful of the Count's wrath, refused. Frantically anxious to terminate the pregnancy Sonya jumped off a chest of drawers, and when this did not have the desired result repeated the performance—all to no avail.

By this time her mental balance was so precarious that self-mutilation, or worse, held no terror for her. From merely threatening to do away with herself or mooting suicide in overwrought diary jottings, she had graduated to real, if inept, suicide attempts when the intensity of her quarrels with Tolstoy reached fever pitch. And there was plenty for them to quarrel about. Over the years her husband's quest for a truly spiritual mode of existence had crystallized in a Tolstoyan code of conduct that made life with him a veritable trial. Sonya's diary entry, 'He turned to Christianity; the martyrdom was mine', hid a kernel of truth beneath the hyperbole. Tolstoy's renunciation of aristocratic land ownership with its social pretensions and sharp financial practices was motivated by commendable idealism, but in execution it imposed a grave burden on his wife-cum-estate administrator. The problems Lyovochka's spiritual odyssey posed for Sonya ranged from the merely embarrassing to the downright exasperating. At her 'at homes' for the local gentry he would mingle with the fashionably accoutred guests dressed in a grey peasant blouse; when it was a question of giving the children guidance for life, he told one daughter: 'It is more important for you to take care of your room and cook your own soup than to make a good marriage'; once when Sonya complained of mounting expenses he informed her curtly that he could not take an interest in such matters. When in the aftermath of the 1905 Revolution marauding peasant bands threatened life and property, Sonya requested and secured armed police guards for the estate; these remained for two years, during which Tolstoy agonized over opposing the violence of the deprived with the counter-violence of the state.

The other-worldliness he preached he likewise practised, wearing laboriously fashioned home-made shoes, chopping wood and working in the fields. Although he repented of his one-time resolve to take up the contemplative life, he did submit to the extreme discomfort and privations of a pilgrimage. Having set out dressed *muzhik*-fashion in bark shoes with pack on back and staff in hand, he found on arrival at the monastery the pilgrims' cells so filthy that sheer nausea forced him to drop his disguise—whereupon the abbot allotted him quarters befitting an aristocrat.

The experience—the start of an ever-deepening disenchantment with the Church which culminated in his excommunication—did not, however, wean Tolstoy from his perception of dirt (in less than stomach-heaving dosage) as concomitant to a state of grace. When the authorities jailed one of his disciples for alleged subversion, he, whom officialdom treated with kid gloves, felt a pang of envy. He said, 'I would like to be put in prison; a real prison—good and stinking!' Still, what the authorities failed to provide he supplied in good measure himself. 'Getting him to wash', Sonya confided to her diary, 'is like pulling teeth. I'll never get used to the dirt and the bad smell.' But what exasperated and saddened her even more than the sage's neglect of his body was what she considered a perverse misuse of his mind. She deplored his involvement in the village school at Yasnaya Polyana, Tolstoy's pet project of social reform, and considered even the composition of educational texts (in which she gave her husband valuable assistance) a wasteful diversion of unique gifts that should have gone into the creation of high art, i.e. novels. As was to be expected, she found his pursuit of the simple life via boot-making and chopping wood even more reprehensible. When it came to literature she was prepared to subordinate her own, not inconsiderable, talents—as an author of short stories and childrens' tales as well as a translator—entirely to the promotion of his. It was all the more hurtful to her when Tolstoy returned to narrative writing after a long period given over to the composition of politico-philosophical tracts that the fruit of his labours should turn out to be the egregiously misogynist 'The Kreutzer Sonata'.

In his attitude to women Tolstoy the man had always stood at a slight tangent to Tolstoy the artist, creator of Natasha in *War and Peace* and of Anna Karenina. We had already seen how in the sexual sphere he derogated the female, whether married or not, as the temptress dragging man down into sin. In other spheres too the writer, who entitled one of his works 'The Fruits of Enlightenment', upheld the prevailing patriarchal consensus. He believed the proper function of women to be the managing of the household, the bringing up of children and the diversion of their husbands. (A corollary of this, his conviction that they had no place in literature, caused Sonya's afore-mentioned neglect of her own talent for writing.) Tolstoy employed the most specious reasoning to downgrade women. They were, he argued, only capable of two emotions: love of husband and love of children; the former, he concluded with devastating logic, produced their love of dress and the latter their love of money.

'The Kreutzer Sonata' abounds with misogynist insights, pre-eminently a *bon mot* about marriage being a legalized form of prostitution. Other revelations the author puts into

the mouth of his spokesman-hero are 'women revenge themselves on men by playing on their senses' and the Essene-
inspired 'to do God's will we must refrain from repro-
ducing.' When the story, with its obvious personal over-
tones, appeared, Sonya felt as if she had been stripped bare
in public and dragged through the mud. 'Everyone', she
recorded in the diary,' feels desperately sorry for me, from
the Emperor down.' It must have been some compensation
for her, though, that in the privacy of the shared bedroom she
had insisted on retaining to test Tolstoy's adherence to the
Essene creed the apostle of sexual abstinence proved unable
to practise what he had preached on the printed page.

Ere many moons were out, however, Tolstoy, long sans
teeth, entered the seventh—sans taste, sans everything—age
of man, and sex, which had been yielding steadily to money
as the main bone of contention between the fractious spouses
anyway, became a dead issue. The financial background is
quickly sketched in. Basically the sources of Tolstoy's wealth
were twofold: income from the estate, and royalties from his
writings. Neither of these gave him an easy conscience. Estate
ownership ill-suited the arch-critic of property; as for royalties, they made his books dearer and therefore less accessible
to the broad public he wanted to reach and reform.

Sonya had always looked askance at his reform projects as
the hare-brained schemes of a deluded do-gooder. Although
she let herself be impressed into some of his pedagogic
enterprises, she remained deeply sceptical of the whole
exercise. 'Now', she wrote, 'he has a new hobby: teaching
Christian truths to the village children. They repeat after him
like parrots—but they'll turn into thieves and drunkards all
the same.' When one of the more father-fixated of her daughters announced to the assembled family that she wanted to
become a schoolteacher and devote herself to the *muzhiks,*
Sonya declared vehemently: 'You were born counts and
countesses, and counts and countesses you will remain!'

Given the cast of her mind one can imagine the pained
outrage with which she reacted to Tolstoy's schemes for
divesting himself of his wealth. Convinced, not entirely
without justification, that he was prepared to plunge the
family into (relative) poverty in pursuit of an otherworldly

ideal, she determined to fight him *à l'outrance*. There ensued a remorseless intra-marital tug-of-war during which Sonya's desultory stabs at suicide as a weapon of last resort were mirrored by Tolstoy's half-hearted attempts at flight. One point at issue was settled when Tolstoy, eager to be free of the stigma of property, arranged to have ownership of Yasnaya Polyana entirely made over to Sonya and the children (who thereupon engaged in protracted haggling over the division of the spoils).

The transfer of the estate of the family still left the royalties issue unresolved. In the early '90s Tolstoy announced in letters to the newspapers that he was waïving copyright to all his works published since 1881, thereby freeing any publisher who issued a reprint from having to pay him royalties. This gesture of self-abnegation provoked a fearful scene. Sonya screamed that the family needed the money he was giving away and that he was acting in this manner to publicize his own vendetta against her and the children. He riposted by calling her the most stupid and greedy creature he had ever met and accused her of perverting the children with 'her roubles'. In the war of attrition that followed Sonya had few effective allies. Most of the family, being grown up, had dispersed, whereas Tolstoy had a devoted group of disciples living at Yasnaya Polyana. The chief of the latter was one Chertkov, who stood in a relationship to Sonya that resembled Iago's to Desdemona. (Thus he told Tolstoy that he pitied him because, unlike himself, he was not married to 'a peerless spiritual companion'.) Sonya, her mind affected by battling a husband who had replaced the family by disciples in his affection, convinced herself that Chertkov was exercising a homosexual attraction on the near-senile Tolstoy. She went to the lengths of having a priest exorcize Chertkov's evil spirit from her temporarily absent husband's study—while simultaneously showing sufficient business acumen to set up her own publishing firm, for which she solicited start-up capital as well as the widowed Anna Dostoevsky's expert advice. By this means she set about the publication of Tolstoy's notebooks. To pre-empt the falsification of their content—since Sonya was liable to delete references unfavourable to herself—a team of disciples, headed by

Chertkov and Tolstoy's (afore-mentioned) daughter Sasha, set to and in the course of some marathon writing sessions made copies of all the relevant passages, which they then deposited in a bank at Tula.

The struggle for control over Tolstoy's writings was to continue without respite up to his very end. The octogenarian writer, for whom the keeping of a personal journal was a psychic necessity, commenced a new diary entitled 'For Myself Alone', which he tried to hide from Sonya's prying eyes by secreting it inside his shirt or boot-leggings. By ceaselessly ferreting around she nonetheless discovered it one day, shortly after having received a publisher's million-rouble offer for exclusive rights to Tolstoy's pre-1881 works (which included *War and Peace* and *Anna Karenina*) after his death. What she read in the diary convinced Sonya that he had made a will excluding her from the inheritance of his literary estate. Imbued with the notion that she was defending her childrens', and grandchildren's, very birthright, she strained every nerve—even threatening suicide—to make Tolstoy change his will, but he would not yield.

The tension between them became insupportable and in the end the 82-year-old semi-invalid, who had already had several strokes, decided on headlong flight from his dissension-racked home. Accompanied by his daughter Sasha and a servant, he set out on his stumble into the wilderness that ended in the station-master's cottage at Apostovo. His valedictory note to Sonya, 'My departure will cause you pain, but I couldn't do otherwise', plunged her into a frenzy of suicidal grief. Then in a precipitate change of mood she set out in pursuit of the moribund runaway. Reaching Tula to find the last train to Apostovo gone, she exerted her authority as a countess to have a locomotive fired up and a special train readied. At Apostovo Tolstoy's guardians, fearful of the effect of her proximity on the patient, denied her access to him until he was too close to death to recognize her. Then kneeling by his bedside she kissed his forehead and said, 'Forgive me.'

Thus ended a pain-suffused marriage in which husband and wife professed mutual love to the last, notwithstanding the fact that his conduct often left her teetering on the verge of suicide, and hers had driven him to flight on several occasions—till one proved terminal.

Clara Rilke

One of the major controversies that preoccupied the late Victorian middle classes was about the purpose of art. There were those who argued, with Tolstoy, that a work of art only derived validity from its social purpose, while their opponents rallied to Gautier's war-cry of *'L'Art pour l'art'*. Taking art-for-art's sake one step further, some dilettanti claimed, only half jokingly, that they were turning their very lives into works of art. The diverse manifestations of aestheticism provided a ready target for the barbs of satirists—*pace* 'the greenery yallery, Grosvenor Gallery, Foot-in-the-Grave young man' in Gilbert and Sullivan's *Patience*; a French contemporary had a character in one of his plays say, 'As for living, we let our servants do that for us.'

A European culture hero who furnished a text-book example of a life lived for art was Rainer Maria Rilke. The better to serve the muse this 'Edwardian' German poet spent a large part of his life sliding out of the obligations which family bonds and love relationships ordinarily impose on individuals. In Rilke's perception an artist was the executor of God's unfinished creation. By coincidence he himself constituted a particle of unfinished creation, being prematurely born, and often in indifferent health. The circumstances of Rilke's birth made his mother, already overwrought by the previous still-birth of a daughter, subject him to a psychologically damaging over-protective upbringing. She dressed him in girl's clothes till he went to school, and afterwards had him escorted on all his walks to and from that institution.

The Rilkes belonged to the dominant German minority in Habsburg-ruled Prague, the father coming from a military family and the mother from the propertied classes. Dissatisfied with marriage to a man both socially and culturally inferior—a marriage which ultimately ended in separation—Frau Rilke, the author of a slim volume of poems, abreacted her frustration by a display of snobbishness and exaggerated piety. She expressed her snobbery by permanently affecting 'dowagers' black' and, when entertaining, by pouring drinks from *vin ordinaire* bottles disguised under quality labels—and her religiosity by dragging her reluctant son to church where she made him kiss Christ's wounds on the wooden cruxifixes. Rilke's father had, after his discharge from the army, obtained a humdrum position in the Civil Service which offered scant scope for promotion. This rankled— as did the memory of the coveted officer's commission that eluded him during his service with the colours. Intent on the vicarious fulfilment of this ambition through his son, he sent young Rainer to a military preparatory school, and then to the Imperial Cadet Academy at Weisskirchen in present-day Czechoslovakia. (This academy, incidentally, made more of a mark in the annals of literature than of warfare. Robert Musil, another alumnus of Weisskirchen, used it as the setting for *Young Torless*, a study in adolescent sadism. For Rilke his years at the academy were a primer of horror which helped shape his literary personality.)

Despite the evidently low esteem in which he held the Cadet Academy and his subsequent rejection of soldiering as a career, Rilke remained sufficiently intrigued by the military mystique to compose *The Lay of Cornet Christoph Rilke*, a paean to the heroism of a putative eighteenth-century ancestor, who died at 19 fighting the Turks. (The *Lay* was to achieve huge sales in Germany and Austria during the Great War, when Rilke's poor physical shape, aided by judicious string-pulling, helped the 40-year-old escape front-line service.) The poet's interest in his antecedents was motivated by more than the simple search for a forbear round whose brief life an epic poem might crystallize. According to a dubiously authenticated family tradition the Rilkes had distant aristocratic forebears, and the poet was given to imaging himself the scion of a Carinthian noble line. At the same time, he made a veritable cult of poverty in poems transfiguring the poor into beings closest god in all creation. This spiritualized approach to poverty chimed in with his concurrent receptiveness to all emanations of 'Holy' Russia.

He toured that huge country, around 1900, with the redoubtable Lou Andreas-Salomé as his companion and guide. Hugenot-descended, Russian-born Lou Andreas-Salomé was a highly unusual female—a New Woman virtually before the term had been invented. Fifteen years earlier she had caused a sensation by living in a platonic *ménage à trois* with Friedrich Nietzsche and another man. Since she was both intellectual and beautiful, both men desired her, but she had a chastity fixation: having grown up as the only daughter in a family of sons, she claimed to look on all men as brothers. Nietzsche, whose offer of marriage she rejected, took this very much amiss, describing her retrospectively—with characteristic finesse—as 'a dry, dirty, nasty smelling monkey with false breasts'.

Lou had preserved her virginity throughout her subsequent marriage to Professor Andreas—a marriage contracted, after the elderly suitor's suicide attempt, on the express understanding that it was not to be consummated. (Their deep companionate relationship did not lack drama either. One afternoon a rattle in Andreas's throat woke Lou from her sleep: she had dreamt she was choking him for trying to take possession of her.)

The 21-year old Rilke fared quite differently at the hands of this woman fifteen years his senior. Not long after their first encounter they slept together; 'we became man and wife,' Lou wrote afterwards, 'even before we became friends.' She also corrected the prentice poet's overheated style and gave him an entrée to literary circles in Berlin, but would not let herself be tied down to a permanent relationship. Nonetheless, she remained a quasi-maternal, frequently consulted friend of Rilke's for many years.

Cut adrift from Lou after their Russian trip, Rilke settled, for want of anything better to do, at Worpswede, an artists' colony situated near Bremen. Here his aesthetic and erotic sensibilities were powerfully stirred by two aspiring women artists, one a practitioner of painting and the other of sculpture. The painter, Paula Becker, was blonde and vivacious; the sculptress, Clara Westhoff, dark and contemplative. To Rilke they appeared like two facets of a single personality, appealingly innocent in their bohemianism. He hymned Clara as 'doubly beautiful when listening to me read', and Paula as 'gentle and slender in her white virginity'. In reality Paula could no longer, thanks to an affair with the Worpswede painter Otto Modersohn, lay claim to the last mentioned attribute. Modersohn was married, but his wife's death, a few months after Rilke's arrival at Worpswede, obviated the need for the affair to remain clandestine. Paula let Rilke into her secret with the words:

> I did not tell you because I thought you knew. You always know and that is so beautiful. And today, I had to put it into words for its baptism, laying it reverently in your hands for you to stand godfather.

(Exalted metaphor-laden phrases formed the currency of daily speech in Rilke's circle; Lou Andreas-Salomé recalled the first rapture of their affair thus: 'We were like brother and sister, but from primeval times, before incest became a sacrilege.')

With Paula Becker set to become the wife of the widowed Modersohn, Rilke rather hurriedly married Clara Westhoff (who may have been pregnant). It is possible that he was pressured into marriage by her parents. At any rate, he fell ill—but the Westhoffs would brook no postponement. The ceremony over, the newly-weds travelled to a sanatorium in Saxony, where, strange to relate, they spent their honeymoon. Rilke's bout of ill-health was a psychosomatic reaction to the responsibilities of marriage, which he perceived, deep down, as an invasion of his privacy; he was already incubating the notion that, ideally, marriage ought to be a union in which each partner acts as the self-appointed guardian of the other's solitude. But the discrepancy between ideal and reality was to preoccupy him more in future; what faced him within a few short weeks of leaving the sanatorium was the news from Prague that his study subvention from a wealthy uncle had terminated with the marriage. Clara was now definitely pregnant and these two parallel developments deepened the misgivings about the married state he had already entertained at the time of the wedding. Undeterred by the eventual birth of a daughter (named Ruth) he set about persuading Clara that separation would benefit them both as artists, since it would give their individual potential scope to unfold and flower. Rilke's gospel of the self-sufficiency of the poet seems to have fitted in with Clara's own artistic credo since she made no demur; in fact, the letters in which she announced the dissolution of the matrimonial home to family and friends sound as if they had been written by him.

After their separation, Rilke remained on friendly terms with Clara; for instance, working as Rodin's secretary in Paris he arranged for her to study under the great sculptor. (Baby Ruth was meanwhile looked after by the Westhoffs.) Rilke's letter inviting Clara to Paris had stated characteristically: 'Let us make no preparation—which would entail responsibility for the outcome—but just work. . . . Our lofty aim remains to give everything to art and nothing to life.' (Apropos of art, life and Rodin: while the latter could teach Clara art, there was nothing instructive about living that the sculptor—whose path was littered with discarded mistresses, from Camille Claudel to Gwen John—could impart to Rilke.)

Rilke actually found it easier to convince his separated wife of the rightness of his action than he did other women of his acquaintance. Lou Andreas-Salomé criticized his sliding out of conjugal and paternal responsibility; in Paula Modersohn-Becker's estimate he had imposed his personality on Clara 'like a cloak for her king to walk over'. But none of this censure could erode Rilke's rock-like conviction that the dissolution of his marriage had been justified because it avoided a 'dangerous, hopeless standstill'. When Paula Modersohn-Becker died in childbirth at 31, the poet saw it as vindicating his philosophy: 'She slipped back', he wrote, 'from the first beginnings of great artistic achievement into family life, and then into the fate of an impersonal death she had not prepared for herself.'

What Rilke was meanwhile preparing for himself was a life of ceaseless peregrination—from Russia to Spain, and North Africa to Scandinavia, with frequent stays in Italy—so that the impact of those places on his vibrating consciousness might generate poetry. The financial problem involved was to some extent solved by Rilke's knack for eliciting patronage and hospitality, especially from titled and wealthy women. As a long-stay visitor of solicitous hosts, he sampled in turn Duino Castle (seat of the Princess Taxis), Capri, and a Swiss château. Since his stay with the Taxis, for instance, spawned the *Duino Elegies*, one of the masterworks of twentieth-century poetry, the hosts tended to feel honoured by his sponging on them. But Rilke's attractiveness to women extended beyond the ranks of those wealthy enough to dispense patronage. An astonishing number of ladies of limited means, but frequently with double-barrelled names suggesting elevated provenance, fell victim to Rilke's insinuating manner—expressed through dedicatory poems or exquisitely stylized letters (in French)—which they mistook for tokens of intense attachment.

In his encounters with attractive women, he often gave the impression of desiring a relationship in the full sense of the word—only to shrink back from committing himself at a crucial moment. What lay behind these bewildering oscillations was not sexual abstemiousness, but the self-anointed poet-priest's horror of involvement with another person. The choice before him, as he saw it, was the clear-cut one of either becoming a little human, or of ceasing to write; his very deficiencies as a man were the sustenance of his work.

Rilke's cavalier manner of asserting the primacy of his vocation over all other considerations was exemplified by his 'affair' with Mimi Romanelli, a Venetian society beauty and accomplished pianist. When, shortly after making her acquaintance, Rilke asked for a photograph and in a letter addressed her as *belle et admirable, il est bien naturel que je vous aime*, she attached a literal meaning to his words. Soon after, though, came the customary withdrawal, which Signora Romanelli took so badly that she nearly suffered a breakdown. On Rilke's next visit to Venice, the young woman's brother felt impelled to intercede with him on her behalf. The poet returned a dusty answer: 'You overrate me!', he expostulated 'I am no support, I'm only a voice.' And to Mimi, he wrote reproachfully: 'How different my life would have been these last days if you had undertaken to protect my solitude—protection I stood much in need of.' Then, compounding the offence, he went on to suggest that they jointly read the verse of the sixteenth-century poetess Gaspara Stampa, whom he dubbed a great lover because she had risen above the need to see her love requited. This unilaterally aborted affair could almost serve as a paradigm for all of Rilke's dealings with women after his separation from Clara.

He never let it come to a complete rupture, however, by the device of transforming these former potential lovers into friends, with whom he maintained intimate contact by means of a voluminous correspondence. With one solitary exception the women involved showed themselves prepared to go along with this scheme perfectly adapted to the disposition of their platonic seducer, and in so doing they felt comforted. To Clara, the first woman who had colluded with him in this manner, Rilke once wrote consolingly, 'Though you and I live many days journey apart, is there not a real house around us, invisible only to the outside world?' Her answer to this rhetorical question remains a matter for conjecture; similarly one can only guess at her reaction to Rilke's absence from their daughter's wedding, for which he apologized in the most perfunctory manner.

In 1926, a few short years after the unattended wedding, Rilke died of leukaemia in Switzerland. At the funeral his patroness, Princess Maria Taxis, placed a laurel wreath on the tomb inscribed *'Au poète incomparable'*. Few would quarrel with that evaluation of Rilke—but it might usefully be supplemented by an observation of his fellow poet and sometime friend Marina Tsvetayeva: 'Love lives on words and dies with deeds.'

Jarmila Hašek

In the extensive spaces of Eastern Europe bounded by Russians on one side and German-speakers on the other, there are about half a dozen countries with a combined population of over 100,000,000. These countries have long histories and rich, many-hued cultures. Musically they enjoy world-wide prestige, thanks to composers like Chopin, Dvořák, Smetana, Janáček, Liszt, Bartók, Kodályi and Enescu (not to mention conductors or instrumentalists). With regards to literature, however, the situation is drastically different. No native writer, resident in those countries, except one, has ever left his imprint on the consciousness of the Western reading public. (Kafka, writing in German, does not count.) The one exception was Jaroslav Hašek; in his *The Good Soldier Švejk* Hašek created an archetypal figure that is as much part of the world's literary heritage as Cervantes' Don Quixote or Mark Twain's Huck Finn. The creator of Švejk was born at Prague, capital of Habsburg Bohemia, in the 1880s, into a family precariously poised between working and lower middle class. Their failure to gain, and keep, a secure foothold among the petty bourgeoisie stemmed from the apparently congenital alcohol-addiction of most male Hašeks. As an adolescent Jaroslav exhibited none of his—ultimately fatal—addiction to drinking (and its counterpart, eating), but already then aspects of the fully-grown wayward character he eventually evolved into were becoming noticeable. He would leave home on a sudden impulse and, without a word to his parents, embark on months-long hikes through the country-side. Yet if he was irresponsible, he was at the same time preternaturally street-wise. Though penniless, he nonetheless kept body and soul together on his wanderings by playing on Catholic-Protestant rivalry in the saving of souls. In every village he came to he would knock at the door of the Catholic and Protestant presbytery in turn and claim he had just been turned away by the other; in consequence, he never went short of food or a bed for the night.

Such fertility of invention was to prove useful to Hašek the writer. It did less for Hašek the man because it impaired his grasp of reality—but on the threshold of manhood the development of his story-telling faculty mattered more than any other consideration. Having started his working life as a clerk in an insurance office, he walked out on his job one lunch-time, thereafter drifting into freelance journalism. The paper that offered him most scope for placing articles was *Animal World*; eventually he obtained regular employment there. At around this time he met Jarmila, the subsequent first (and only legitimate) Mrs. Hašek. Jarmila was a pince-nez-wearing, fashion-conscious blue stocking with brothers who were painters—for which reason she, at least initially, took a tolerant view of Hašek's bohemianism. However her father, a self-made bourgeois, saw him simply as an out-at-elbows anarchist. Hašek both loved Jarmila and behaved irre-sponsibly towards her by borrowing money which he never repaid. Her parents wanted the relationship ended, and she twice ran away from home to escape their strictures. In the end, though, everything seemed to turn out for the best: Hašek was offered the editorship of *Animal World* and the lovers married.

The newly-weds formed one of the most ill-matched couples imaginable. Jarmila was timid, prudish and inclined towards melancholy; Hašek convivial, anarchic and always craving to perpetrate some really shocking deed. At first he reined in his wonted conviviality by spending evenings at home; in effect, all this reformation amounted to was that he had beer brought from the pub instead of drinking it there. At work he subverted the dignity of editorship, regaling readers of *Animal World* with 'thoroughbred werewolves for sale' advertisements, and reporting the discovery of the fossil of an antidiluvian flee. Not surprisingly, the proprietor of the paper dismissed him, after which he opened kennels, which the authorities, alleging irregularities, speedily closed down. This debate prompted Jarmila to move back to her parents' house, whereupon Hašek made a bizarre suicide attempt that landed him in a mental home. Even there his capacity for invention did not desert him. He told his father-in-law he had gone into the institution to cure himself of alcoholism. After his discharge, Jarmila, who was still, despite everything, in love with Hašek, allowed herself to be impregnated by him; her consequent pregnancy obliged her parents to let them move together again.

The father-to-be had meanwhile returned to his favoured *métier* of freelance journalism. In search of colourful copy he frequented bars and whorehouses and was easily drawn back into his former inebriate nocturnal lifestyle. Things reached such a pitch that upon his mother's death it needed Jarmila's prodding—and her redemption of his black trousers from the pawnshop—to make Hašek attend the funeral at all, and to do so in suitable attire. Eventually their child, a boy, was born; they christened him Richard. On a subsequent Sunday Jarmila's parents paid them a visit and Hašek, saying the happy event called for a liquid celebration, went out to fetch some beer. He never came back. Concluding, after some hours, that he had walked out of Jarmila's life for good, the parents took her back to their house, where the child grew up fatherless.

For the next few years Jarmila, whose feelings for her wayward husband survived even his desertion, remained in ignorance of Hašek's whereabouts. Then, during the Great War, the rumour circulated in Prague that Hašek, by now a minor celebrity in his home-town, was fighting in Russia. This enabled Jarmila to tell little Richard that his father could not come to see him because he was away bearing arms for Emperor Franz Josef. On the Eastern Front, meanwhile, Czech soldiers, Hašek among them, were going over *en masse* to the Russians. He, however, differed from the majority of his compatriots, who from 1917 onwards fought against the Bolsheviks, by throwing in his lot with them. Hašek's commitment to the Revolution was one he took uncharacteristically seriously. The Bolsheviks gave him a chance to use his journalistic gifts by propagandizing foreign prisoners-of-war and Red Army men. He edited a newspaper at Ufa, a town in the interior of Russia bitterly fought over in the Civil War. At the Ufa printing works he met an employee, Shura Lvova, to whom he began to pay court. He kept the existence of his first family secret from Shura, signing a declaration that he was single and childless when they underwent a marriage ceremony in 1920. By this time Shura had joined the Communist Party, while he was secretary of the Party cell of a Red Army division. Not long after their marriage, strikes presaging a revolutionary situation broke out in Czechoslovakia. When news of this reached Hašek he hastened back to Prague with Shura, his new wife. By the time the couple arrived in the Czech capital, however, the authorities had by firm action averted the hoped-for revolution. In consequence, far from playing the rôle in the transformation of Czechoslovakia Hašek had conjured up in his imaginings, he found himself politically isolated, financially insecure and legally under threat—for, heedless bigamist though he was, he had a horror of being thrown into jail. At first he relied on his impish humour to keep reality at bay, for instance telling acquaintances that Shura, née Lvova, the Communist ex-printworker was a fugitive Russian aristocrat related to Prince Lvov (the first post-Tsarist Prime Minister). When his mood darkened he talked of suicide, but in the main he relied on alcohol to alleviate his sense of disappointment; once, in a drunken stupor, he knocked Shura to the floor. The months spent re-acclimatizing to Prague were the gestation period of *The Good Soldier Švejk*. In the meantime, though, a living had to be earned. Hašek appeared in cabaret, hired by a club-owner in the expectation that he would titillate his audience with sensational revelations about Soviet Russia; when Hašek did not live up to these expectations, his contract was not renewed. One positive result—also, in a way, for Hašek—of the cabaret publicity was that Jarmila found out about his return to Prague. She, now a secretary at the Chamber of Commerce, sent him a letter saying she had always believed he would survive the war and expressing the wish to see him again. Their reunion after over ten years, and a World War, was fraught with emotion—emotion heightened by Hašek's revelation of his second marriage, which he described as a 'frightful misunderstanding'. Jarmila told him of Richard growing up as the darling of the family, and agreed, despite everything, to keep in touch–though secretly, because she was, once again, fearful of her parents finding out about them. In her next letter she employed code in case it fell into Shura's hands, calling Richard the little bourgeois; she enclosed a page from his exercise book which read: '. . . our concierge is a tailor. My papa is a writer and is a legionary in Russia; he may be dead.' Then, after requesting a Russian memento for Richard, to show him he was not completely forgotten, she asked Hašek to confess to Shura that he had a son. On being told, Shura felt deeply hurt; it was one further blow to add to Hašek's drunken binges (from one of which he failed to return for three whole days), and to her isolation, both as a non-Czech speaker and a Russian surrounded by émigré compatriots who hated her as a Communist. At the next rendezvous Jarmila brought Richard along without, however, telling him who her journalist acquaintance was, and the father addressed the son in the formal second-person plural throughout.

In a letter sent shortly afterwards Hašek wooed Jarmila with a mixture of promises and pathos: 'I'll give up drinking', he wrote, 'as I had done in Russia. I still love you, please let me meet you if you're not ashamed of me.' He had good reason to insert the last conditional clause. Years of excessive drinking and over-eating—his notion of an in-between-meals snack was to walk about with a large brine-filled jar of pickled cucumbers under his arm wolfing them down one by one—had given his face the appearance of a peeled watermelon and his body the dimensions of a balloon. This regimen naturally affected his health, and stress compounded the symptoms of physical decline when the judicial authorities contemplated bigamy proceedings against him. Suffering severe stomach pains, he was haunted by the fear of cancer; the attack passed, however. Jarmila, who had kept up their secret trysts, finally let herself be persuaded to set up home with him. This arrangement was terminated soon afterwards, when Shura discovered herself to be pregnant and pressured Hašek to return to her. Shura's pregnancy turned out to be no more than a fiction designed to get him back. Jarmila did not feel entirely chagrined at this turn of events, having seen herself merely fulfilling the rôle of nurse during their cohabitation.

Throughout all this time Hašek had struggled to maintain the flow of instalments of *The Good Soldier Švejk*, irrespective of distractions (many of them, of course, of his own making). Now he accepted the argument of his publisher that he needed a tranquil writing environment, and moved to the picturesque and remote Castle Lipnice. Actually he did not so much move as abscond to Lipnice, behind Shura's back. Characteristically, he subsequently felt conscience-stricken about his disappearance and wrote Shura an explanation, but, equally characteristically, he had no sooner posted the letter than, repenting of his action, he tried the retrieve it—much to the annoyance of the village postmistress.

1922 saw him back with Shura in Prague. Fairly soon, though, their reunion was marred by Hašek going on a gargantuan drinking spree with his brother Josef (who eventually died of alcohol poisoning). The epithet gargantuan could equally well be applied to Hašek himself who by this time weighed close on twenty-four stone. Although suffering from loss of appetite he thought a reduced food intake would reflect on his manliness and therefore continued, out of a peculiarly Czech form of machismo, to force himself to overeat. The punishment he had long inflicted on his body was visibly beginning to take it's toll, but the unmistakable onset of ill-health coincided with an upturn in Hašek's financial fortunes. Royalties from *The Good Soldier Švejk* began to flow in, making the recipient entertain—for the first time in his life—notions of himself as a man of property.

Leaving Shura yet again, he returned to Lipnice, where he bought a neglected little house at the foot of the castle. Here Hašek inhabited just one threadbare room which he also, despite steadily deteriorating health, used as a venue for convivial drinking bouts. Heedlessly persisting in his self-destructive mode of life throughout a bitter winter, he went down with pneumonia in the New Year and died of heart failure soon after. Neither Jarmila nor Shura attended the funeral of the husband for whom desertion had remained an ever-open option throughout two marriages—a man who, in his biographer's words, was a 'creative egocentric psychopath incapable of helping himself'.

IV

Composers' Wives

Elvira Puccini

THE posthumous world première of Puccini's *Turandot* took place at Milan in the spring of 1926, a whole year behind schedule. The composer having died with the last two scenes of the opera merely sketched in, the job of completing the score had devolved upon the mediocre Franco Alfano, who, justifiably overawed by the magnitude of the task, had proceeded in a dilatory manner. Several postponed premières had served to heighten the general expectancy, so that when, on 25 April 1926, Toscanini leapt on to the dais in La Scala's orchestra pit to launch *Turandot* upon the waiting world, the atmosphere in the packed auditorium was electric. (Politics had generated contributory high voltage backstage. The La Scala directors had invited Mussolini to attend the première. He had accepted on condition that the Fascist anthem was played before the performance, whereupon Toscanini told them they had better engage another conductor—and since he was Puccini's musical executor, his will had prevailed over the Duce's.) The performance given by a less than ideal cast before a raptly attentive house was a triumph. Puccini's occasionally dissonant score elicited ever louder and longer ovations as the tale of the stone-hearted princess transformed by love unfolded on stage. Then, at the point in the Third Act where the slave girl Liu snatches up a dagger to stab herself, Toscanini lowered his baton, turned to the audience, and said in a husky voice: 'Here the maestro laid down his pen.' The huge house, which was hushed as the curtain descended, exploded into thunderous applause moments later. Toscanini, who had retired to his dressing room, felt too overwrought to return to the pit. The next night he conducted

74

the opera in its entirety, i.e. with Alfano's tacked-on ending. Shortly afterwards he cancelled his remaining engagements for the season and went on extended sick leave.

By macabre coincidence the point at which Toscanini had rung down the first night curtain marked not only the death of Puccini, but also, indirectly, that of a servant girl of his which he had—equally indirectly—caused. The roots of that tragedy stretched back to the early years of the composer's career. In the 1880s when, poor and struggling for recognition, he still resided on and off in his native Lucca, he frequently visited a married ex-schoolmate who owned a provision shop. This man was an amateur singer; his wife Elvira, who was similarly interested in music, used to play piano duets with Puccini. It did not take her long to realize that she preferred the impecunious composer to her complacent shopkeeper husband. Shortly after the birth of her second child Elvira fled the matrimonial home and, accompanied by her firstborn, moved in with Puccini. The steep upturn in the composer's fortunes a few years later appeared to confirm the rightness of that impetuous course of action, but Elvira's satisfaction at this welcome development was tempered by her simultaneous discovery of Puccini's unbridled addiction to womanizing. The man, who, in one opera after another, paid moving tribute to women's supreme capacity for sacrificial love, in fact prided himself on his promiscuity—as evidenced by his dictum, 'I am a mighty hunter of wild-fowl, beautiful women and good librettists.' (Incidentally, librettists were not tacked on to this ripe bit of bombast just for the sake of its triad form: whenever Puccini completed one opera he would begin a frantic search for suitable subject-matter for another, approaching numerous writers in the process; his entire leisure-time reading subserved the selfsame object.) As for his other two preferred types of quarry, there was a link between them that might have furnished the plot for a Rossini *opera buffa*. Puccini's fellow wild-fowlers, with whom he would carouse in a lakeside hut dubbed Club La Bohème (for obvious reasons), often helped him concoct alibis involving fictitious hunting and boating trips in order to hoodwink Elvira as to the real reasons for his frequently night-long absences.

Later on, when Puccini's conducting engagements in various European capitals necessitated repeated trips abroad, he could, of course, avail himself of the opportunity for philandering without having to resort to subterfuge to allay the suspicions of his increasingly jealous partner. Elvira's jealousy was compounded by a recurring morbid fear that, since Puccini was not tied to her legally, he might—notwithstanding the fact that he had fathered a child upon her—just abandon her if the fancy took him. It was a wholly imaginary fear. Prey to worries of this kind the woman once renowned for her dark-blond hair plaited into a helmet, hour-glass figure and stately deportment coarsened into a thick-waisted matron who, barely 40, began to dress in unbecoming black. To add to the impression of prematurely middle-aged embitterment she treated the neighbours in the village to which the successful Puccini had moved with ill-disguised condescension.

He, meanwhile, held advancing age at bay by having a pharmacist friend from Lucca provide him with a steady supply of tablets, lotions, hair dyes and—naturally—aphrodisiacs, the last-mentioned being needed to demonstrate that his reach had not outrun his grasp, as well as to convince Elvira that he was not wasting his vital juices on others. Another, vastly costly item of the composer's consumption that needed steady replenishing were 'fast' motor cars. One day, having made his chauffeur take unnecessary risks, he had a nasty accident; the resulting compound fracture of his right leg left him bedridden for weeks. In the new situation Elvira grew into the rôle of an endlessly solicitous nurse, and this brought them closer together. Helped by the fact that Puccini's immobility precluded any philandering, they soon experienced something akin to a second honeymoon, with Elvira discarding her black attire for ribbons and furbelows. When it transpired that the invalid required a longer bed rest than anticipated, she engaged a village girl, Doria Manfredi, to assist her as maid-of-all-work. Doria, a homely-looking 16-year-old endowed with the twin virtues of diligence and equanimity, proved a real find. She worked all the hours the Good Lord had sent, nursing, laundering, ironing and waiting at table; when, in addition, it became clear over a period of time that no word of gossip ever passed her lips, she became accepted as virtually a member of the Puccini household.

This household had meanwhile added the cachet of respectability to that of wealth. Elvira's husband having died in 1904, Puccini lost little time in regularizing his liaison with the 'relict'. But, alas for the newly fledged husband's peace of mind, in human relations A frequently does not lead on to B. Marital status, which might have been expected to make Elvira a happier person by banishing the spectre of abandonment forever, in fact made her harder to live with. Once invested with, so to speak, legal title to her husband, she grew possessive to a degree that bordered on the insane.

When Puccini had at last recovered from his leg injury he, of course, resumed his amorous forays into the various European capitals and centres of operatic life. His amours were usually what our coarser age terms one-night-stands and involved chorus girls or shop assistants (although the evidence suggests that he also had a heartfelt brief *affaire* with a London society hostess, who remained a supportive friend for years thereafter).

In one of his letters to Elvira from abroad Puccini articulated his personal creed concerning profane and sacred love in explicit, if euphemistically couched, terms:

> All artists cultivate these little gardens in order to delude themselves into thinking that they are not old and finished and torn by strife. You imagine immense affairs; in reality it is nothing but a sport to which all men, more or less, dedicate a fleeting thought without, however, giving up that which is serious and sacred—that is the family. . . .

On another occasion he wrote that it was possible to compose a march after drinking a pail of wine, 'but for a love duet one must have a warm heart and a cool head'. By acting on this casuistic philosophy with its inbuilt mental reservations, Puccini managed to have the best of both worlds—respectability at home and licence at abroad—for a good part of his adult life, at whatever psychic cost to Elvira. Her jealous tantrums were a constant trial, but thanks to the restorative powers of aphrodisiacs—dependence on which even made him consider monkey gland injections—he contrived to discharge his minimal conjugal obligations, while continuing to cut a swathe through the chorus lines of the opera houses of Europe. For all that one major bugbear continued to haunt him during recurrent, often prolonged, musically fallow periods: the want of good libretti to reignite the damped down fires of his creativity. At such times he felt too debilitated for the pleasures of the chase—whether after wildfowl or women—fully to assuage his melancholy.

The problem of 'composer's block' was, of course, not unique to Puccini. A colleague and virtual contemporary of his, Richard Strauss, experienced similar intermittent moods of sterility. Strauss, however, had such an insouciantly egotistical streak in his make-up that when he ran short of external inspiration he turned to his own person as a fit subject for musical treatment. (Such solipsism was a genetic trait; his father had described himself as the best horn-player in the world, adding 'that is not a boast, but an admission'). When Strauss composed his *Symphonia domestica*—which, scored for ninety-six players, gave a new meaning to the term domestic—he declared with matching complacency: 'I don't see why I shouldn't compose a symphony about myself; I find myself just as interesting as Alexander or Napoleon.'

Strauss and Puccini shared many attributes. For one, they both stood in direct line of succession to their respective countries' newly deceased 'national composers'—Wagner and Verdi. For another, both were self-centred, money-grabbing and catatonically indifferent to the moral dimension of politics. (Strauss accepted the presidency of the Nazi Reichsmusikkammer, Puccini honorary membership of the Fascist Party.) Thirdly, and most germane to our subject, they both married possessive women given to outbursts of morbid jealousy.

There was one crucial difference, though, as regards the latter: whereas Elvira Puccini had abundant reason for jealousy, Pauline Strauss had absolutely none. Richard Strauss was a model bourgeois—an uxorious husband and smugly dutiful paterfamilias in life as well as (*pace* the *Symphonia domestica* with its Papa, Mama and Baby themes) imagination. None of this prevented the overbearing Frau Pauline—who, once miffed by the Parisians' cool reception of her husband's work, exclaimed, 'It's time we came back here with bayonets'—from using a trivial incident involving mistaken identities to blow up a gale-force matrimonial storm. One day, while the composer was away on tour, she opened a letter addressed to him which read 'Darling love! Do get me the tickets. Your faithful Mitze' (followed by the sender's surname and address). Having clapped eyes upon this missive she, without any further ado, ordered her lawyer to institute divorce proceedings, and refused even to open the letters an increasingly mystified Strauss sent back from his tour. Once back in Berlin the latter managed, through adroit detective work, to disentangle the skein of mistaken identities behind the incriminating letter, and calm eventually returned to the Strauss household. Several years later the composer, stuck for suitable subject-matter and rummaging in his memory, called the ludicrous episode to mind and decided to turn it into an opera—with a libretto written by himself. The resultant work called *Intermezzo* (and incorporating the letter incident and Pauline's tantrums almost verbatim) has kept its—admittedly secondary—place in the operatic repertoire up to this day.

For Puccini, in contrast, the crisis provoked by an overjealous spouse provided the very opposite of material for an *opera buffa*. One night a coughing fit had interrupted Elvira's sleep a little before midnight. The piano in Puccini's study, normally in use when he was composing, was silent, but voices were audible downstairs. Impelled by manic suspicion she leapt out of bed and, still in her nightgown, flew down the stairs—to come upon Puccini engaged in conversation with the maid Doria by the open door leading into the garden. In an access of raging jealousy which the composer was powerless to calm she accused the stunned girl of adultery with her husband. Protestations of innocence only increased Elvira's fury which, expressed in gutter language, drove Doria to her room; there the ashen-faced, trembling girl locked herself in while her mistress spent the next hours frantically hammering at the door. Early next morning she escaped to her mother's house, to which Elvira eventually followed her, repeating her accusations. In the afternoon the much-provoked wife pursued the hapless girl through the village streets calling down the curses of heaven on her timidly bowed head. The locals, only too well aware of Puccini's proclivities, gave credence to Elvira's story and almost prevailed upon the priest to drive Doria from the village. The Manfredi brothers, for their part, made threats against the life of Doria's alleged seducer, and Puccini found it expedient to visit Paris for a performance of *Tosca* at the Opéra-Comique.

On his return he learnt that Doria had immured herself in her mother's house and was refusing to touch any food. He contrived, at some personal risk, to see her, but she was now beyond the reach of her proffered solace. A few weeks later, reduced to a near skeleton, she took poison and died in agony; her mis-spelt suicide note was a last protestation of innocence. When the consequent autopsy found her indeed to have been *virgo intacta*, local opinion turned so vehemently against her persecutor that Elvira, fearing for her life, did not set foot outside the house for days. For Puccini who had once again removed himself—this time to Rome—this reversal of public sentiment meant that on his return he attracted sympathy as the object of demented jealousy in place of the former censure.

When the Manfredis instituted proceedings against Elvira for persecution and defamation of character, she announced she would contest the action. Still locked into her paranoid delusions she claimed to possess proof of Doria's illicit liaison with her husband. Puccini's simultaneous attempts to dissuade the dead girl's next-of-kin from bringing the action and Elvira from contesting it having failed, the case came to trial. Not surprisingly the judge found Elvira guilty and sentenced her to five months jail, a fine and payment of the costs. Thereupon Puccini made his wife replace her lawyer with one of his own choice, who appealed the sentence. During the run-up to the hearing of the appeal the composer approached the Manfredis, offering them 12,000 lire to drop the lawsuit. To his intense relief Doria's brothers accepted the offer; they spent the money on putting up a monument to her, and acquiring a comfortable lakeside house for themselves.

Having succeeded in putting an end to the seemingly interminable repercussions of the whole unhappy affair, Puccini remained conscience-stricken. Each year on the anniversary of Doria's death he would—unless he was abroad—walk alone to the cemetery to place a bunch of flowers on her grave. He also conceived another, more widely resonant mode of expiation. When, years later, he embarked on the composition of his final work *Turandot*, he transposed Doria, the maid-of-all work, into the character of Liu the slave girl, metamorphosing a suicide caused by psychotic jealousy into self-immolation through transfiguring love.

But art is one thing, life quite another. Soon after the clamour surrounding the Doria Manfredi case had died down, Puccini was pursuing his clandestine amours with the same avidity as before. A major reason for his chagrin at the outbreak of hostilities in 1914 was that war restricted his freedom to travel abroad and to spend the nights in anonymous hotel bedrooms. In the later war years he carried on a lengthy liaison with a German officer's wife, who resided just inside Switzerland and whom he visited so often that the frontier guards suspected him of spying. For all the pain this ceaseless philandering caused Elvira, she evinced a fierce loyalty to him. When it was rumoured that Mascagni, composer of *Cavalleria rusticana* and long-term friendly rival of Puccini, had been nominated for the Senate, she vowed she would renounce Italian citizenship and emigrate over such a slight to her husband. (He was in fact eventually made a senator—an honour he affected to disdain by signing letters to friends *sonatore*, i.e. musician, a pun on *senatore*.)

Thus the Puccini marriage continued routinely on the terms of the unequal bargain he had outlined in the aforementioned letter about all artists needing to cultivate 'a little garden'. How tragic that this inequitable bargain, which metaphorically poisoned the life of one woman, should have been the gratuitous cause of another one taking literal poison. And how apt that Puccini, the beneficiary of the bargain, should, while composing *Turandot*, have laid down his pen at the precise point of his—imaginatively transposed—surrogate victim's death.

Lina Prokofiev

A budding operatic soprano need not have professional singers for parents—but it helps. Nor is it essential for her to be a good linguist, but that, too, can be helpful. Lina Codrina's parents were both singers. Her facility in languages came from a Spanish father and a part-Polish, part-French mother who spoke some Russian; she herself grew up from the age of 10 in English-speaking New York. This gift of tongues, which was nearly to cost Lina her life after the Second World War, propelled her into romance at the end of the First. In 1918, when she was 21, Lina and some fellow music students went to a Carnegie Hall concert given by the pianist-composer Sergei Prokofiev; soon after she became personally acquainted with the totally apolitical and self-absorbed artist, whose 'Classical' Symphony had already brought him fame in his mid-twenties.

Tall, stiff, with white-blond hair, Prokofiev was attracted to the petite Mediterranean-looking Lina both on account of her appearance and her linguistic facility. She also felt drawn to him, though he made little attempt to disguise his egotism. The romance encouraged by Lina's mother—a personal acquaintance of Rachmaninov—matured over the next few years. So did their respective careers. Prokofiev composed the opera *The Love for Three Oranges* and had his ballet 'The Buffoon' staged by Diaghilev's Ballets Russes at Paris; she performed a song cycle of his at Milan, and made her operatic début—as Gilda in Verdi's *Rigoletto* at La Scala—in 1922. In the same year Prokofiev, who had been commuting across the Atlantic for his collaborative effort with Diaghilev, moved back to Europe. He set up home with Lina at Ettal, near Oberammergau (in Bavaria). She became pregnant in due course, and a son, Sviatoslov, was born to them in 1924. In between those two events they went through a civil ceremony; the marriage certificate listed him as having a Nansen passport (for stateless persons) and her a Spanish one. Prokofiev's statelessness—the consequence of having left the new-born Soviet Union in 1918—bothered him. This was not on account of his somewhat indeterminate legal status, but because, despite his years in the West, he still felt profoundly Russian. This attachment to his native country made him maintain close contacts with ex-colleagues, such as the composer Nicolas Miaskovsky, who were still living there. Director of the Moscow Conservatoire under the Soviets, Miaskovsky maintained a regular correspondence with the exile in which, presumably out of fear of the censor, he minimized the extent to which Russian life had deteriorated since the Revolution. This resulted in the politically unversed Prokofiev remaining quite ignorant of the situation inside the Soviet Union. Returning there briefly in 1927, after a ten years' absence, he arrived at the tail-end of a period of experimentation, when avant garde works like Shostakovich's *The Nose* and Alban Berg's *Wozzek* had received Russian premières, and failed to grasp the way the cultural climate was changing.

Back again in the West he was forced by the decreasing yield from his composer's royalties to undertake more hours as a concert-pianist. The family was now living in Paris, where in 1928 Lina bore him another son, Oleg. The following year he left her alone again to undertake a second lengthier trip to the U.S.S.R. on which he renewed acquaintance with ex-colleagues from pre-war St. Petersburg Conservatoire days. Lina, neither privy to these friendships, nor emotionally attached to Russia—although she knew the language—felt their paths beginning to diverge. At the same time acquaintances like the composer Nicolas Nabokov (cousin of Vladimir) observed that Prokofiev 'could be as boorish with his wife as with his friends'.

The early '30s brought an upturn in the composer's financial circumstances. They could afford to hire governesses and cooks, and among visitors invited to their leased summer villa near Biarritz were celebrities of the standing of Chaliapin and Chaplin. Back in Paris, however, Prokofiev still insisted that the family inhabit a furnished apartment—the reasons being that he wanted to keep the option of an eventual return to Russia open.

Two simultaneous developments helped strengthen the

prodigal's penchant for returning. For one, Stalin had dissolved R.A.P.M. (the Revolutionary Association of Proletarian Musicians), who were always sniping at Prokofiev as a bourgeois who had emigrated after the Revolution, and had set up the comprehensive Composer's Union in their place. For another, Prokofiev was persuaded that whereas in France he faced competition from the likes of Ravel and Honegger, in the Soviet Union he would bestride the musical scene like a colossus. On his next trip to the country he definitely decided on the move, though he took a few more years to implement the decision. He came to regret it eventually, but the first person to pay the price was Lina. She, a Westerner in every sense of the word, sophisticated, polyglot, a member of *le tout Paris*, had exchanged the 'city of lights', her home for over a decade, for Moscow—drab, provincial, austerity-ridden, and (the year being 1936) fear-infested.

In one way, of course, the move had been long prepared for: *en famille* the Prokofievs had customarily spoken Russian. Furthermore, even as residents of Moscow they enjoyed a vastly more comfortable life-style than ordinary Muscovites. As for fellow members of the 'privilegentsia', such as Composers' Union colleagues, they envied Prokofiev's access to foreign travel and the cornucopia—a streamlined blue Ford car, tailored clothes, patent leather shoes—he garnered abroad. Not that those material advantages could totally make up for the shock to the composer's system when barely months after returning, he saw Shostakovich victimized over his allegedly 'pornophonic' opera, *The Lady Macbeth of the Mtsensk District*. The witch-hunt of his only potential rival made Prokofiev retreat into the world of childlike imaginings: he composed *Peter and the Wolf*.

While her husband approximated to being a Socialist (at least in his fetish of work) Lina was a socialite; she escaped from the drabness and insecurity of Soviet life into socializing with foreign embassy personnel and other non-Russians—a highly suspect activity in Soviet eyes that was to cost her dear. Another motive behind Lina's intense pursuit of social contacts was that she and Prokofiev, who in the past had often spent time apart from necessity, were now doing so from choice. The reason for this suggests itself: the marriage, as evidenced by ever louder sounds of altercation emanating from the Prokofievs' apartment, was heading for the rocks. Lina, who had opposed the move in advance, regretted it bitterly afterwards, and felt that she had been sacrificed to Prokofiev's personal ambition. Nor did the children constitute a strong marital bond since Prokofiev had, in the words of one acquaintance, 'a distant, even military relationship to them'.

As the marriage headed towards collapse Europe edged closer to war. In 1938 Prokofiev collaborated with the film director Eisenstein in the creation of the government-commissioned patriotic epic, *Alexander Nevsky*. But while Stalin was with one hand mobilizing the country's psychological defence, he was undermining it with the other. The purges, so destructive of Soviet morale continued; their victims in 1939 included the theatre director Meyerhold.

Since Meyerhold had been a collaborator, as well as close friend, of Prokofiev his death shook the composer profoundly. In search of recuperation and of the peace needed for compositional labours, he spent that summer, *sans famille*, at a rest home for intellectual workers in the Caucasus. One of the other guests there was an intense young woman exactly half his age, by the name of Mira Mendelson. The two became acquainted; Mira, a student of literature and a would-be writer, felt intrigued, and privileged, when Prokofiev talked to her of how Romain Rolland's Beethoven biography was influencing his current compositions. He, in turn impressed by her well-informed devotion to the Russian literary heritage, was probably, as composers are wont to do when they meet people with a literary bent, appraising her as a potential librettist. Mira would certainly be a better helpmeet for Prokofiev than Lina, whose skills as a polyglot hostess had no place—outside an anthropological museum—in 1930s' Moscow. Since what Stalin demanded of Soviet composers was the creation of epics that tapped into the national cultural heritage, the bookish and doting Mira represented precisely the sort of collaborator Prokofiev could have wished for. In addition she was 24, as compared to Madame Prokofiev's 42 years. In other respects, though, the balance of advantage lay with Lina who had better looks, more poise and greater vivacity—not to mention dress-sense—than her rival. But all those personal considerations paled finally into insignificance beside one existential fact: Russian-born Mira had grown up as a child of the October Revolution and her Jewish father, an academic specialist on Marxist economics, was a Party member in good standing. As against that Lina was a foreigner who, in the paranoid atmosphere of the purges and war fever, aroused suspicion by a heedless display of Western preferences and attachments. Even Russian-born Prokofiev was looked at askance as a former emigré who had since returning kept one foot in the West by means of foreign tours. The truth of the matter was that the composer, politically ignorant and with a seventeen-year gap in his experience of Soviet reality, felt confused and vulnerable after witnessing the witch-hunt against Shostakovich and the arrest and death of Meyerhold. Under the circumstances he could not be blamed entirely for turning to Mira Mendelson as someone equipped with the antennae—not to mention the Party connections—required to stave off danger to himself.

After an eighteen-month openly conducted 'courtship' the composer finally left his family early in 1941 to move in with Mira and her parents (while continuing to support Lina and the boys financially). A few months later war impacted on Russia with such devastating force that in a matter of weeks the authorities evacuated leading artistic personalities from endangered Moscow to places of safety in the remote south. Prokofiev and Mira travelled together with Miaskovsky, Chekhov's widow and other luminaries to the Caucasus; Lina and the boys perforce stayed behind in Moscow.

Apart from the hardships the war imposed heightened activity on the three main protagonists of our story. Prokofiev, in addition to much else, composed the music for Eisenstein's *Ivan the Terrible* and worked on *War and Peace*, for which Mira was distilling the libretto from Tolstoy's novel. Lina meanwhile did interpreting and translation work for foreign diplomats, particularly the U.S. Embassy in Moscow, whose work-load the war-time alliance had enormously increased. By 1943, with the Germans in irreversible retreat, the assorted artistic evacuees, including Prokofiev and Mira, were returning to Moscow again. Even though the composer was now within easy reach of his former family, he hardly ever saw them. His stay in the capital was not to be a prolonged one, however. Prokofiev suffered from—undiagnosed—high blood pressure. During the last war winter he had a dizzy spell, took a fall and got badly concussed. He required months to get back on his feet and was never properly fit again. This semi-invalidity made him and Mira, his ever attentive nurse, spend increasing periods of time in country dachas and rest homes after the war.

The post-war years for Russia hardly signified a return to peace in the full sense of the word. Superimposed on war-time scars which would take years to heal, the Soviet body politic showed new self-inflicted wounds. Soldiers who had been German prisoners-of-war were sent to Siberia as collaborators with the enemy, and the unfolding Cold War against the West took its toll among members of the artistic community. First of all writers like the poetess Akhmatova came under the lash, soon followed by composers. Prokofiev, who had already suffered a major blow—cancellation of the première of *War and Peace* (Part II)—was, in company with Shostakovich, Khachaturian and Miaskovsky, pilloried as a formalist, i.e. a snobbish, decadent obscurantist. Like Shostakovich, who, 'implicated' in the *The Lady Macbeth of the Mtsensk District* scandal a decade earlier, had subtitled his next work 'a Soviet composer's reply to justified criticism', Prokofiev abased himself before his accusers. 'Formalism', he declared in a public statement, 'is alien to the Soviet people. It leads to the impoverishment and decline of music.' He went on to promise that his work in progress, the opera *The Story of a Real Man*, would contain 'clear melodies and harmonic language'.

In his private life, meanwhile, all was disharmony. Mindful of the premium the Soviet establishment, in its puritanical post-war period mood, placed on marital respectability, he married Mira after seven years' cohabitation, in January 1948. (The legality of this second union was dubious since his first had never been dissolved—Lina having persistently resisted demands for a divorce.) At any rate, the marriage had been in January; in February Lina was arrested and charged with espionage for a foreign power. At her trial a K.G.B. agent gave evidence that she had been frequenting the American and other foreign Embassies. In the xenophobic Cold War climate of the time the sentence—twenty-two years in Siberia—had the inevitability of Greek tragedy.

It is not known whether Prokofiev reproached himself for having deprived Lina of the protection of his name by divorcing her—in whatever way it was done—so he could marry Mira. The circumstantial evidence points to the fact that the composer at no point attempted to exert such marginal influence as he, a Stalin Prize winner, possessed to help his former wife. (We must remember, though, that in the same fear-shadowed year, 1948, a Soviet public figure with far more clout than Prokofiev, namely Prime Minister Molotov, stood supinely by while his wife was hauled off to the Gulag for frequenting the Israeli Embassy.) Another shock event that coincided with, and darkened, Prokofiev's second honeymoon was the death of the film director Eisenstein, whom he had esteemed no less highly, as a man and an artist alike, than Meyerhold. He must have been saddened to remember that the fruit of their last collaborative effort, *Ivan the Terrible*, Part II, had withered on the vine (i.e. been denied a showing in Soviet cinemas). Prokofiev's new opera, *The Story of a Real Man*, did not fare very much better. However, by the time of its first production—and negative reception—he was already busy at work on the music for the ballet *The Tale of the Stone Flower*. Assisted by Mira—librettist, amanuensis and nurse—Prokofiev kept moving on and upward on the treadmill of creation, in spite of his gradually failing health. With headaches and dizzy spells getting worse, he finally succumbed, aged 62, on 5 March 1953, the same day as Stalin died. Because of this macabre coincidence there was a few days' delay before the news of his death reached the Soviet public, or the world at large.

Shortly after Stalin had passed from the scene, his successors set up the Pospeliev Commission (named after its chairman) to investigate breaches of 'Socialist legality' affecting Party high-ups and their families. As a result of the commission's labours, prisoners like Polina Molotov were soon released from incarceration in Siberia. The great mass of less well-connected camp inmates, however, had to wait till Khrushchev's 'amnesty' three years later before being let out of the Gulag. Their number included Lina Prokofiev. She, the socialite, had astonishingly withstood the rigours of Socialist re-education through labour. Eventually she was allowed to leave the Soviet Union. She came to Britain, where one of her sons, Oleg, was working as an artist. (The other, Sviatoslov, practised architecture in Moscow.) Over here she attracted some notice by recording the narrator's rôle in *Peter and the Wolf* with the Scottish National Orchestra in 1986. She died in 1989, year of the demise of Stalinism in Eastern Europe, thereby echoing the coincidence of her husband's death with that of Stalin himself.

V

Wives and Secretaries

Friederike and Charlotte Zweig, Mamaine and Cynthia Koestler

THIS chapter is about the suicide pacts of two married couples who, though distant in time and place, shared many common characteristics. In each case the husband was a writer who had been married before and the wife was the husband's secretary. Both husbands were older than the wives, who of their own volition submerged their lives totally in those of their marriage partners. In consequence when the husbands resolved to commit suicide, the wives (each with years still ahead of her) joined willingly in the act of self-extinction. In addition both husbands were Central European Jews, but that is where the similarity ends. Stefan Zweig grew up in the long drawn-out sunset of pre-1914 Europe, Arthur Koestler in the hectic iconoclastic '20s. Zweig probed the convolutions of the human psyche; Koestler quarried for ideas, political and scientific. In personality and life-style they also differed markedly: Zweig, a high-minded aesthete, practised grand-seigneurial aloofness amidst his collection of books, musical MSS and other memorabilia; Koestler, the *bohémien* polymath, wallowed in intellectuality, while seeking the *frisson* of public campaigning, sexual aggrandisement and alcoholic excess.

Of Zweig it can be said, probably with greater truth than of most, that he had been born with a silver spoon in his mouth. As the second son of a wealthy Viennese textile manufacturer, he enjoyed privilege unencumbered by responsibility. A polyglot family background gave him linguistic facility which leisurely travel enhanced further. Translations and

90

travel impressions led him on to creative writing. A steady output of novellas, essays and poems established him, not yet 30, as a well-regarded man of letters with an assured income. At around this time he met Friederike von Winternitz, a minor writer who was to become his first wife. Though married, and a mother, Friederike felt so drawn to the aspiring *littérateur* that, with her two small daughters in tow, she left von Winternitz to set up home with him. In the First World War, Zweig veered from short-lived patriotic fervour to a deeply-felt pacificism; his drama *Jeremiah*, performed in Switzerland in 1917, caught the mood of war-weary Europe and earned him an international reputation. In the 1920s, as, thanks to a steady output of novellas, biographies and literary studies, his fame spread still further, he acquired a large house with a beautiful outlook at Salzburg. Here Friederike catered for a stream of visitors—including international celebrities like H. G. Wells, Ravel and Bartók—supervised the household, and brought up the children, while Zweig immersed himself in what he dubbed the *Betrieb*, or literary production line. There were tensions below the surface, however. When engaged on a literary project, Zweig could grow insufferably tetchy over the incompetence of secretaries, the noise of the children, or Friederike's frantic socializing. Though extremely hard-working, he would take off, on a whim, every now and then and undertake solitary train journeys to Italy or the South of France. These jaunts did not lead to lapses from marital fidelity, though Zweig, a well-dressed, *soigné* figure with a much photographed face, enjoyed being recognized and deferred to by female readers encountered en route.

In the early 1930s the political horizon darkened on both sides of the Austro-German border that almost skirts Salzburg. Germany was engulfed by Nazis, and in Austria the right-wing Catholic Dollfuss[1] set up a dictatorship. The Socialists tried to stop him by a resort to arms and went down to defeat. In the aftermath of the fighting, in a government-decreed search for illegal weapons, the police raided Zweig's house at Salzburg.

1. Engelbert Dollfuss (1892–1934): Austrian statesman who replaced parliamentary democracy by Catholic authoritarianism.

This was a ludicrous exercise, since the apolitical Zweig had no connection whatever with the Socialists; moreover, as a pacifist, he totally opposed the use of arms. He considered the police action an assault, both on his privacy and his reputation. Outrage at the raid and apprehension of the ominous developments in nearby Germany made him impatient to shake the dust of Salzburg off his feet; having, by coincidence, embarked on a biography of Mary Stuart as his next writing project, he went to London to settle down to the labour of researching the life of the Scottish queen. Friederike accompanied him briefly to assist in flat-hunting and the selection of a suitable secretary. By the time of her return to Salzburg the *Betrieb* had been started up again in an apartment at Portland Place, within reach of the British Museum, to which a 26-year-old bilingual, German and English speaking, secretary reported every morning.

The latter, a German-Jewish refugee by the name of Lotte Altmann, was a well-educated, earnest young woman, who proved a perfect helpmate to the author; she seemed presciently aware of his needs and fell in uncomplainingly with his every whim. To Zweig, Lotte represented a welcome change from Friederike, who was even now adding to the past catalogue of her perceived shortcomings as hyperactive hostess, argumentative spouse and indulgent mother of boisterous daughters a marked reluctance to sell the Salzburg house. To Friederike maintaining the house meant continuity with a past whose passing she regretted; besides, the Austrian housing market was still, a few short years after 1931, in a depressed state.

The work on Mary Stuart having proceeded apace, Zweig decided to winter on the Riviera with Friederike while putting the finishing touches to the manuscript. As he needed secretarial assistance for that, he got Friederike to send Lotte a letter inviting her formally to join them at Nice. In reality Zweig had already started an affair with the doting young woman, but he felt propriety demanded such subterfuge. He affected indifference in her presence, for instance by telling Friederike not to point out the scenery to Lotte since she lacked all appreciation of beauty.

In the spring he and Lotte went back to England, and

Friederike returned to the children in Vienna and to the unresolved problem of the house sale. Convinced that she was obstructing the transaction to thwart his plans for taking up permanent residence in England, he kept pressing her to sell up, even on unfavourable terms; eventually they divested themselves of the property, at a heavy loss, in 1936. In the same year Zweig incubated the plot of the novel *Beware of Pity* (which, like half a dozen other works of his, was turned into a film). The title was uncannily appropriate, for soon after the sale of the house he informed Friederike that he wanted a separation. At the same time the author, who in *Letters from an Unknown Woman* had shown deeply compassionate insight into the female psyche, felt constrained to soften the blow; he therefore wrote: 'I am convinced this is the only way out, yet I feel deep pain. Please think of me only as your best friend.'

Friederike was persuaded to file for divorce, in the Austrian courts, on grounds of mental cruelty—with her daughter testifying that Zweig would lock himself in his study and refuse to speak to anyone—and obtained a decree nisi. In the meantime the grains in Europe's hour-glass were running out. The event Zweig had foreseen with dread, the Nazi take-over of Austria, took place. As disaster followed disaster, there was one glimmer of good news: Friederike and the girls found refuge in France. Soon after, Hitler's attack on Poland started the Second World War. By this time Zweig, fearing Nazi bombs on London, had removed himself to Bath. Here in the first week of the war, he and Lotte had a Register Office wedding. The ceremony over, they wrote a joint letter to Friederike in Paris asking for forgiveness and inviting her to come and visit them in their new home. Zweig's pangs of conscience about the cast-off Friederike soon paled into virtual insignificance beside his depression over steadily worsening news. In the first war winter he mourned the deaths of four dear colleagues—Freud, Schickele,[2] Toller,[3]

2. René Schickele (1883–1940): German Expressionist poet, novelist and dramatist.
3. Ernst Toller (1893–1939): German-Jewish Expressionist playwright and poet.

Joseph Roth[4] (the last two by their own hands)—within twelve months. The news about Jews under German occupation was dreadful. When the Nazi steam-roller reached the Channel coast in May 1940, Zweig grew frantic with fear of an imminent invasion of Britain; by June he and Lotte sailed from Liverpool to New York. Arrival in the relative safety of America did not restore his peace of mind, however. Living in a New York hotel, he began to neglect his appearance and spent hours dozing fully dressed on his bed. Lotte was incapable of generating the 'antibodies' required to fight his particular disease. An asthma sufferer herself, she lacked both physical and emotional stamina, telling a visitor: 'What can I do for Stefan, except allow myself to be dragged along with him?' Her words proved prophetic, but only after a further passage of time. For the moment Zweig switched from a depressed lethargy to concentrated activity which, however, did not indicate a lessening of his depression. He was composing the autobiographical *The World of Yesterday*, a lament for a Europe which, thanks to Hitler, had vanished as completely as the Inca Empire. In the process he worked Lotte so hard that Friederike (who, escaping to America from Unoccupied France, had met up with them again) remonstrated with him—to which he replied: 'Hard work is good for her health.' In fact, concern for Lotte's health was one of the reasons Zweig adduced for their final move to Brazil (a country, where he, moreover, enjoyed extraordinary esteem). There, in a villa near Persepolis, Zweig went through the motions of resuming the literary *Betrieb*, while Lotte learnt sufficient Portugese to give the servants instructions. But Zweig's depression was too deep-seated for normality to be restored. One weekend in January 1942, having sent the servants away and put their affairs in order, they both took Veronal and departed this life in a gesture of Zweig's devising. On the funeral pyre of the civilization that had nurtured him Lotte, half his age and grand-daughter of a rabbi (i.e. teacher of a faith which abominates suicide), thus committed *suttee* according to the Hindu precept that a husband's death

4. Joseph Roth (1894–1939): Austrian Jewish novelist whose work is suffused with nostalgia for the Habsburg Empire (*Radetzky March*).

removes the *raison d'être* for his wife's existence.

When fellow emigrés and literati received the news of Zweig's *felo-de-se* their grief was mingled with a sense of betrayal. Thomas Mann judged it a dereliction of duty committed in selfish disregard for the demoralizing effect it would have on the refugee community. Forty-odd years on from that time of trial, how is one to interpret Lotte's final gesture? Admittedly she was an asthmatic, but one now at last exposed to a benign climate. It was not the case that she (like some refugees without living next-of-kin) desperately needed companionship. She had a close-knit family consisting of mother, brother and sister-in-law in London, and a niece in New York. Nor was Zweig the 'older man' of romantic fiction who, by a combination of experience and vigour, casts a spell over young women; 'don't think', he once told Friederike apropos of Lotte, 'that I am still a lover.' One is forced to the conclusion that Lotte belonged to that (alas still numerous) section of womankind who, endowed with receptivity to the higher things in life, simultaneously labour under a sense of personal inadequacy; in consequence, they think the only way they can further the cause of art is to serve one of its practitioners as handmaiden—and, if need be, as human sacrifice. Of course, Lotte's asthma also predisposed her towards introspection, but this factor, like her roots in the German-Jewish middle class who deemed *Bildung* (culture) the highest good, are only incidentals adding grace-notes to an old, old story.

To move on to Arthur Koestler from Stefan Zweig is to explore a talented individual with a gift for perversity at, so to speak, a higher level. Koestler was both more predictable and difficult than Zweig. He also knew—in the Biblical sense—far more women. Koestler could be described as a solipsist given to intermittent flashes of self-knowledge. Occasionally he would admit that his behaviour, particularly towards women, had been reprehensible—only to proceed to trace it back to the woman who had cast her shadow over his formative years, i.e. his mother.

It cannot be gainsaid that Madam Koestler, a Viennese

Jewess married to a struggling Hungarian business man, was an egregious personality. Throughout Arthur's childhood in Budapest she forbade him the company of other boys out of a mixture of fear of contagious diseases and disdain for the benighted provincials among whom she, the *grande dame* from Vienna, was forced to reside. (Sixty years later, in Hampstead she would still boast of her select family circle, to which that *parvenu*, Dr. Freud, had been pleased to gain admittance.) After attending a Budapest gymnasium Koestler went on to the Technical University of Vienna in the early 1920s. Here the budding polymath garnered fragments of knowledge that later led to his employment as science editor of a Berlin newspaper. Journalism took him to Russia where the encounter with Soviet reality dealt his newly acquired Communist faith a severe blow. He continued nonetheless, in face of the rising Nazi tide, to cleave to the Communist Party. Hitler's accession drove him from Germany. In the mid-'30s he worked for the Comintern propaganda machine in various European countries (and also contracted a brief marriage with a fellow Communist Jewish refugee from Germany). As a journalist reporting on the Spanish Civil War he narrowly escaped execution by the Francoists and grew totally disenchanted with Communism. Caught up in the collapse of the French army in 1940, he managed to make his way to England, where he quickly attracted attention with a series of books. The most influential was *Darkness at Noon*, a fictitionalized study of Stalin's purges, whose impact on public opinion resembled that of *Animal Farm* or *1984*. Drawn into the literary life of war-time London, he made the acquaintance, at a party hosted by *Horizon* editor Cyril Connolly, of Mamaine Paget who was to become his second wife. Mamaine, an ex-debutante with artistic interests working in the Ministry of Economic Warfare, felt immensely drawn to the intellectually high-powered and polyglot Koestler. Within a year they were discussing marriage. Koestler declared himself in favour but also totally opposed to having children, whereupon Mamaine said she refused not to have children; however their marriage, contracted soon afterwards, remained childless. This was to be a source of great sadness to Mamaine. Another impediment to her married happiness was Koestler's refusal to put down roots anywhere. His compulsion to move on every few years involved Mamaine in living, at different times, in Wales, France and—most unhappily—in the United States. Even North Wales (chosen by Koestler for its resemblance to Austria), where Mamaine felt happy, was not good for her asthma. There were, of course, compensations going beyond the enjoyment of her husband's company: holidays (both hedonistic and rugged), receptions, publication parties and, above all, converse with the likes of Bertrand Russell, Sartre, de Beauvoir, Camus and Malraux. However, there was no guarantee that Koestler's encounters with his peers would necessarily end in amity. Combative, even when sober, Koestler would provoke practical brawls and personality clashes. Once he punched Camus in the eye and, on another occasion, when taken to a police station for sleeping off a hangover in his car, he did the same to the *commissaire* and landed in court.

But men were not the only targets of Koestler's easily roused ire. In 1949 Mamaine's twin sister Celia received a letter from her in France.

> Dear Celia,
> We've been beautifying the house to some extent with paper and curtains, which has been hard work and has reduced K to a near breakdown with exasperation. He always gets like this when painters and workmen are around and always thinks he will never be able to lead a quiet life and work again. Considering how he loathes it he has been most good-tempered, and we have had no major rows, except for one yesterday, which was my fault, because C.B. rang up and said could he drop in in the afternoon, and owing to my usual pathological inability to think of excuses for putting people off whom one doesn't in the least want to see (I don't like C.B. and know that Arthur loathes him) I said okay. When I told K he went quite mad with fury and struck me a stunning blow on the head.* I didn't hit him back as (a) violence seems undignified, and (b) because to hit someone much stronger than oneself is obviously useless and highly dangerous; but vowed to myself to take strong measures against him. However, half an hour later he had quite recovered and apologized, and I had put C.B. off, so all was well.
> I am reading *The Naked and the Dead*, which seems excellent. K thinks it is simply wonderful.

I have asked Macmillans to send you K's Palestine book—I
do think it's awfully good—an example of how history should
be written. . . . Love, M.

* This is only the third time in our life together that he has
done this—three times too many, of course, but considering
how berserk he goes, surprisingly few!

This was not the first occasion during her life with Koestler
Mamaine had communicated her distress. In 1947, barely two
years into their cohabitation, she had written from Wales:
'Lately Koestler seems to be nagging more than usual. . . . I
am terribly depressed.' Though it may not have been much of
a consolation, Mamaine did not long remain the only female
recipient of her husband's abuse. South African-born Cynthia
Jefferies, who had started work as Koestler's secretary in
Paris in 1949, and accompanied the couple to the U.S.A., was
by 1951 the object of Arthur's phobia, with all his irritability
directed against her. At times during their American stay
inanimate objects served as lightning conductors:

> He suddenly worked himself up into a rage and knocked
> over the kitchen table . . . also broke a couple of chairs and
> a lamp. . . . He almost broke his foot kicking at things and is
> now limping about. He has hardly spoken to me since, i.e. for
> two days. . . . There was no apparent reason for his outburst
> nor for his behaviour since. . . .

Actually Mamaine knew the deeper reason: it lay in Koestler's
irrationality. He was (she once wrote) the sort of man who tells
someone who wants spaghetti, 'no have ravioli—it's better',
only to say when the other agrees, 'No, have risotto—that's
better.' The story of their first separation bore out the truth of
the analogy. Early in 1951, while still in the States, the Koestlers
had a fearful row which ended in their agreement to separate.
At least Mamaine thought they had agreed to separate, but
afterwards Koestler behaved as if nothing had happened. A
few months later they returned to Europe, spending part of
the summer in France. The end of the summer brought the end
of their marriage. They separated in earnest—a development
Mamaine had not merely envisaged but actually elevated into a
sacrifice for a higher good in advance. 'I shall consider my life
well spent', she had told her sister eighteen months earlier,

since I've spent six years of it with Arthur. . . . I greatly believe in him as a writer and would do anything, even leave him if necessary, to help him fulfil his destiny. I should count myself and my life of little importance in such a case.

After the separation, Mamaine returned to London where she bought a small house near his, and they met weekly, though the paths of their lives diverged. In spring 1954 Mamaine's asthma got worse. Taken into hospital, where Koestler visited her, she died after two months, aged 37. Mamaine's death upset Koestler greatly, with remorse engendered by recollection of his treatment of her compounding the grief. As a timely antidote Cynthia, who had kept in constant touch with both of them, wrote from the States assuring him that he had nothing to reproach himself with. By this time Cynthia had undergone various traumas of her own. Having virtually been in love since he first hired her as a secretary in 1949, she had become severely depressed after her employment—and with it the contact with Koestler—ended. During 1952 her depression had reached a pitch where she toyed with the idea of suicide. (Her own father, a surgeon, had died in that fashion when she was 10.) Then, in 1953, she had entered into an ill-considered marriage which lasted all of six weeks. Subsequently she had started a relationship with a man who turned out to be in analysis.

When Koestler, back at work after the exorcism of mourning, wrote her of his current literary project and described his current secretary as unable to spell and awful at shorthand but nice, Cynthia replied: 'On reading your news your poor old ex-slave couldn't help feeling a twinge of jealousy.' Fairly soon she received a telegram from Koestler offering her temporary employment. She took the next plane to London to immerse herself in the MS of *Reflections on Hanging*, the centrepiece of the campaign for the abolition of capital punishment in which Koestler was currently investing his considerable energies as propagandist and lobbyist. The manuscript completed, Cynthia returned to New York where the man she was involved with confronted her with the news that his psychoanalist had advised postponing any decision about his future life until he was out of analysis. The situation was, however, transformed by another cable from Koestler, currently grappling with the project of *The Sleepwalkers* (Copernicus, Galileo, Kepler), offering her a permanent job. She jumped at it.

From that time onwards they were always together, marrying ten years later, in 1965. As had happened in the relationship with Mamaine, Koestler laid down the ground rules, the chief being that their union was to have no issue. Adherence to this rule obliged Cynthia to undergo two abortions, but she made no demur. Regarding another cause of Mamaine's unhappiness—the *déraciné* lifestyle—Koestler had by now decided to be an Englishman with a permanent home in London, supplemented by a chalet in the Austrian Alps.

Since Cynthia was, moreover, a more accommodating, not to say subservient, spouse than her predecessor, there was far less friction in the relationship. The third Mrs. Koestler even contrived to maintain a display of equanimity in face of her husband's routine philandering by taking the view that she was privileged to share his life at all. As Koestler grew older concerns not previously uppermost in his mind began to occupy him. One was what is roughly defined as the paranormal, i.e. telepathy, precognition, psychokinesis, etc. the study of which he wanted to be pursued as rigorously as of any 'other' branch of science. Another of his newly acquired interests concerned voluntary euthanasia. Believing that the decision whether and when a terminally ill person should depart this life was a matter not for the state or the medical profession but for the individual concerned, Koestler assumed the Vice-Presidency of the Voluntary Euthanasia Society. His adoption of the last-named cause owed a great deal to personal circumstances. At 70 Koestler contracted Parkinson's disease and, although the condition was temporarily stabilized, progressive deterioration set in. Leukaemia added to the problems and by his seventieth-seventh year Koestler was reduced to a human wreck. Determined to act before he became incapable of any action, he made his quietus, in the company of Cynthia, by means of a barbiturate overdose washed down with brandy. At the time of the double suicide Cynthia was 55 and apparently enjoying perfect health. In her typewritten addition to Koestler's farewell note she had written: 'Despite certain inner resources I cannot live without

Arthur.' Her *Liebestod* aroused intense controversy. Koestler incurred severe posthumous censure for alleged overweening self-aggrandizement in condoning, and possibly even encouraging, his wife's demonstration of loyalty unto death. Koestler's defenders contended that his death would have disposed the surviving Cynthia towards suicide in any case. They argued that her father had ended his own life and that she had actually contemplated suicide during an earlier crisis. Koestler's detractors claimed that in that case he should have enjoined his best friends to keep a close watch on her during the traumatic early stages of bereavement.

As the argument rumbled on Koestler's chief champion, the similarly Hungarian-born humorous writer George Mikes, alleged that Cynthia welcomed death because she had been suffering from cancer. Why, asked the detractors, had she not mentioned that fact in her suicide note?—to which Mikes made the rejoinder that she wanted it kept secret. If so, it was a secret that she had taken to her premature grave. What is no secret is that Koestler made her happy. Even concerning the first half dozen of the thirty-odd years they knew each other, when he often treated her badly, she was persuaded in retrospect that he tried to force a rupture in her own best interests—since he considered himself a reprobate who was bound to disappoint her starry-eyed expectations.

VI

Dancers

Isadora Duncan

THOUGH the Fitzgeralds, Scott and Zelda, ran her a close second, Isadora Duncan was the greatest romantic ever to come out of America. This is not to be wondered at since every detail of her background (from birth in San Francisco midway between gold rush and earthquake onwards) resembled a romantic cliché. Her charming, déclassé father descended from an Independence War general but was careless with other people's money—and affections. The mother, a divorcee trapped in genteel poverty, worked all hours teaching piano and knitting to provide for the family—and still regaled the children with renditions of Mendelssohn and Schumann in the evenings. The children, when small, did door-to-door selling of mittens and caps their mother had knitted; later on, they helped her conduct classes in social dancing at the Duncan home. This was how Isadora, the youngest, discovered her vocation.

After gaining a varied experience, including a stint in vaudeville, over several years, she felt ready at 22 to display her combined skills as a dancer and choreographer before metropolitan audiences. In the same year, 1899, in which she staged *The Happier Age of Gold* at New York, she produced her characteristic definition of dance as 'seeking the divine expression of the human spirit through the medium of the body's movement'. But since, in Isadora's view, ballet represented a perverse deformation of that expression, she also conducted a search for the well-springs of dance in her studio.

> For hours I would stand quite still, my two hands folded between my breasts, covering the solar plexus. I was seeking

and finally discovering the spring of all movement. The method taught at ballet school produces an artificial mechanical movement not worthy of the soul. I, on the contrary, sought the source of the spiritual expression to flow into the channel of the body, filling it with vibrating light.

For all the stir Isadora created by her performance (not to mention her pronouncements) no theatre manager, bar one, seemed interested in arranging a tour for her. The exception was Lois Fuller, who had previously managed a group of Japanese actors at the Paris Exposition. Isadora signed up with her, but found the lesbian antics of Fuller's all-female troupe hard to take. The tour, nonetheless, led onto better things because in Vienna she encountered an impresario who had the nous required to put her on the map. He booked her into a theatre at Budapest where Isadora, dancing to such patriotically flavoured compositions as Liszt's *Rákóczi March* and Strauss's *Blue Danube*, scored a solid run of sold-out performances.

She found Hungary a rewarding experience in other respects, too. She fell totally under the spell of its music, declaring that one gypsy playing on a dusty road in Hungary was worth more than all the musicians in the world. Furthermore she fell head over heels in love, the object of her affections being the romantic lead of the National Theatre, with whom she was quite besotted. After a while, though, she realized that marriage to him would relegate her to the position of a junior partner expected to bask in the reflected glory of her husband. Giving precedence to artistic self-realization over emotional fulfilment, she terminated the affair at considerable psychic cost. She spent several weeks in hospital followed by a stay at Franzensbad, a spa frequented *inter alia* by women seeking abortions. (Whether Isadora went there with that object in mind cannot now be established with any degree of certainty.) When she recovered she proceeded to Munich where she became a star, her chief fans being the local University students. After each performance, they would unhitch the horses from the dancer's carriage and pull it through the streets to her hotel, where they intoned a serenade beneath Isadora's window. In Munich she also met Siegfried Wagner, who, together with his mother Cosima, had taken over the direction of the Bayreuth Festival.

There was talk of engaging Isadora to dance the Bacchanale in the Bayreuth production of *Tannhauser*. This in fact happened, but only several months later. Meanwhile, there followed an interlude during which all the Duncans went to Greece, where they mooted a characteristically impractical project to build a temple.

Back in Germany, Isadora once again fell in love with someone who could not bring her happiness. The man, an art historian, married to the daughter of Cosima Wagner, viewed their encounter as a platonic sharing of ideas and emotions, whereas she hankered after a full-blooded relationship. She had not long recovered from that bruising experience when the stage designer Gordon Craig impacted on her life by rushing into her dressing room one night after a performance and exclaiming, 'You're wonderful! But why have you stolen my ideas?' Craig, illegitimate son of Ellen Terry, pioneered new techniques in directing and designing plays. A dynamic, volatile personality and inveterate bohemian, he eventually fathered ten illegitimate children, two of them on a woman musician he intended to marry. While he (obviously) loved women, he was averse to seeing them occupy leading positions in the theatre. This patriarchal attitude and his inconstancy—in turn magnified by Isadora's jealous suspicions—did not make for an easy relationship, but their affair nonetheless continued for two years. Early in the Craig years, which Isadora was to look back on as the happiest period in her life, she went to dance in Russia. During her stay there she met Stanislavsky and such luminaries of the world of ballet as Anna Pavlova and the choreographers Petipa and Fokine. The last-named dubbed her 'the greatest American gift to the art of dance who reminded Russians of the beauty of simple movements'. Isadora, far from reciprocating the compliment, indicted ballet for separating gymnastic movements of the body completely from the mind and deforming the beautiful bodies of women.

Back in Berlin again, she disposed of sufficient funds—partly from tour earnings, partly from donations—to realize her cherished ambition of establishing a residential dancing school for girls. She purchased a villa in the lakeside suburb of Grunewald and adorned its high-ceilinged main hall and the dancing rooms with statues and bas-reliefs of young girls dancing, running and jumping. Among the staff she engaged was her sister. Each of the pupils, who originally numbered forty, slept in a *Himmelbett*, so-called on account of its head-board picture of an angel playing a musical instrument, and its white muslin curtains with blue lace ribbons. Fairly soon, though, Isadora had to halve the intake. In the course of a visit to the Grunewald villa Kaiserin Auguste Viktoria had registered shock at the sight of the childrens' bare limbs—whereupon the school's own Board of Patronesses had censured Isadora. Stung, the dancer saw fit to go over to the counter-attack. Towards the end of a lecture on 'Dance as the art of Liberation' at the Philharmonic Hall she launched into a peroration asserting, decades in advance of women's lib, the right of every woman to love and bear children as she pleased. A few weeks later she dropped into an arithmetic lesson at her school and asked the pupils what was the greatest thing in life. The girls answered with one voice: 'To dance'. Isadora shook her head. Perplexed, the girls suggested 'To paint', 'To sculpt', 'To compose'. Once again Isadora shook her head; then, raising a forefinger, she announced 'To love', and left the classroom.

The explanation for her mystifying interruption of school routine lay close to hand: she was pregnant with Craig's child. As her pregnancy became more obvious, she secreted herself in an all but inaccessible house perched atop the North Sea dunes in a Dutch village. Although Craig visited her there, she felt his remoteness, and this preyed on her mind to such an extent that she made an inept attempt to drown herself. From suicidal depression, her mood swung to ecstatic happiness at the time of the arrival of child, a girl. After the delivery she told Craig that now she knew 'the tremendous love surpassing the love of a man'. Later she penned a statement which women's libbers may abhor but will ignore at their peril: 'Oh women, what is the good of us learning to become lawyers, painters, or sculptors, when this miracle exists?' Gordon Craig, for whom childbirth hardly partook of the miraculous, had a say in the naming of the child as Deirdre—beyond which he discharged none of the obligations of a father.

Isadora resumed touring. She went to Russia once again, taking a homosexual along with her as an *ersatz* lover designated to wipe out the memory of the absconded Craig. The Russian tour yielded mixed results; she secured Stanislavsky's backing for the establishment of a school at Moscow on the lines of the Berlin one, but the project remained stillborn nonetheless. The United States tour took Isadora back to the land of her birth for the first time. She told journalists come to interview the famous returnee: 'Walt Whitman said "I hear America singing"—*I* see America dancing.' She also formulated a 'patriotic' theory about the provenance of her art. Far from having its roots in Ancient Greece, she claimed that her style of dancing arose out of the hoedown-type celebrations staged by the pioneers with covered waggons who opened up the continent. Returning to Paris she met and launched herself upon an affair with a Europeanized American whose wealth and apparent readiness to use it on her behalf made Isadora dub him her Lohengrin—the knight who in Wagner's opera comes to the rescue of the heroine. Isadora's 'knight' was Paris Singer, a son of the billionaire inventor of the sewing-machine (and, incidentally, a brother of the Princess de Polignac).[1] Paris Singer was married with five children, but lived apart from his wife. He took Isadora and little Deirdre on a yacht trip to Egypt and heaped equivalent luxuries, including the purchase of a palatial Riviera villa, upon them in France. But he turned out to be a less adroit promoter than Diaghilev, with whose Ballets Russes Isadora was currently—the year being 1910—having to compete for the favour of the dance-orientated Parisian public.

Her ability to perform became in any case progressively curtailed as she found herself bearing Singer's child. A boy, christened Patrick, was duly born, and Isadora had perforce to bid the stage a temporary adieu. The life of a chatelaine, which Singer would have liked her to pursue, held no appeal for her, however. She had an *amour* with a pianist, which aroused Singer's rage and led to a rupture, although their affair was not thereby brought to a clear-cut, unambiguous

1. Princess de Polignac, née Winnaretta Singer (1865–1943): leading Parisian patroness of avant guarde music in first half of the twentieth century.

end. Isadora still seemed to draw him as a woman, though his interest in her ideas and schemes—above all that for establishing a network of residential dancing schools—had always been perfunctory at best.

By this time some alumni of her Berlin school had reached an age and level of terpsichorean skill that made it opportune for them to perform in public. Isadora arranged for them to appear in Paris where they were promptly nicknamed '*Les Isadorables*'. Before they could be exposed to public scrutiny, however, she needed to undo some of the harmful effects of her sister's teachings at Grunewald. That accomplished, the girls and Isadora jointly scored a great success at the Chatelet Theatre—*Pace*. One review read: 'The delighted audience applauds and applauds, freed of all everyday worries and care, left with no other thoughts but those of grace and youth eternal.'

These plaudits encouraged Isadora to resuscitate plans for establishing her own theatre at Paris. Her hopes soared when Singer, who was known to contemplate the purchase of real estate near the Champs Elysées, put out feelers for a reconciliation. They had a 'family reunion' with the children that took the form of lunch at an Italian restaurant. Afterwards Singer went off on business and she prepared for a rehearsal. The children meanwhile were entrusted to the chauffeur who was to drive them home. En route going uphill from the Left Bank the engine stalled. He got out to crank up the motor, having, by mistake, put the gear into reverse. To his horror, as he started the engine, the car accelerated away from him and plunged over the embankment into the Seine, and the children were drowned. The tragedy devastated Isadora. Taking flight from the place of trauma, she rushed to Greece to immerse herself in nursing victims of the recent Balkan War (1913). Presently, though, she felt so overwhelmed by the squalor in which the refugee camp hospitals were mired that she moved on again—this time to Italy. Here she drew some comfort from the company of the tragedienne Eleanora Duse, a friend dating back to the Gordon Craig years. Later, while nursing her grief in seclusion near Viareggio, she was seized by the notion of having a stranger father a child upon her. With a young sculptor as 'sperm donor', she had no difficulty in conceiving again, but at the end of the pregnancy malign fate dealt her another blow. The child died at birth.

Isadora's personal tragedy coincided with the global one of the outbreak of the Great War. She returned once again, to her native—and still neutral—America. Here she promoted herself, as well as the Allied cause, by performing a dance, draped in a red shawl, to the accompaniment of the *Marseillaise*. Once again, she seemed poised for a major breakthrough. She recruited pupils whom she trained for joint performances in a theatre put at her disposal by a wealthy backer. To simplify matters she quartered the girls in improvized dormitories within the theatre building, but in so doing she contravened fire department regulations. The girls were accordingly turned out of their quarters; when this was done shortly before a scheduled performance of *Oedipus Rex*, Isadora vowed to leave the country, which she now denounced as irremediably philistine.

Back in war-torn France she adapted her repertoire to the exigencies of the situation, dancing César Franck's *Rédemption* and Tchaikovsky's 'Pathétique'. For the remainder of the war she commuted between France and the States, having unsatisfactory love affairs with her accompanists in both countries, and effecting a final break with Singer in the latter.

Isadora's first destination, once peace made unrestricted travel across Europe possible again, was Greece. She went to Athens to train dancers for a huge Dionysian Festival commissioned by the King. This monarch, alas, died (in consequence of a bite from his pet monkey), and his successor's government cancelled the festival on economy grounds. Back in western Europe Isadora commuted between Paris and London performing Tchaikovsky's *Marche Slave*, which she had, under the impact of the recent Russian Revolution, transformed into an evocation of servitude and rebellion. The Soviet envoy to Britain saw her dance *Marche Slave* in London, in consequence of which Anatoly Lunacharsky, the Soviet Commissar of Education invited her to come to Russia. His offer—'We will give you a school and a thousand children as pupils'—was one she found hard to resist. However, arriving in malnourished, shivering Moscow, Isadora was soon made to realize the impracticability of the grandiose ambitions she had entertained en route. The official attached to her explained why prevailing circumstances made it impossible to fulfil the promise contained in Lunacharsky's invitation. Instead, he advised: '. . . start with small groups of children in the workers clubs and gain their confidence.' In reality things worked out a bit better than that. The authorities actually enabled Isadora to start a subsidized small school for fifty children. However, this venture was shortlived: with the introduction of Lenin's New Economic Policy in 1921 the subsidy was withdrawn and the pupils' parents could not afford the fees Isadora needed to charge.

In the event, her greatest experience in Russia was not a public, but an intensely personal one. Past 40, she found—or thought she found—love once again in the person of the young poet Sergei Yesenin. He was a village intellectual, transplanted to the big city, who had shown precocity both in his poetic output (which aligned him with the Imagist school) and his love life. By the time the 26-year-old met Isadora he had gone through two marriages and fathered three children. Their affair was quite strange, not only on account of the sixteen-year age difference between the lovers, but because they had no language in common.

Although Isadora had resolved never to marry again, circumstances conspired to make her go back on that resolution. Yesenin had for some time hankered after a trip abroad—a plan in which Lunacharsky concurred because he wanted him to broaden his horizons and establish contacts with foreign publishers. When Isadora, on news of her mother's death, decided to return to the West, they married and obtained joint travel documents. (Under pressure from Isadora, Lunacharsky had instructed the official registrar to enter her age as 37—to chime in with Yesenin's 27—on the marriage certificate.) As the newly-weds' plane taxied along the runway at Moscow Airport a car drove up, from which two men leapt running in pursuit of the departing aircraft. They were Imagists who had intended to snatch Yesenin away from Isadora, whom they considered a baleful influence on his muse.

The unpunctual kidnappers were not the only Russian literati who had little good to say about Isadora. When she and Yesenin called on Maxim Gorky in Berlin, the grand old man of Soviet letters took exception to the flip manner of Isadora's discourse on political matters: 'This lady', he said, 'praises the Revolution the way a theatre lover praises the première of a play.' He also expressed profound and seering criticism of her as a performer.

> Her dance seemed to me to depict the struggle between the weight of Duncan's age and the constraints of her body, spoilt by fame and love. These words are not meant to be offensive to a woman. They merely speak of the curse of old age.

While Gorky read the signs of dilapidation through love and age on Isadora's body, Yesenin's Peter Pan face was acquiring the pallor of blotting-paper under the combined influence of alcohol and insomniac nights. Because the Berlin trip coincided with the climacteric of Germany's post-war inflation, a new world far more louche than the Moscow of the N.E.P. period opened up before the poet's bloodshot eyes. The German capital teemed with taverns, bars and nightclubs in which the motto, 'Anything goes', was given literal interpretation, and the poet, simultaneously released from the constraints of his home environment and of convention, gave his libido free reign. Overdosing on drink and pornographic 'live performances', he conducted nightly safaris that could be described as pub-crawls combined with brawls. And, since roughing up fellow drinkers did not suffice to still his rage, Yesenin not infrequently smashed items of furniture in his and Isadora's hotel rooms. At last it was time to move on from entertainment-crazed Berlin to New York in the grip of prohibition. The 'demon drink' belonged to a whole cluster of bogies that prompted apprehension in the post-war United States, with the fear of Communism running it a close second. The latter spawned such bizarre notions as that Isadora and Yesenin were coming to America to spread Soviet subversion. This had the risible result that Sol Hurok, the impresario arranging Isadora's tour, was stripped naked at Ellis Island (where he had gone to meet his client) lest he help her to smuggle political contraband into the country. A little way into her American tour Isadora, labelled the Red dancer by sections of the press, in despite of Sol Hurok's plea to avoid further trouble, made a curtain speech expounding her aesthetic to a Boston audience.

> If my art is symbolic of anything, it is symbolic of the freedom of woman and her emancipation from the hide-bound conventions that are the warp and woof of New England puritanism. To expose one's body is art; concealment is vulgar. Nudity is truth, it is beauty, it is art. Therefore it can never be vulgar, it can never be immoral!

And, waving her red silk scarf above her head, she cried: 'This is red, so am I. It is the colour of life and vigour . . . you don't know what beauty is!' Then she tore her tunic down to bare one breast and cried out, 'This—this is beauty!' While a large part of the audience rushed to the doors, Yesenin, who in America decked himself out in a black Cossack tunic, with cartridge loops on either breast and a silver dagger dangling from his belt, opened a window backstage from which, shouting a Bolshevik catchphrase in Russian, he waved some kind of red material. Next day the mayor forbade all subsequent appearances of Isadora in Boston. This set the pattern for the rest of the tour, on which, though some performances were cancelled, Isadora danced to sold-out houses, made defiant curtain speeches and was promptly denounced by the local mayor. She relished the controversy and attendant publicity, but meanwhile Yesenin was becoming ever more difficult to live with, as, drunk on prohibition liquor, he would wreck their apartment and threatened to attack everybody in sight, including Isadora. In America, where there were no fellow Russian literati as there has been at Berlin, he felt desperately frustrated over Isadora's sketchy grasp of Russian, since he could only compose poetry under the stimulus of having an audience instantly on hand. The combination of press attacks and her husband's violent rages caused Isadora to terminate the tour precipitately, and the ill-matched couple set sail for Europe.

Back in Russia their moribund relationship soon received its death blow. One night when Yesenin came upon Isadora in her bedroom crying over the photographs of the dead children, the poet who had experienced such (to him) irritating scenes before, snatched the album out of her hands and hurled it into the fireplace. At the same time he is alleged to have shouted, 'I'm your husband—your man'—an expression of his suspicion that the considerably older Isadora looked upon him as a substitute for little Patrick (whom he, indeed, resembled). Isadora's chagrin over this scene, and Yesenin's subsequent departure—which this time turned out to be for good—was partly assuaged by the offer of a Ukranian tour, eventually followed by one through the Soviet Asiatic Republics. Soon after, she left Russia for France, though even then her contacts with the Soviets continued. She would visit the Paris Embassy to try and arrange the transfer of pupils from her Moscow school, that they might train the thousands of French girls she hoped to deploy in pageants under the auspices of the *Parti Communiste*. A political innocent—as well as hopeful self-promoter—throughout her life, Isadora at one Soviet Embassy reception button-holed a low-ranking Italian diplomat, whom she overwhelmed with expressions of admiration for Eleanora Duse, her one-time lover the nationalist poet Gabriel D'Annunzio, and for Mussolini.

While she was engaged in these and other schemes, news reached her from Russia that Yesenin, still officially her husband, had married for the fourth time. A little later she heard of his suicide—committed after he had drawn blood from his own wrist, with which to write a poem. The news caused the press to reprint old stories about their turbulent relationship. In response she fired off a telegram to the news agencies: 'There was never any quarrel or divorce between Yesenin and myself. I weep over his death with anguish and despair.' Her use of the phrase 'anguish and despair' was more than mere dramatic locution. Friends now often heard her speak of committing suicide, but discounted the possibility—because in the next minute she would discourse on her plans for starting a school in Paris or staging Communist Party pageants.

Another project of hers was a dance performance based on Liszt's Dante Symphony. To devise the choreography she went down to Nice, where, in the summer of 1927, she had a studio. There she became infatuated with a young garage mechanic whom she, with characteristic hyperbole, likened to a Greek god. One evening she let him take her for a drive in a Bugatti. Shouting '*Adieu mes amis—je vais au gloire!*' she settled into her seat, which, in the low-slung racing car was barely a few inches above the ground. Since, moreover,

Bugattis had no mudguards, the fringes of her thick shawl fell into the spokes of the wheel at her side. As the driver started the engine, the first turn of the wheels broke Isadora's neck. With the 'Greek god' beside her, she had gone to glory.

Romola Nijinska

Question: what have Igor Stravinsky, Richard Strauss, Eric Satie, Manuel da Falla, Maurice Ravel, Claude Debussy, Sergei Prokofiev, Jean Cocteau, Leon Bakst,[2] Alexandre Benois,[3] André Derain,[4] Henri Matisse and Pablo Picasso in common? Answer: they were all associated with the Ballets Russes.

The Ballets Russes, matrix of modern ballet, was, thanks to Diaghilev's creative flair, enriched and energized by everything innovative and stimulating in early twentieth-century culture—from Symbolist poetry and Cubist art through a cult of the erotic (L'Après-midi d'un faun) and the exotic (Sheherazade), to sophisticated primitivism (The Rite of Spring). Mirroring Wagner's Gesamtkunstwerk concept, Diaghilev integrated dance with drama, painting and music to an unprecedented degree. Although the Ballets Russes acted as an artistic powerhouse for two whole decades (from 1909 till Diaghilev's death in 1929), its golden years were the immediate pre-war seasons when the above ballets were premièred. As a flexible itinerant troupe Diaghilev's dancers scored over their static rivals, such as the St. Petersburg-based Marinsky Company, by daring innovation and star appeal, while falling short of the latter's uniformity and high-precision finish. Diaghilev's first star ballerina was Anna Pavlova, but their ways soon parted. His first, and greatest ever, male star was Vaslav Nijinsky. The mongol-featured, undersized (5 ft. 4 in.) Nijinsky truly became a legend in his own lifetime. (The myth persists: which other dancer has had a racehorse named after him?) He was credited with the ability to stand

2. Leon Bakst (1866–1924): Russian-Jewish artist, chief set designer for Ballets Russes (Sheherazade, Daphnis et Chloé).
3. Alexandre Benois (1870–1960): Russian painter and set designer for Ballets Russes (Les Sylphides, Petrushka).
4. André Derain (1880–1954): French painter, one of the originators of Fauvism.

still in mid-air. The *Sunday Times* described him as peerless; in Rupert Brook's opinion seeing him dance was to watch a miracle.

Nijinsky was the third child of Polish dancer parents who subsequently separated. The father started a second family, occasionally returning to the first. On one such visit to St. Petersburg he threw young Vaslav into the Neva to teach him to swim. This sort of behaviour and the life-long institutionalization of Nijinsky's elder brother points to a genetic defect in the family (at any rate among the males). At 9 Nijinsky entered the Imperial Ballet School where he did well, though he proved slow at book-learning. He made no friends at school, but always felt close to his sister Bronia, an aspiring ballerina. When, aged 18, he graduated to the Marinsky's *corps de ballet*, he was drawn into a sleazy coterie of St. Petersburg socialites by a colleague who introduced biddable young men to wealthy homosexuals. Nijinsky formed an attachment first with a Russian prince, who initiated him into the luxurious world of night-clubs, parties and shopping trips to the jewellers Fabergé, and subsequently with a Polish Count. At the same time his career prospered. He attracted the notice of the talent-scouting, and similarly inclined, Diaghilev, who engaged him as principal dancer for the first Paris season of the Ballets Russes in 1909.

The Russians were a revelation to the West. The French critics outdid each other in lauding them, none more than Nijinsky whom they called a 'prodigy' and a 'veritable god of the dance'. Since his sister Bronia also belonged to Diaghilev's troupe, Madame Nijinska had come to Paris to chaperone her; it amused company members to see the mother escort her daughter from the theatre each night apparently oblivious of the fact that her under-age son was going home with his elderly lover (Nijinsky was 20, Diaghilev 38, but looked older).

Though artistically successful, the Ballets Russes seasons were beset by financial difficulties, intrigue and the clash of artistic egos almost from the start. In 1910, the fatigued and near-bankrupt Diaghilev came close to abandoning the whole project; what kept him from doing so was, in part, his desire to create opportunities for Nijinsky to express his genius through choreographing ballets as well as dancing in them—although this meant parting company with his previous chief choreographer, Fokine. Nijinsky's new creations, *L'Après-midi d'un faun* and *Petrushka*, won widespread acclaim (even if some audiences jibbed at the overt eroticism of the Faun).

By 1912 Nijinsky's way of life had become immensely glamorous—he danced at the coronation gala for George V when the Covent Garden auditorium was festooned with 100,000 roses—but also quite rootless. The Marinsky, to which he had previously always returned from his seasons with the Ballets Russes, had dismissed him (for being indecently attired in the Benois-designed *Giselle*), and he was leading a nomadic existence, moving from place to place with the Ballets Russes. That year the company's tours took them to the twin capitals of Austria-Hungary. Among the audience at the Budapest opera house was a 19-year-old girl, of aristocratic background, by the name of Romola de Pulsky. She felt herself so attracted by the glamour emanating from Nijinsky that she took it into her shrewd, as well as pretty head, to make a play for him. It seemed a fairy-tale ambition—an anonymous member of the audience at a second-rate opera house setting her cap at the lover of a homosexual Maecenas encompassed by beautiful ballerinas—but Romola could deploy single-minded persistence as well as, thanks to her family, the contacts needed to put her plan into operation. Daughter of an art-loving aristocrat (who had died) and an ex-actress mother, she had a brother-in-law who sang at the Vienna Court Opera. Through her Viennese contacts she secured an interview with Diaghilev whom she asked for admission to the Ballets Russes as a fee-paying student. Quizzed by the perspicacious impresario about her feelings towards Nijinsky, she threw him off the scent by pretending enthusiasm for Adolphe Bohn (the lead in the *Polovtsian Dances*). Once attached to the company as an *élève*, she cultivated the friendship of the ballerina Miriam Ramberg—the subsequent Marie Rambert—with whom Nijinsky had built up a degree of intimacy. (Diaghilev's suspicion of this budding relationship made him ask one of his assistants to keep an eye on them during rehearsals when he himself was away.) Miriam Ramberg had no inkling of Romola's feelings for Nijinsky and felt rather flattered to have the sophisticated young society lady solicit her company and confidence. She acted, all unknowing, as the conduit for transmitting information about Nijinksy's interests, feelings and general state of mind to Romola—information that stood the latter in good stead when she eventually made his personal acquaintance. This happened in a cursory way on the boat-train taking the company from Paris to London, but blossomed into a much closer relationship when, aboard the SS *Avon*, they set out on a South American tour in mid-1913. The relaxing long drawn-out sea-journey under sunny skies wrought a sea-change in Nijinksy: he who had left Europe as the 24-year-old lover of the middle-aged Diaghilev disembarked in America as the heterosexual bridegroom of a girl barely out of her teens. The transformation owed a lot to Romola's allure as well as astuteness. However, these qualities alone might not have done the trick had there not been some company members, and hangers-on, aboard ship only too eager to further the amorous intrigue. The matchmakers' commission they hoped for was the discomfiture of Diaghilev, whose autocratic methods and financial recklessness had made him many enemies.

The chief go-between in Romola's service was Baron Gunsbourg, who had a ballerina mistress. Best man at the subsequent wedding, the Baron had also, two days before the ship's final landfall at Rio de Janeiro, asked Romola's hand in marriage on Nijinsky's behalf. Employing a proxy not only accorded with the bridegroom's extreme punctiliousness—though invited, he refused to sleep with Romola in advance of the wedding ceremony—but also had a more mundane reason: the lovers had no language in common. In the words of one biographer:

> . . . at the Buenos Aires church the Austro-Hungarian bride was led up the aisle on the arms of a Russian-Jewish friend and united to a Russian-Pole whose language she did not speak, in a ceremony performed in Latin and Spanish.

Gunsbourg's translator's services were again required after the wedding when Nijinsky, feeling honour-bound to reveal the darker aspects of his past to his new wife, made a clean breast of his association with Diaghilev and of his brother's insanity. The latter fact did not suggest a hereditary taint to him; he told Romola that, after five years entirely devoted to art, they would have a child, 'the supreme fulfilment of marriage', and settle down in a permanent home. In fact, they had a daughter, Kyra, within the year. The extent of Nijinsky's naïvité was even greater than that: he actually expected Diaghilev to give the marriage his blessing and to continue their former creative relationship as if nothing untoward had occurred. What happened when the impresario received the news, which he did at Venice, was the very opposite. Nijinsky's treachery, for that is how Diaghilev regarded it, dealt him a devastating blow. Drunk with grief and rage he had close colleagues take him to Naples, where he abreacted his bitterness in frantic bacchanalia. Then he executed his countermoves. He had Nijinsky dismissed (on a technicality) while the company were still on the Brazilian leg of the tour. On a 'talent-spotting' trip ot Moscow, he recruited 18-year-old Léonide Massine to replace the renegade on stage, as well as in his affections, and he reinstated Fokine as chief choreographer of the Ballets Russes.

Meanwhile, what of the prime mover in the drama, whose poaching on Diaghilev's preserve had set these various developments in 'train'? Romola, already aware in Brazil that her womb was full of Nijinsky's seed, filled her mind with paranoid suspicions, even before his dismissal by the impresario. She interpreted any fortuitous mishap (a rusty nail on stage, a falling piece of scenery) as deliberate— a Diaghilev-inspired accident-on-purpose to injure, maybe even kill, her husband.

Soon enough Nijinsky and the Ballets Russes parted company. Returning to Europe Romola took comfort from Bronia's and her dancer husband's readiness to help Nijinsky start a new ballet company. This was to be based on London whose public, with the Oscar Wilde scandal still in mind, welcomed her reclamation of Nijinsky from the love that dare not speak its name. But the new venture failed for a variety of reasons, one of them, in fact, being variety: the Palace Theatre management inserted the ballet in the middle of a music-hall programme.

The resulting fiasco took its toll of Nijinksy's savings and his nerves. To recuperate, he and Romola left for a holiday in the Alps during which Kyra was born. The outbreak of the Great War overtook and trapped them in Budapest, where they were obliged to stay with Romola's mother and stepfather. Relations between them rapidly deteriorated to the point where the mother denounced her son-in-law to the police as a spy, alleging that the balletic notation with which he occupied himself in his enforced idleness, was a code for recording military secrets.

The Nijinsky's virtual internment ended in early 1916 when, thanks to the intervention of various European crowned heads, including the Pope, they were allowed to cross into neutral Switzerland. Some time before their release, an exchange of letters between Diaghilev and Nijinsky had led to a formal reconciliation; on the dancer's arrival in Paris he immediately got ready to rejoin the Ballets Russes currently on tour in the U.S.A. When he reached New York, Diaghilev met him on the quayside with kisses of welcome, and in return Nijinsky placed Kyra in the other's arms. This affecting scene attracted useful publicity, but the two men had become too estranged from one another to breathe new life into the bones of their erstwhile fruitful relationship. In addition Romola's morbid suspiciousness placed heavy obstacles in the way of the smooth running of the company. Among the ensemble were two Tolstoyans who befriended and often chatted to Nijinsky. Having something of a religious bent, he was susceptible to their influence and actually took to wearing Russian peasant-type shirts. When, after the U.S. tour, the company moved to Madrid prior to another American season and the Tolstoyans continued to engage her husband in earnest discourse, she suspected another plot. Once again she saw Diaghilev's hand behind an attempt to finish off Nijinsky—this time by converting him to Tolstoyanism so that he would either turn vegetarian and become too enfeebled to dance, or forsake his career altogether to work on the land.

Persuaded that Diaghilev was contriving her husband's ruin to smooth the path for his current lover Massine, she got Nijinsky to withdraw from the scheduled South American tour, whereupon Diaghilev had the Spanish authorities arrest him for breach of contract. Speedily released, Nijinsky had a furious altercation with the impresario that severed the last remaining links between the two men. Obliged to sail for South America he danced with the company at Buenos Aires in late 1917. It was to be his last public appearance—writing *finis* to an international career of eight years' duration, which, despite its brevity, engendered an abiding myth. From South America the Nijinskys returned to Switzerland and rented a villa close to where Friedrich Nietzsche had spent his reclusive final years of sanity. Here the dancer rested, planned future ballets, and read Nietzsche's *Ecce Homo*; then, like it's author, he suddenly lapsed into madness. He appeared in the village, adorned with a big golden cross and peremptorily told passers-by to go to church; he arranged a private solo performance at his villa at which he brooded instead of dancing; he announced he had given up the ballet for good and was returning to Russia—then convulsed by revolution—to work on the land. Romola consulted the famous Swiss pychiatrist Professor Bleuer, who pronounced Nijinsky 'incurably insane'. She placed him first in Bleuer's institution and then the Steinhof mental home in Vienna, but his condition showed no improvement; on the contrary, when Madame Nijinska and Bronia—his closest confidante since childhood, who had just escaped from Soviet-occupied Kiev—came to see him at Vienna in 1921, he failed to recognize them. Two years later Romola brought him back to her apartment in Paris. Here Diaghilev visited Nijinsky and asked him to dance for the Ballets Russes again, only to be told, 'I cannot, because I am mad'—a sadly lucid statement under the circumstances.

From the early 1920s onwards Romola acted as breadwinner for both of them. She set up a one-woman 'cottage industry' catering for the persistent widespread interest in Nijinsky by means of articles, lecture tours and a less than objective biography. Arising out of the latter a film project was mooted by Alexander Korda, who subsequently reneged on the deal, however. Because of her preoccupations and for medical reasons, Nijinsky was institutionalized again. The late '30s found him in the above-mentioned Swiss clinic, where insulin treatment ameliorated his condition by ridding him of hallucinations. Romola took this for a hopeful augury only to have her hopes cruelly dashed when, on a mountain walk near the sanatorium, he tried to push her down a precipice. After the outbreak of the Second World War, she again took Nijinsky to her native Budapest—only to be met with the same lack of sympathy on her parents' part as previously. Thanks to contacts in high places they nonetheless did not fare too badly till 1944, when the Germans occupied the country, and Romola, apprised by a friend, the German conductor Furtwängler, of the Nazi extermination of mental defectives, had to fear for Nijinksy's life. She therefore moved him from Budapest to the comparative safety of the Austro-Hungarian border. Here they lived in caves with battles between the Wehrmacht and the Red Army raging round them. Liberated by the advancing Russians, whose language he spoke, Nijinsky fleetingly reverted to his former self: in the evening, as the soldiers swilled vodka and strummed balalaikas round the camp fire, he—whose feet had remained earthbound for a quarter of a century—danced with them. It was to be his brief swan-song as a dancer.

Taken to England by Romola, he gently vegetated, dying in 1950. Three years later, at the instigation of Serge Lifar, his remains underwent ceremonial reburial in France. Lifar, *premier danseur* of inter-war Paris, who had raised funds for Nijinsky's treatment in excess of Romola's capacity, reserved the adjacent plot for himself; in consequence, on Romola's death in 1978, she received burial apart from her husband. This may seem rough justice on a wife who, throughout most of their marriage, was Nijinsky's bread-winner, custodian and part-time nurse. On the other hand, a strong case could be made out for saying that she received her just deserts. Impelled by the ambition to use Nijinsky's fame to lever herself upwards into the top stratum of European society, she had pursued and married the dancer with total indifference to the consequences, either for the Ballets Russes or himself. Nijinksy's precariously balanced mind collapsed under the cumulative strain of severance from his patron-cum-mentor Diaghilev and the burden of having to act as simultaneously impresario, administrator, choreographer and principal dancer for his own company. His subsequent collapse after only four, out of thirty-seven, years of marriage snatched the glittering prize of social pre-eminence from Romola's grasp, although she could still compensate for half a lifetime's sick-room attendance by feeding off the Nijinsky legend emotionally as well as financially.

If there is such a thing as a war of the sexes in which women are either victims or victors, then Romola de Pulszky must be counted among the latter—with the crucial qualification that her victory belonged to the Pyrrhic variety.

VII

Actresses

Helene Weigel

AFTER Richard Wagner's widow Cosima had been directing the Bayreuth Festival with considerable success for several years, someone asked her why she had not overseen the production of her composer-husband's operas during his lifetime. After a brief pause she answered, 'In those days I served!' A similar reply could have been given by Helene Weigel—actress-wife of Bertolt Brecht and director of the Berliner Ensemble after the latter's death—concerning the fifteen years they spent in exile, during which she had been little more than his deceived spouse, domestic factotum and rearer of children.

Like Cosima, Helene Weigel combined an enormous capacity for subordination with tough-mindedness. Product of a progressive Viennese *lycée* (whose headmistress, a Jewish feminist, briefly employed Kokoschka and Schoenberg to teach her girls art and music), she had trained as an actress. Soon after her Berlin début in the early 1920s she had met Brecht, an up-and-coming playwright who was married and living in Munich at the time. Not long after their meeting he left provincial Munich for the German capital, which during those brief 'golden Weimar years' closely approximated to the cultural metropolis of Europe. Unable to find lodgings in Berlin, he moved in with the accommodating Helene Weigel, who, aware of a playwright's need for privacy, promptly vacated her studio attic and took a furnished room nearby. Although she had moved out she frequently returned to her former bed, in consequence of which she soon presented Brecht, already the father of a daughter in Munich, with an illegitimate son. Simultaneously he was creative in all sorts of directions—writing, discussing and incubating plays, trying out avant garde methods of production, dabbling in film, and so forth. In those diverse activities he always worked with collaborators, some of whom he subsequently rewarded by acknowledging their co-authorship. It is not much of an exaggeration to ascribe authorship of part of his *oeuvre* to an informal collective centred on Brecht, and, since most of his co-workers were female, one biographer coined the epithet 'sexual collective' in describing them. (This is not meant to signify that every female drawn into Brecht's field of force was inevitably bedded by him—though the great majority undoubtedly were.)

What was it that made Brecht, an unprepossessing, badly dressed and sometimes downright malodorous man so irresistible to women even before he had achieved celebrity status? The novelist Lion Feuchtwanger,[1] whose friendship with Brecht went back to the early Munich days, describes him thus in his 1930 *roman à clef Success*:

> Of course, this fellow was always unshaven. The way he made his hair grow over his forehead had a kind of naïve coquetishness. He smelt like soldiers on the march. When he sang his crude ballads with his shrill voice, women swooned. . . .

What bound the members of the 'sexual collective' to Brecht was a common dedication to radicalism alike in art, politics and personal relations; concerning social mores nothing was considered more outmoded than the institution of marriage. In 1927 Brecht divorced Marianne Zoff, his first, Munich-based, wife from whom he had long lived apart—and then, eighteen months later, to everybody's surprise, he married Helene Weigel. Surprise is actually too feeble a term for denoting the reaction of the sexual collective. When, armed with a bunch of flowers, he broke the news to Carola Neher (Polly in the film version of *The Threepenny Opera*) and added, 'It couldn't be avoided—but it doesn't mean anything', the actress beat him around the face with the flowers he had just presented to her. Hers was a mild reaction. Elizabeth Hauptmann, his chief literary assistant-cum-mistress, made

1. Lion Feuchtwanger (1889–1958): German-Jewish novelist and playwright eventually domiciled in the U.S. (*Jew Süss, The Oppermans*).

an unsuccessful suicide attempt; another literary member of the collective promptly got herself engaged to an incompatible suitor.

What motivated Brecht to marry Helene Weigel at the risk of severe censure by others? Three answers suggest themselves: he admired her acting ability; she was a devoted helpmeet and mother (bearing him another daughter the following year); lastly, and just as importantly, as a Communist Party member she laid claim to a comprehension of socio-political processes he was only groping towards in the year of the Wall Street crash. The worldwide depression triggered by the crash helped hoist the Nazis into power. On Hitler's accession in early 1933 the Brechts fled Germany with the help of friends who smuggled their children out of the country. There followed fifteen years of peripatetic exile— involving writing 'for the drawer' for him, and immersion in domestic tasks to the virtual exclusion of acting opportunities for her. The first way-station on their emigrants' odyssey was Denmark. Here, in a surprisingly short time, the sexual collective was reconstituted with a mixture of German emigré and indigenous Danish members. One of the latter was Ruth Berlau, an actress with writing ambitions and left-wing sympathies who was married to a doctor; she eventually left her husband and her homeland to be closer to Brecht in his next long-term haven of refuge, America.

In the United States the Brechts mainly lived in Hollywood, where he obtained low-level employment as a script-writer, while Ruth Berlau alternated between New York and Washington, D.C., which afforded her opportunities for political and literary work. In 1942—Brecht happened to be writing *The Caucasian Chalk Circle* at the time—Ruth was expecting a child by him. This coincidence influenced his delineation of the character of Grusche, the heroine of the play and the most overtly appealing female in the Brechtian canon. (In the play the maid Grusche takes care of a princess's child cast adrift in a revolution and saves it at the risk of her own life and marriage prospects.) Brecht endowed Grusche with more appealing features than originally intended in an effort to encourage Ruth to go ahead with the pregnancy.

He succeeded in this—as well as in keeping the pregnancy secret from Helen Weigel. The child was duly born, but died soon afterwards. Its death was only one of a series of blows Ruth Berlau sustained in the course of a long association with Brecht which ultimately left her the most pathetic and ill-used member of the sexual collective.

During the years of their American exile Helen Weigel remained locked in her *hausfrau* rôle, while Brecht had to console himself with the thought that the plays he was writing would eventually achieve performances after the war. This hope was in part fulfilled by the post-war première of *Galileo* (in translation by Eric Bentley) on Broadway. However, the play which starred Charles Laughton—who, incidentally, had fallen in love with the inveterately heterosexual Brecht—failed to impress either the critics or theatre-going New Yorkers. Not long after, the playwright was cited before the Committee for Un-American Activities. Although he managed to nonplus his would-be inquisitors with characteristically cryptic answers to their questions, it was time to quit America, with whose language and way of life he had in any case—unlike his erstwhile musical collaborator Kurt Weill—never bothered to familiarize himself.

The Brechts accordingly returned, via Switzerland, to East Germany, whose government put a lavishly subsidized company and a permanent theatre at the playwright's disposal. The Theater am Schiffbauerdamm in East Berlin gave Brecht the opportunity for staging the key part of his *oeuvre* written in exile which had never seen the light of day. By the same token it offered Helene Weigel a chance to tread the boards again after an all-too-long absence. Here she 'created' the parts of the Princess in *The Caucasian Chalk Circle*, of the Mother in Brecht's Gorky adaptation and, most memorably, of Mother Courage in the play of the same name. In addition to achieving prodigies on stage, Helene Weigel rendered her husband valuable assistance in overseeing the manifold activities of the company, officially known as the Berliner Ensemble. However, by this time, the early 1950s, they were husband and wife in name only, and Brecht was contemplating divorce—although he never crossed that particular Rubicon. He had long ago stopped loving Helene, though he esteemed her as the mother of his now grown-up children, theatrical helpmeet and ideological drill-sergeant when he felt beset, as he increasingly did, by political uncertainty. Part of him admired, while another deplored, her masculine (or, some would say, native Jewish) ability to drive a hard bargain; when leaving Denmark she had, for instance, secured a higher price for their house than they had paid originally. Given the etiolation of the Brechts' matrimonial bond, it was only natural that the playwright's apotheosis as head of his own theatrical company should be accompanied by a reconstitution of the sexual collective. Old co-workers like Elizabeth Hauptmann and Ruth Berlau were now, so to speak, supplemented by a number of aspiring theatrical hopefuls. One such was Käthe Reichel, a gifted and overly ambitious young actress, whose demands for extra rehearsal time roused the ill-will of her colleagues. Brecht, for his part, lavished loving attention on her and called her his 'dear clamp'. (Shades of Luther's wife, the ex-nun Käthe, whom the reformer had punningly dubbed his *Kette*, or chain.) Another recruit to the sexual collective was Isot Kilian, actress wife of the dissident East German academic, Professor Harich. Brecht, whose sexual mores had always been informed by what may be termed nonchalant consumerism, sent Harich a letter in which he suggested *expressis verbis* that he divorce his wife and remarry her again in two years' time. Harich's reaction to this piece of monumental impudence is not recorded. He had, at any rate, matters of graver consequence to ponder at the time, being involved in oppositional activities which resulted in him spending the next ten years in jail.

Brecht, too, was multiply preoccupied. He reputedly abre-acted his own disappointment with the régime on whose extraordinary largesse his theatre (with its unheard-of nine months' rehearsal time) depended in quips like: 'If the authorities disapprove of the people why don't they dissolve it and elect another one?' He was, moreover, in bad health, and at the Schiffbauerdamm he encountered problems inseparable from any large organization, as well as others specifically of his own making. Ruth Berlau was a reproachful presence that might be marginalized but could not be entirely ignored. She had been creatively and emotionally involved with Brecht for the best part of twenty years, and although she continued to occupy an important post as pictorial archivist of the Berliner Ensemble, she felt neglected and ill-used. The man who had fathered her dead child had bought a house near Copenhagen 'for them', but she knew that he intended it for her alone and refused to be put out to grass. Brecht often let entire weeks elapse without seeing her, after which he expressed shocked surprise at the deterioration in her appearance and demeanour. This woman, formerly possessed of formidable talent as political activist, actress, writer and photographer, was now reduced to making embarrassing gestures of protest at her relegation to the archivist's limbo. She screamed abuse, slapped faces, threw stones at windows and drank ever more heavily. Brecht, whose *obiter dicta* on love include the ineffable comment, 'there's no pleasure in taking when the bill is presented afterwards', received letters from her which he opened like a basket of vipers.

In the mid-'50s the already ailing playwright recruited yet another young member into the sexual collective. Käthe Rülicke by name, she was an assistant director and the extra-curricular (i.e. non-professional, non-amorous) rôle Brecht assigned to her was to act as his personal confidante in the Ruth Berlau case. All these emotion-fraught complications had the potential, as Helene Weigel well knew, to impair the efficient working of the by then internationally famous Berliner Ensemble. In a situation in which she, too, was to a considerable extent an injured party, she displayed remarkable sangfroid. When a Polish guest director began to make advances to Isot Kilian she summoned him discreetly to her office; there she intimated to the would-be interloper that it upset Brecht if other men paid too much attention to the women he loved. In late 1956 Brecht died, aged 58, and was buried at his own request without the elaborate *pompes funèbres* that customarily attended the demise of important personages in Eastern Europe. In drawing up his will he had previously sought to discharge the debt owed to some of the women who had shared his work and his bed: the royalties from *The Threepenny Opera* were to go to Elizabeth Hauptmann, those from *The Caucasian Chalk Circle* to Ruth Berlau, those from

The Mother to Käthe Rülicke, and some from his poems to Isot Kilian. Alas, because of a legal nicety, the intended division of Brecht's literary estate was destined to remain in the realm of good intentions. Isot Kilian, whom Brecht had despatched to get his last will authenticated by a notary had, on finding that official's waiting-room crowded, left without obtaining his all-important signature on the document—and thereby rendered it invalid. It is said that at the great man's burial five black-clad females stood beside the grave, of whom four were crying and one laughing; the one who laughed was the widow. Because of the defective will Helene Weigel inherited, in addition to the directorship of the Berliner Ensemble, the whole of Brecht's very considerable estate. Having displayed rare forbearance of rivals during her husband's life-time, she now revealed an unsuspected mean streak by assigning paltry sums to her other four intended co-legatees. Only in the case of Elizabeth Hauptmann, the co-author of some of Brecht's 1920s' plays and indispensible assistant thereafter, did the adamant widow let herself be persuaded, by her husband's publisher Peter Suhrkamp, to make remotely adequate provisions for services rendered.

The woman we have called Brecht's Cosima survived the death-induced termination of what had long become her *mariage blanc* for fifteen years, directing the Berliner Ensemble till her own death in 1971.

Lida Baarova

The mutual attraction between men of power and beautiful women—or, simply, women projecting beauty as actresses or dancers—is a well-attested fact. It can be traced back in history at least to Byzantium where Emperor Justinian took the circus artist Theodosia as his consort. Our own century has shown the prevalence of the phenomenon in countries with the most divergent power structures—Communist, Democratic and Fascist. It occurred both in Communist China (see p. 27), and Russia, where Marshal Bulganin[2] pressed his

2. Nikolai Bulganin (1895–1975): Soviet statesman, economic and military administrator.

unsolicited attentions upon the singer Galina Vishnevskaya like some corseted Czarist Guards' officer caught in a time warp outside the Marinsky stage door. In the United States President Kennedy enjoyed closer contact with Hollywood even than Ronald Reagan by bedding exemplars of tinseltown pulchritude who allegedly included Marilyn Monroe. In Fascist Italy Mussolini pursued an extra-marital liaison with the actress Clara Petacci, who was caught at his side in the hour of reckoning and shared his ignominious end. The Third Reich, too, engendered an adulterous romance wherein power served as an aphrodisiac and gave the glow of love a phosphorescent tinge. The couple involved could have been dubbed Beauty and the Beast, if the man had not looked too insignificant for the latter epithet. Short, frail, ugly of countenance, and clubfooted, Joseph Goebbels was variously nicknamed 'poison dwarf', 'shrunken Teuton', 'Wotan's Mickey Mouse', 'Mahatma Propagandhi', or '*Kaulquappe*: tadpole'; tadpoles, it was said, consist only of *Maul* (mouth) and *Schwanz* (tail, or penis).

According to folklore, the Propaganda Minister's *Maul* was so huge that when he wanted a mouth organ, the tallest tree in the Black Forest had to be cut down. As to the tadpole's only other bodily organ, the vox populi noted that the only virgin left in Berlin was the stone angel atop the *Siegessäule* (Victory Column). There was more than a grain of truth in that remark because, when it came to womanizing, Goebbels led the field among the Nazi high-ups. Since a great deal of patronage over stage and screen was in his gift, many aspiring actresses shared his 'casting couch' in furtherance of their career; other women slept with him because power exerts the same attraction on the impressionable as a magnet does on iron filings. Although the eugenically conscious, family-oriented Nazi ethos deprecated promiscuity, Goebbels' sexual peccadilloes tended to be shrugged off as casual flings. Even his wife did not take them too seriously; with five pregnancies and two miscarriages to her account during the first seven years of their marriage, Magda Goebbels probably thought her spouse needed occasional outlets for his free-floating sexual energy. What was more, in public the Number Three in the Nazi Party showed his wife unusually non-macho signs of affection, such as calling her 'angel' or 'sweeting'. As a blonde, Magda conformed to the ideal Nazi stereotype, even though her soigné deportment and dress-sense set her apart from the distinctly homespun—not to say clod-hopping—model of femininity in vogue during the Third Reich. Hitler, the erstwhile Alpine backwoodsman repelled by the cosmopolitanism of Vienna now turned omnipotent Führer, wanted German women to be unglamorous, domesticated and broad-hipped (for childbearing); at the same time, a non-sexual impulse—maybe the pursuit of a fantasy about court life—made him seek to surround himself with women who exuded glamour. Society, or more precisely, what passed for society in the Third Reich, used to gather at receptions and on Party occasions, where the male participants tended to be uniformed Nazi high-ups and frock-coated or lounge-suited diplomats and businessmen; often the females in evidence were stage or screen performers whose company Hitler and Goebbels favoured. (Goering, too, had married an actress.)

At one such social occasion during the 1936 Party Rally at Nuremberg the 20-year-old Czech movie star Lida Baarova was present. Despite her youth Lida had appeared in films for several years—most recently opposite the matinée idol Gustav Froehlich in *Barcarole*—and was currently living with Froehlich. (By coincidence, both Goebbels and the actor had lakeside villas on the outskirts of Berlin and were thus almost neighbours.) When Goebbels met the actress, he was instantly smitten; her dark hair, high Slav cheekbones and husky voice all captivated the man who a few short years later would pour poisonous invective on 'Slav subhumanity'. Smitten, he pounced at once. Saying that he wanted to discuss Fräulein Baarova's career prospects with her, he took her into a private room in the Party Rally building. Three minutes before the interview had to end—Goebbels was due to address the Rally immediately afterwards—he planted a kiss on Lida's lips. She barely had time to help him erase lipstick traces with her handkerchief before he was off, orating before the huge Brown-shirted throng. In the course of the ecstatically received peroration he occasionally focused his gaze on the actress (seated, among other *Prominente*, in front of the auditorium) and wiped his mouth with his handkerchief. This overt signal of love, sent out during a rhetorical performance which had the international press corps scribbling away furiously, impressed Lida profoundly. So did Goebbels' subsequent assiduousness in sending her flowers accompanied by *billets-doux* and offers of other, more substantial, presents.

The affair flourished. The lovers held clandestine trysts either at Lida's small apartment off Berlin's Kurfürstendamm, or in a pavillion on Goebbels' lakeside estate. Gustav Froehlich put no obstacles in their way, although the Third Reich rumour mill put out the report that the actor had slapped Goebbels' face. This was a total fiction; Froehlich, who had divorced his Jewish wife after the Nazi take-over, would hardly have tangled with one of the most powerful and malign men in the new power structure. (The fictitious slap, incidentally, inspired the punning bon mot, *'Ich möchte einmal fröhlich sein'*, which could mean, 'I would like to be happy once', or 'I would like to be in the actor's shoes'.) As to the other injured party involved, Magda Goebbels, her attitude to the affair was both less complaisant and more vacillating. When she first got to hear of the liaison, she dismissed it as just another one of her wayward husband's customary peccadillos. Later she changed tack and viewed the *amour* as so serious, not to say ineluctable, that she invited the other woman to tea and made a bid for her friendship and co-operation. Amid the tinkle of Meissen cups in the sumptuous ministerial residence, she suggested to the nonplussed actress that they address each other in the familiar *Du* and would brook no denial. She said she knew how much Goebbels loved Lida, and wanted to be treated by her as a sister and not as a rival; for her own part she was quite prepared to condone the *affaire* as long as it did not drive a wedge between the children and their father. But three into two simply will not go. Magda's compromise suggestion was unworkable, even if—a very big if—she had intended it seriously in the first place.

With the lovers continuing to see each other, gossip about the affair appeared in the foreign press, and this had obvious implications for Germany's carefully fostered image in the year she played host to the Olympic Games. Goebbels, who had never hidden his sneering contempt for many of his colleagues, was in turn bitterly hated by the likes of Himmler, chief Party ideologue Rosenberg,[3] and Food Minister Darré. The last-named, in a characteristically Nazi locution, described Goebbels' scandalous *amour* as 'squirting pus' on the clean waistcoats worn by himself and other morally upright Nazi leaders. Darré went on to warn his anti-Goebbels allies that something had to be done to stop further emission of such 'pus'. However, what he and his partisans were up against was the fact that the Propaganda Minister enjoyed a close rapport with the Führer, who in turn stood in the same relation to his satraps as that of the sun to the solar system. Goebbels unique closeness to Hitler stemmed from a two-fold nexus between the two men. For one, Hitler had a shrewd appreciation of the extraordinary gifts Goebbels brought to the manipulation of the German national consciousness in the Nazi interest. For another, the Goebbels' Berlin apartment provided a congenial setting for the notoriously insomniac Hitler to while away his evenings and nights; the key rôle in providing him with that 'home from home' was of course played by Magda Goebbels, the chief victim of the Baarova *affaire*.

It so happened that a leading Nazi official close both to Goebbels and his wife had a powerful personal motive for exposing the *affaire*. This was Karl Hanke, State Secretary at the Propaganda Ministry and an officer in the SS. Hanke had the key to the Minister's mailbox, which enabled him to monitor the correspondence between Goebbels and his astonishing tally of mistresses. In addition he had the motivation to ferret out the thirty-six names that appeared in his resultant 'Leporello album'.

Previously an unquestioning devotee of his brilliant Minister, Hanke had been outraged by this miasma of libertinage, and claimed, as an SS man, to feel duty-bound to combat such corruption. One means for venting his sense of outrage was the organization of a hostile claque at the première of

---

3. Alfred Rosenberg (1893–1946): German Nazi ideologist; war-time administrator of the occupied Eastern territories, he was hanged at Nuremberg.

the new Lida Baarova film, *A Prussian Love Story*. The claque punctuated the screening with whistles and catcalls; when the star took a bow at the end, she was greeted with shouts of *'Ministerhure'*.

By coincidence Hanke also coveted the highly personable Frau Minister, whose own interpretation of the marriage vows, incidentally, had not always been of the strictest. As a token of his devotion Hanke handed Frau Magda a copy of the thirty-six-name list (a facsimile of which also landed on the desk of SS Reichsführer Himmler). The State Secretary's capacity for moral outrage was matched by his foresight: using the persuasive powers conferred by his SS rank, he had already obtained the agreement of some of the thirty-six sex partners of the Minister to give evidence in court in case of divorce proceedings being instituted. As for Frau Goebbels, she inclined more and more to the view that her husband's conduct left her no other alternative.

At this point Goering, the Number Two in the Nazi hierarchy, brought the matter to Hitler's attention. The Führer, who had only some weeks earlier dismissed the Reich Defence Minister, Field Marshal von Blomberg,[4] for marrying a 'woman with a past', was exceedingly wrath to hear of his Propaganda Minister's entanglement with Lida Baarova; the last thing he wanted was another scandal that put the moral probity of his satraps in question. He accordingly summoned Goebbels to the Chancellery and read him the Riot Act. Confronted thus, Goebbels for the first and last time in his political career, hesitated about putting self-advancement above all else. He declared himself ready, for the sake of love, to resign his ministerial post and take up some distant ambassadorship—maybe in Tokyo—but Hitler would not hear of a divorce. He ordered Goebbels to sever all links with Lida Baarova and observe a six-month moratorium before contemplating any change in his marital arrangements.

From here on Lida's fortunes changed drastically. Goebbels curtly informed her of the end of their *affaire* in a phone call from Goering's residence, and had to exert his famed

---

4. Werner von Blomberg (1878–1946): German general and minister, dubbed 'Rubber lion' for kotowing to Hitler.

rhetorical skills—within the hearing of the other—to talk her out of the suicide she threatened. Her latest starring vehicle, Dostoevsky's *The Gambler*, disappeared from all German cinema screens overnight, and all her pending film contracts were cancelled. After keeping her under close surveillance for three months, the Police Chief of Berlin finally told her to go back to Prague in the interest of her own safety.

But the actress's return to Czech obscurity did not signify the total elimination of romance from the case. Hanke wanted to marry Magda as much as ever and continued importuning Hitler to let divorce proceedings go ahead. (The happy dénouement envisaged by Hanke, in which he ultimately replaced his current superior not only in the marriage bed but also the ministerial chair, would also have been most welcome to Darré, Rosenberg and other members of the anti-Goebbels cabal.) However, nothing would persuade Hitler to drop the ace propagandist at the precise time—the run-up to the Second World War—when his skill in poisoning the wells of truth with printer's ink and agitating the air-waves to drown out the cries of the victims was needed more than ever before. The estranged Goebbelses were accordingly commanded to have a reunion at the Berghof (Hitler's Bavarian mountain eyrie) which provided what is nowadays known as an excellent photo opportunity. The cover photograph in the next issue of the *Berliner Illustrierte* showing Goebbels and Magda, both po-faced, on either side of a smiling Hitler finally stilled talk of an impending marital breakup that had been heard for the previous eighteen months.

Outwardly things thus resumed their normal course. Behind the scenes, though, both spouses had ample grounds for dissatisfaction. Magda had not forgiven Goebbels his infidelity, and he had to suffer the continued presence of his sworn rival Hanke at the Propaganda Ministry. In addition, he chafed under the enforced severance from the woman he came close to sacrificing his career for. Within days, however, history contrived to present the thwarted lover with an opportunity for abreacting all his frustration. When in November 1938 the grief-crazed son of a Jew deported to the no-man's land between Germany and Poland shot a Nazi diplomat in Paris, Goebbels threw himself heart and soul into organizing the vicious retaliatory pogrom the régime unleashed upon defenceless German Jewry. With the extinction of independent Czechoslovakia and the attack on Poland providing additional therapy, he was able to slough off the depression that had dogged him after the break with Lida. Meanwhile, too, the marriage had knitted together sufficiently for another Goebbels child (their sixth) to be born in 1940.

By this time Karl Hanke had moved from the Propaganda Ministry and been made Gauleiter of his native Silesia. At the tail-end of the war the deranged Führer even appointed Hanke successor to the 'defector' Himmler. Goebbels did not desert Hitler, but, like him, committed suicide (in the company of Magda and their six children). A few days later Hanke was shot by Czech partisans—compatriots of Lida Baarova. She survived the war and lived on in Prague, still cherishing the memory of her one-time lover.

Jane Fonda

According to an old wives' tale, if an expectant mother undergoes a traumatic experience, the nature of that experience can influence what sort of person her child will grow into. If we substitute father for mother in that bit of folklore, we may, with judicious suspension of disbelief, hit upon the key to the grown-up Jane Fonda's character-development.

Around the time of Jane's birth in 1937, Henry Fonda was heavily involved in the shooting of the Spanish Civil War movie *Blockade*. The film's director, Lewis Milestone, and its script-writer, Clifford Odets,[1] intended the film to be a means of arousing cinemagoers' sympathies for the threatened Republican cause. (Milestone had directed *All Quiet on the Western Front*, a film which undoubtedly influenced the thinking of its mass audience.) However, as the shooting of *Blockade* proceeded, the studio heads, who were fearful that Mussolini and Franco would embargo their entire output in retaliation, decided to emasculate the film. Milestone and Odets were replaced and the script neutered. The version

---

1. Clifford Odets (1906–63): American dramatist and script-writer reared in the theatre of social protest (*Waiting for Lefty, Golden Boy*).

of *Blockade* that finally reached the screen mentioned neither Franco nor the Fascists and conveyed only the most anodyne message. This experience and other similar ones had a profoundly depressing effect on Henry Fonda, whose recurrent theme in conversation with Hollywood friends hereafter was the necessity of selling out in order to survive. Towards his family he expressed his bitterness through withdrawal into silence and melancholy.

Personally he had little to feel melancholic about. *The Grapes of Wrath* was one of the cinematic sensations of 1939, and in the following year his wife Frances bore him a son, Peter. For all that, their first child, Jane, grew up in a household where affluence and conspicuous socializing camouflaged an emotional vacuum at the heart of things. Then in 1943, Henry, whose remoteness from the family created that vacuum, went into the U.S. navy. The situation now improved, only to deteriorate again after his demobilization. In 1947, feeling frustrated on several counts in Hollywood, he took Frances and the siblings East and switched to work in the theatre. Before long he started a liaison with another much younger woman, and proceeded to compound that hurt to his wife by telling her he had been unhappy throughout their thirteen-year-long marriage. The 'revelation' plunged Frances into a nervous breakdown. 1950, Jane's thirteenth year, proved her unluckiest. Her mother was away in a sanatorium where—the siblings were told one day—she died of a heart attack. (In reality Frances had slashed her throat.) Eight months later her father married again. Soon after, her brother, while purportedly examining a shot-gun on a friend's estate, discharged a pellet that penetrated his liver. However, thanks to surgery and three blood transfusions, Peter pulled through; in addition the siblings' new 'mother', who was Jane's senior by only eight years, showed great warmth towards them. Things therefore settled down somewhat, at least as far as Jane was concerned. She spent several uneventful years at a prep school en route to Vassar College. Peter had livelier prep school days—so lively, in fact, that having been expelled from two schools in succession, he was made to stay with a maternal aunt in Omaha.

Meanwhile, Henry Fonda's third marriage (he had had

another wife before Frances) showed signs of giving way to a fourth; the siblings' new stepmother was Jane's senior by a mere five years. At Vassar Jane evinced a lively interest in men, but though sexually hyperactive, fulfilled minimal study requirements. She also attended drama workshops, which led on to her stage début at 20, with her father, in *The Male Animal*. At the time Henry Fonda disapproved of Jane's acting ambition, saying—with unconscious irony—that he wanted a more normal life for his children. Actually her acting ambitions had not yet been fully formed; that only happened, when after quitting Vassar, and tasting life on the Left Bank of Paris she returned to New York and formed a strong friendship with Susan Strasberg.

From New York, where she did modelling and mingled with fashion editors and photographers, she went to Hollywood and indulged in a beatnik phase. Back in New York again, she enrolled at the Actor's Studio (headed by Susan's father, Lee Strasberg), where the 'Method' style of acting had gained world-wide renown with the elevation of Marlon Brando to superstar status. At the Actor's Studio she formed a very close attachment with a budding director, the Greek-descended Andreas Voutsinas. This attachment had an amorous component (though Jane kept another affair going for a while), but both placed greater emphasis on perfecting their craft. In effect, Voutsinas became a sort of Svengali to Jane's Trilby—the first of a number of domineering men in the life of the latter-day feminist.

Soon after, Joshua Logan gave her her first film part in *Tall Story*. Her second screen appearance in *The Chapman Report*—a movie inspired by Dr. Kinsey's researches into the sexual mores of American society—earned her enthusiastic reviews. At the same time she attracted considerable publicity by expressing personal views on sex and marriage which echoed the theme of the film. Undoubtedly influenced by the sight of her father's disintegrating fourth marriage, she denounced matrimony as a constricting and outmoded institution which would have no place in her scheme of things. Such subversive sentiments, which, a few years earlier, would have scandalized a Hollywood establishment responsible for the Green Code and the Hays Office, at that time (the year was 1961) simply swelled the chorus greeting the dawn of the Age of Aquarius. The Fonda tribe entered the decade of the '60s in an appropriate state of interpersonal disarray; the fourth Mrs. Fonda was leaving Henry, Peter had dropped out of college (to try acting), and Jane was living with Voutsinas, whom her father loathed both on and off stage. As if to prove Henry's professional objection to Voutsinas, a play which he had persuaded Jane to take to Broadway flopped miserably—but she still clung to the man whom every one else now merely regarded as drama coach to an up-and-coming star.

Ultimately, though, as Jane swam into Roger Vadim's orbit, her first 'Svengali' vanished from view. Vadim, a Frenchman of Russian extraction, was a cinematic showman with a penchant for audience titilation, who had simultaneously conferred stardom and marital status on his three previous leading ladies: Brigitte Bardot, Anette Strayberg and Catherine Deneuve. Vadim cast Jane (a fluent French speaker since her Left Bank days) in *La Ronde*, a tale of a sexual merry-go-round. Even though, following precedent, he had made her his mistress, he did not scruple to jazz up the bill-boards for *La Ronde* with a depiction of Jane's naked posterior. She started a legal action, which he defended by shuffling off responsibility for the poster on to the advertising agency contracted to promote the film. Living with Vadim broadened Jane's outlook in several directions. She joined her lover in pot-smoking sessions and on a trip to Moscow where Cold War preconceptions fell from her eyes like scales; through him she also met Roger Vailland, a Marxist intellectual, who had a strong influence on her thinking. In 1965 she and Vadim got married. Afterwards she went to Hollywood to star in *Cat Ballou*; during her stay she personally witnessed the explosion of black frustration and anger in the Watts ghetto.

The reality of racial tension was again forcibly brought home to her the following year, while she was on location for Otto Preminger's *Hurry Sundown* in a Louisiana townlet. The local Ku-Klux-Klan threatened Preminger because his black actors did not use the segregated swimming pool, but instead of submitting to the threat he hired special police. Then, one afternoon, a little black boy ran up to Jane in the main street to hand her a flower and she picked him up and kissed him. She could see the passers-by freeze with horror—and within the hour the sheriff ordered the company to leave town 'for their own safety'. The process of Jane's politicization had commenced—helped along by Joan Baez's protest against the Vietnam War and, possibly, by her brother's arrest on a charge of possessing marijuana. (Peter was not convicted and went on to make his cinematic début with the biker film *Wild Angels*, a forerunner of *Easy Rider*.) The following year Jane Fonda, while starring nude in her husband's science-fiction extravaganza *Barbarella*, came politically of age. In France again, where she commuted between fashionable St. Tropez and Paris, she evinced keen interest in the Tribunal on American war crimes in Vietnam convened by Bertrand Russell, Jean-Paul Sartre, Simone de Beauvoir, James Baldwin and others.

In 1968 Jane had a baby daughter whom she named Vanessa in honour of her English actress colleague and fellow radical Vanessa Redgrave. In that year she essayed her first socially significant rôle, in *They Shoot Horses, Don't They*, a movie about a six-day dance marathon of Depression days. In order to prepare herself for the part of Gloria (who speaks the classic no-hoper line, 'The whole damn world is just like Central Casting; they've got it all rigged before we ever show up'), Jane took a beach house in Malibu where she lived in barefoot hippy style and drained herself of energy. Though her performance aroused admiration among her colleagues, she missed out on the hoped-for Oscar—but consoled herself with the 'best actress' award of the New York film critics.

As the '60s drew to a stormy close, the name Fonda was writ ever larger on the Hollywood firmament, in newspaper headlines and on American TV screens. While the road movie *Easy Rider* catapulted Peter to overnight fame, and to equivalence with Bob Dylan within the counter-culture, Jane experienced a St. Paul-on-the-Damascus-Road-type illumination. She returned from a trip to India (during which she had read Hermann Hesse's indictment of human cupidity, *Steppenwolf*) clear in her own mind that she needed to leave Vadim. This was to be a first move in a wider re-direction of her life prompted by the realization that the pursuit of fame represented a dead end. Jane thenceforth became a political crusader and activist. She plunged into the campaign of some Red Indians for the recovery of tribal lands filched from them by the U.S. in the nineteenth century. She visited the Indian militants illegally occupying Alcatraz Island in San Francisco Bay and smoked marijuana with them. Then she set out with Elisabeth Vailland on a fact-finding cross-country tour of Indian reservations; at Fort Lawson (in the state of Washington), where militants had occupied a disused military facility, she was arrested, but not sent to jail.

Before long two other, more immediately dramatic campaigns absorbed her attention and energy. One, naturally, was the mounting opposition to the Vietnam War. The other concerned the cause of the Black Panthers incarnated in their charismatic co-founder Huey Newton. The Panthers were involved in various fatal shoot-outs with the Californian police, in one of which Newton himself was seriously implicated. Convinced that he had been set up by the authorities, Jane told a meeting: 'Huey Newton is qualified to be President of the United States; he is the only man I have ever met who approaches sainthood.' Though few would echo that particular judgement, her contention that the authorities were bending the truth and the law in order to frame alleged subversives had substance, and was evidenced by F.B.I. chief Edgar Hoover's attempt to implicate the actress herself in financing the Panthers' purchase of guns for the coming revolution. Jane's contribution to the Stop-the-Vietnam-War campaign took diverse form. She toured university campuses addressing anti-war rallies, helped finance 'G.I. coffee houses' (clubs near army bases offering soldiers leisure facilities and politicized entertainment), and organized the F.T.A. (Fuck the army) troupe which provided that entertainment.

She interspersed all this activity with the filming of *Klute*, a movie about prostitution, preparing for which she befriended a number of hookers to study their motivation and life-style. *Klute* finally earned her the Oscar denied her earlier, probably for political reasons, when she starred in *They Shoot Horses, Don't They*. At the award ceremony she calmed nerves all round by announcing, 'There's a lot I could say but this isn't the time or the place.' On other occasions she was not so controlled. Returning from a campus speaking engagement in Canada, she was stopped by U.S. customs who confiscated her address book and 102 vials of drugs. When she tried to go to the toilet, she was stopped by a patrolman, whom she kicked in the thigh while screaming 'Get the fuck out of here, you pig!' She was jailed and let out on bail. The papers meanwhile carried banner headlines 'Jane Fonda arrested on drugs charge'; disappointingly for the press, a police laboratory test revealed that the 102 vials of drugs consisted of vitamin and valium pills.

In 1972 she crossed another frontier by flying to Hanoi, capital of North Vietnam. From there she made a series of broadcasts denouncing the U.S. air attacks on the country, especially the bombing of dykes. Her critics in the U.S. Congress claimed that in so doing she had also crossed the thin borderline between opposition to the war and treasonable propaganda for the enemy, but because of the illegal nature—under the U.S. Constitution—of the war itself, they failed to sustain the treason charge. She also became the target of physical and verbal attacks. Stopping over in Sweden on the return journey from North Vietnam, she attended a demonstration at Stockholm—favourite bolt-hole for American draft resisters—and had a pot of red paint flung over her; back in the United States she was likened to Tokyo Rose (who broadcast Japanese propaganda to G.I.s during the War in the Pacific).

However, by then—the early 70s—American attitudes to the Vietnam conflict were changing. For one, the realization was gaining ground that, contrary to official predictions, the war had become unwinnable. For another, the court-martial of Lieutenant Calley over the MyLai massacre revealed a level of atrocities against Vietnamese civilians which American public opinion felt disinclined to tolerate. Since Jane had previously helped put together a documentary cataloguing U.S. army atrocities in Vietnam through eye-witness accounts of honourably discharged G.I.s—a documentary which all the three major American TV networks refused to screen—she felt completely vindicated. Her sense of having been right throughout the complex South East Asian imbroglio received a further boost by President Nixon's difficulties over the secret bombing of Cambodia and the unfolding Watergate scandal. But, as the ancient Greeks well knew, a sense of hubris invites nemesis. In 1973 the truce that, for all practical purposes, ended the Vietnam War also brought the release of American PoWs. Their tales of torture at the hands of their North Vietnamese captors contradicted the simple black-and-white imagery—saintly Ho-Chi-Minh battling against diabolical Richard Nixon—that had informed Jane's attitude towards the conflict. Her reflex reaction to the torture allegations was to call the released prisoners (whose bodies still bore the stigmata of ill-treatment) liars whom history would judge harshly. When forced to modify her stance, she rationalized North Vietnamese behaviour by arguing that U.S. aggression had forced them to act brutally in self-defence. Overall, though, as Nixon vanished beneath the mudslide of Watergate and the war dragged on ignominiously till the total collapse of U.S.-backed South Vietnam, Jane could claim to have moved with—and not against—the grain of history.

Throughout these alarums and excursions she had also had a busy private life. After a brief affair with fellow actor and anti-war activist Donald Sutherland, she met Tom Hayden, the subsequently most important man in her life. Hayden, though virtually unknown outside the United States, enjoyed—as a '60s figure who had been wherever 'it was at'—considerable fame within the country. Editor of the Berkeley campus daily, civil rights worker in Mississippi, founder of Students for a Democratic Society (and author of the S.D.S. Manifesto with its leitmotif of participatory democracy) in turn, he had last come into prominence as one of the 'Chicago Eight' charged with fomenting a riot at the 1968 Democratic Party Convention. Found guilty at the first trial, he had managed to get the verdict overturned on appeal in 1972. When Jane met him, he had just managed to have himself expelled from the Red Family Commune at Berkeley, for—in the words of his ex-mistress Anne Weills—'manipulating everyone'. With her instinctive respect for adepts at *realpolitik*, Jane did not let Anne Weills' judgement on Hayden colour her own estimate of him—quite the contrary. (Even so, her encounter with Ms Weills, a prominent feminist,

142

had a consciousness-raising effect: when the other woman declared, on public TV, 'Our lives are defined by men, directed by men', Jane concurred, but added, to avoid misunderstandings, that she was no 'separatist'.)

She and Tom Hayden married in 1973, without, however, letting the nuptials disrupt the time-table of their political activities. During the following year, which, in its *embarras de richesses*, saw Nixon resign and Jane return to Hanoi to film her self-financed *Introduction to the Enemy*, they had a boy whom they named Troi. That manifestation of domestic felicity indicated that, though the Haydens were, as yet, unconscious of it, they had passed the peak of their radicalism. Tom was the first to edge back into the main stream. In 1975 he opposed Senator John Tunney in the Californian Democratic Primary election on a platform of 'economic democracy', gaining—thanks to the support of students, disadvantaged Hispanics and show-biz friends—about 40% of the vote.

Soon after, Jane returned to main-line Hollywood by starring in *Fun with Dick and Jane*, a comedy about yuppies who, strapped for cash, turn to fashionable thieving. Her next movie, *Julia*, based upon incidents in Lilian Hellmann's life, by contrast had a deeply serious content (somewhat spoilt by the subsequent discovery that the writer had invented those incidents). Jane's next two films were on the themes central to her and her husband's concern: the Vietnam veteran movie *Coming Home*, and the danger-of-nuclear-meltdown film, inspired by the accident on Three Mile Island, *The China Syndrome*. The latter chimed in with Hayden's championing in his Economic Democracy campaign of solar power as the safest, most ecology-friendly source of energy. Another aim of Economic Democracy was the transfer of the control over corporations from millionaires to 'little people', i.e. employees and small shareholders. Meanwhile, however—and this was not lost on a cynical public—the wife of the anti-millionaire crusader had hit upon a stratagem designed to place her among the super-rich. She, a perennial fitness freak, had devised a programme of exercises (the 'Jane Fonda Workout') which was made available country-wide through a chain of body fitness salons and brought in an impressive income from 1979 onwards. Some of that income was, however, swallowed up by expenses she and Hayden incurred touring the Economic Democracy Roadshow. Designed to publicize Hayden's 'new' approach to politics and economics among broad sections of the electorate, the Roadshow failed to make the desired impact—largely because the public perception of Hayden remained one of a turncoat politician (i.e. an ex-radical trying to make his way inside the system).

Simultaneously Jane's own standing as a political personality took a second knock similar to the one she had suffered over the torture of the American PoWs in North Vietnam. The trigger this time were the Boat People fleeing newly-communized South Vietnam in peril of their lives. Joan Baez, the respected initiator of protests against the U.S. involvement in Vietnam, repenting of her former excessive sympathy for Hanoi, now paid two visits to the Boat People refugee camps and challenged Jane to do likewise. The actress could not, however, bring herself to disavow the régime she had championed for so long and, instead of making the requisite public gesture, extended discreet financial support to the Boat People. She also continued to give financial support to her husband in his quest for elected public office. Thus she devoted some of the proceeds from her women-at-work movie *Nine to Five* to subsidize Hayden's race for the Senate in 1984.

As she celebrated her fiftieth birthday, Jane—once the subject of the Fonda Amendment to the National Security Act in the U.S. Congress—approximated ever more to the classic American ideal. She was eternally young, self-actualized, rich and family-orientated. A good mother and devoted wife, she had also been reconciled both on screen (*Golden Pond*) and off with her father—who will probably be remembered as much for his progeny as for his artistry.

VIII

Journalists

Dorothy Parker

RECEIVED wisdom has it that every comic wants to play Hamlet. Whether every actor cast as the Prince of Denmark yearns to put on a red nose is a moot point; what is less debatable is that the world teems with Hamlet types who hide melancholy and self-doubt behind a comic carapace. One such was Dorothy Parker, the first female wit known throughout the English-speaking world. In a manner of speaking, the seeds of her self-doubt were sewn at the moment of conception: she was the offspring of a mixed marriage, and pained awareness of the Jewishness transmitted by her father stayed with Dorothy throughout life. Not that Jacob Rothschild belonged to the species of immigrant Jew arousing disdain in late nineteenth-century America; U.S.-born, he was a prosperous clothing manufacturer and bourgeois paterfamilias.

Dorothy grew up, surrounded by servants, in a large house in a salubrious New York suburb and enjoyed lengthy holidays at the seaside. When she was 5 her mother died, however, and the orphaning left a deep psychic scar. For the remainder of her childhood she felt absolutely alone—reproachful towards Mr. Rothschild for remarrying, isolated from her rather older siblings, and so hostile to her stepmother that she always referred to her as 'the housekeeper'. The latter compounded her existential offence by intense religiosity; every day when little Dorothy returned from the nearby convent school, with the nuns' incessant talk of Jesus buzzing in her head, she was greeted by her stepmother asking 'Did you love Jesus today?' Jacob Rothschild's behaviour was no less obsessional. On Sunday mornings he often marched his family to the cemetery and lined them up beside his first wife's graveside. When a crunch on the gravel indicated a potential audience, he would take out a large handkerchief and wail: 'We're all here, Elizabeth! I am here, Dottie is here, Mrs. Rothschild is here. . . .'

Dorothy grew into an attractive-looking girl with large eyes and a rich head of dark hair. She attended a college-preparatory and finishing-school, ending her education at 18. A year later Mr. Rothschild died. By this time she had obtained a job, on the strength of some published verse, with *Vogue* magazine and lived in a New York boarding-house. Her next employment was with Condé Nast's *Vanity Fair*, a sophisticated journal which was considered the country's *arbiter elegantiarum*.

In 1917, aged 24, she married—primarily to change her name, she would later say—one Edwin Parker, a Wall Street broker who was descended from a long line of New England clergymen. Shortly afterwards, America entered the First World War and Parker enlisted in the Ambulance Corps. He went through some of the last battles on the Western Front, an experience that intensified his predilection for alcohol; worse still, having access to drugs in connection with his work, he compounded one form of abuse by another.

Post-war he was assigned to occupation duty in the Rhineland, where, with little to do, he drank more heavily than ever. Meanwhile, back in New York Dorothy had graduated to drama critic; she had also become a founder member of a writers' 'club' named—after their stamping ground—the Algonquin Hotel set.

The doyen of the Algonquin set was Alexander Woolcott whose acerbic style—'Reading Proust is like lying in somebody else's dirty bathwater'—Dorothy emulated with little difficulty. Hearing that a certain actress had broken a leg, she quipped: 'She must have done it sliding down a barrister'; challenged to build a sentence around the word horticulture, she came up with: 'You can take a whore to culture, but you can't make her think.'

Even when uttered in private such *aperçus* received widespread circulation in the newspaper columns of Dorothy's literary friends. Soon all manner of outrageous quips circulated as apocryphal Parkerisms; a prime example was the rejoinder allegedly made to a messenger boy sent by the editor to collect overdue copy: 'Tell him I've been too fucking busy—or vice versa.'

When Parker returned to civvie street, she did not refrain from making him the butt of jokes which, if less scabrous, were still wounding. 'Eddie fell down a manhole reading the Wall Street Journal', she would quip to friends, or 'He broke his arm sharpening a pencil.'

Her professional career meanwhile took a sideways turn. Florenz Ziegfeld, whose productions she routinely panned, complained about her to Condé Nast and the latter, mindful of the advertising revenue his papers received from Ziegfeld, instructed the editor of *Vanity Fair* to dismiss Dorothy.

Thereafter she freelanced—a precarious mode of existence not helped by the shaky state of her marriage. Since his 'late' return from Europe, Parker had compounded this offence by recurring bouts of heavy drinking. Finally, in a dramatic reaction, Dorothy moved out of the matrimonial home. 'All I require', she said, 'is an apartment to lay a hat—and a few friends.' In her new 'pad' she also gave house room to a pet dog—the first of many—and a canary she characteristically named Onan, because he dropped his seed on the ground.

Parker had in the meantime decided that to help him dry out he needed to move back to rural New England. He asked Dorothy to accompany him, but she, convinced by now that they were incompatible and that his family was anti-Semitic, refused.

Her life-style now became thoroughly Bohemian. A night owl, she went to speakeasies, artists' studios where hooch was distilled, and a whorehouse frequented by literati with whose Madam she would play backgammon at $20 a game. The acquaintances she made at this time included such cult figures of the 'whoopee years' as George Gershwin and Scott and Zelda Fitzgerald. Her tartness of utterance became a byword. Having attended a house party at the *Saturday Evening Post* editor's country mansion, she wrote, 'Now we know what Philadelphia shirts are stuffed with'—and was never published in that journal again.

If Dorothy's professional activities met with variable success, her emotional involvements had a dispiriting sameness about them. The journalist Charley McArthur, proved an inconstant lover, who, moreover, caused her to have an abortion. (He, the co-author of *Front Page*, was only the best-known of a number of handsome, fickle men who drifted in and out of her bed.)

While *le tout* New York continued to acclaim her insouciant wit, she fell into the tightening grip of depression. Even her best-remembered catchphrase, 'Men don't make passes at girls with glasses', should be read as a pained response—Dorothy was nearsighted—to the cruelty of the male sex. She attempted suicide by slashing her wrists with one of Parker's old razors. However, having phoned room service just before, she was speedily found and taken to hospital. When Robert Benchley, another Algonquin wit, visited her bedside, she had festooned her bandaged wrists with blue ribbons, which she fluttered. His quip, 'You should cut deeper next time', elicited the rejoinder, 'The trouble was that Eddie had not even been able to sharpen his own razors.' Discharged from hospital, she inflicted further punishment on her body by chain-smoking and heavy drinking. An acquaintance called her a masochist with a boundless passion for unhappiness. Though true, it was not the whole truth about Dorothy Parker. While paramours deserted her, the muse did not. She kept writing throughout her unsatisfactory love affairs, producing work in a variety of genres from short stories and plays to poems.

Yet despite her success—the poetry collection *Enough Rope* went into eight printings—she had a second stab at killing herself. This time she took an overdose of pills, and Robert Benchley found her comatose in her apartment. In hospital, gallows' humour prevailed again, at least at first. Seeing Benchley at her bedside, Dorothy poked a tousled head out of the oxygen tent and asked the doctor if she could have a flag for the tent. Her visitor adopted the same bantering tone. 'Dottie', he admonished, 'if you don't stop doing this sort of thing, you'll make yourself sick!' The badinage was pure artifice, however. Benchley had been genuinely alarmed. To knock some sense into his recidivist friend's head he switched to shock tactics. 'If you realised how repulsive you looked,' he rapped out vehemently, 'you'd never try this again. You were lying there drooling, and if you had any considerations for your friends, you'd shoot yourself—but don't be this messy.'

This type of macabre joking was much in vogue among Dorothy's acquaintances. Not long after, at a party for American expatriates in Paris, Ernest Hemingway proposed a toast: 'Here's to Dorothy Parker! Life will never become her so much as her almost leaving it.' The assembled company reacted to this singularly tasteless *aperçu* with embarrassed silence, but Hemingway blundered on, reading out a poem full of anti-Semitic and misogynist innuendo about his absent dedicatee. Dorothy forbore to repay the author of *A Farewell to Arms* in the same coin. In a Hemingway profile for the *New Yorker* she called him the greatest living American writer, whose heroes 'show grace under pressure'. The phrase has entered the language, giving a lie to the notion that all Dorothy Parkerisms are cute or smart. 'Grace under pressure', however, hardly applied to her at the time.

The source of the trouble was, yet again, a faithless lover. John McClain was an athletic-looking broker's clerk who liked to boast of how many women he had bedded. His principal quarry were society hostesses and actresses whose contacts might advance his career. The besotted Dorothy procured a reporter's job on the *New York Sun* for him. He showed her scant gratitude. After several quarrels, prompted by his infidelity, he finally walked out on her with the valediction, 'You're a lousy lay!' She glossed her report of the incident to friends with the quip, 'His body went to his head.' It was surface insouciance: the gradual realization that McClain had left her for good brought on a depression. When mutual acquaintances told him that Dorothy was on the verge of suicide, he scoffed, dismissing it as emotional blackmail she had used on him before. In time she recovered, helped by generous infusions of alcohol and a succession of handsome, tall actors, noticeably younger than herself, who escorted her to first nights and parties.

By the early 1930s, with a string of short stories and three well-received volumes of poetry to her credit, Dorothy

Parker had become something of an American institution—in evidence of which a number of Broadway plays featured her as a thinly disguised protagonist.

In 1933, turned 40, she married 29-year-old Alan Campbell, and indifferent actor with screen-writing ambitions who hoped Dorothy's name would gain them an entrée to Hollywood. The Algonquin set did not think much of Campbell, whose mother in turn went out of her way to wound Dorothy. At parties she would introduce herself to strangers with the formula, 'I am Mrs. Campbell, the mother, not the wife.' However, the marriage worked, up to a point. It did so mainly because Dorothy used the drawing power of her name to secure them employment as a husband-and-wife screen writing team. They settled in Hollywood (despite Dorothy's nostalgia for her old haunts in New York) and chalked up joint credits for fifteen films, including A Star is Born, in the period 1933 to 1938.

Their début in the dream factory coincided in time with the Nazi take-over of Germany. Dorothy had long been something of a political animal, drawn to feminism in pre-war days and demonstrating on behalf of Sacco and Vanzetti in the 1920s. Under the impact of the rise of Fascism she moved sharply to the left and even naïvely proclaimed herself a Communist at times. She set up an anti-Nazi League in Hollywood and enlisted stars like Frederic March and Norma Shearer to its ranks. During the Spanish Civil War she visited Valencia and, on her return, expended much energy on collecting money for Republican relief. Domestically her political efforts focused on unionizing her colleagues in the Screen Writers Guild. Campbell, fearing for their jobs, disapproved of Dorothy's political activities—and she, in return, accused him of cowardice.

Intra-marital relations improved, however, with the couple's acquisition of a farm in Pennsylvania. Here, in peaceful, rural surroundings she became pregnant; more, she began to spin fantasies about an idyllic earth-bound and child-centred existence totally at variance with the life-style she had virtually come to personify in the American consciousness. All too soon, grey reality erupted into the pink haze of her earth-mother day-dreams. In the third month of pregnancy—the first she had allowed to run its full course—Dorothy aborted.

Another miscarriage a year later practically wrote *finis* to the Campbell-Parker marriage, though they continued living under the same Hollywood roof.

Disappointed in all her hopes, personal as well as political, Dorothy grew more cynical than ever. Hosting parties at Beverley Hills, she would greet guests at the porch with, 'How marvellous of you to come!', and then add out of the side of her mouth, 'Do you really want to meet any of the shits in there?'

After Pearl Harbour, when Campbell volunteered for the Air Force, she accused him of desertion, though in her typically contradictory way she was also proud of him. Her own contribution to the war effort consisted, in the main, of the script for Hitchcock's anti-Nazi thriller *Saboteur*. She wanted to do more, but the Womens Army Corps turned her down on grounds of age, and her attempts to become a war correspondent foundered on the authorities' refusal of a passport to the self-declared Communist.

1945 was for her a virtual replay of 1918, with her husband staying on in Europe allegedly on military duty. She told friends that a homosexual lover whom she identified by name was keeping Campbell in London. When in a letter he confessed to an affair with a married, titled Englishwoman she took it badly. The confession both hurt her pride and challenged the myth about Campbell that she had consistently propagated with such quips as: 'I can compete with the girls—but not the boys!'

In 1947 their divorce came through. By this time Dorothy had found a new lover, who disappointingly left her, halfway through a holiday in Mexico, for a younger woman. Showing a streak of paranoia that was to intensify with the passage of time, she ascribed his desertion of her to anti-Semitic prejudice.

Not long after, she and Campbell remarried, thereby proving that their inability to live apart equalled their incapacity for living together. A lot of water had flowed under the Golden Gate Bridge since their first marriage, however. In the grip of anti-Red hysteria, the Hollywood studios would employ Campbell neither in tandem with Dorothy Parker nor on his—untalented—own. Inevitably, the second marriage also collapsed, with Dorothy yet again citing Campbell's homo-sexuality as the root cause of the breakdown.

Professionally she soldiered on, gamely trying her hand at lyrics—for instance, for Leonard Bernstein's *Candide*—in addition to such stand-bys as plays and reviews. *Incredibile dictu*, after a while she and Campbell got together yet again and, the witch-hunt having by now blown itself out, returned to Hollywood. What triggered the move was the chance to script a film for Marilyn Monroe, whom Dorothy greatly admired. The project remained still-born, however, and other screen-writing assignments were hard to come by.

They, nonetheless, kept going on their unemployment handouts and her pay cheques for *Esquire* reviews, plus occasional royalties. They both quarrelled and drank a great deal. In 1962, after a drinking bout, Campbell overdosed on pills. The discovery of his inert body in bed beside her trau-matized Dorothy; even so, she answered an overly solicitous neighbour's question as to what she could do for her with 'Get me a new husband.'

From here on it was downhill all the way. She moved back to a New York that was steadily growing more unlike the city she had known in her heyday. A virtual recluse, she lived in a drab hotel room surrounded by bottles and with a dog for company. When an acquaintance who had introduced her to Campbell some thirty years earlier paid her a visit for old times sake, he encountered a drunken old woman who called him a 'Jew-hating Fascist son of a bitch'. A Jewish friend of hers, calling several months later, was horrified to behold an old crone sitting on a rug strewn with dog faeces and spitting, 'You're a Jew-Fascist. Get out of here!'

Dorothy Parker died in June 1967, aged 74. If one might make so bold as to imitate the Parker style, one might write this *envoi*: It is to be hoped that the full-page obituary which appeared in the *New York Times* on the day after her death softened the blow.

Erika Mann

George Bernard Shaw famously told Mrs. Pat Campbell that he hoped any putative children of theirs would have her looks and his brains—but feared it might fall out the other way round. No such fears troubled Thomas and Katja Mann when they began to raise a family at Munich in the 1900s. Mann looked almost as good as he sounded on the printed page, and Katja combined beauty—painters sought her out as a sitter—with sufficient academic ability to have gained university admission.

It is no exaggeration to say that siblings Klaus and Erika were born with silver spoons in their mouths. Talent and looks did not exhaust the sum of their advantages from birth. The parental home was a riverside villa with pillared balconies; Generalmusikdirektor Bruno Walter[1] lived next door, and he and other members of Munich's cultural élite were frequent house guests. After a none-too-happy stay at a progressive boarding-school Klaus decided, at an age when most boys' interests focus on sport or girls, to become a writer—just like his father and Uncle Heinrich; Erika, Klaus's junior by a year, elected to go to acting school. The siblings showed extraordinary precocity. By 18 Klaus was a regular contributor to *Weltbühne*, a politico-literary journal; Erika, after graduating from acting school, divided her time between appearing on the legitimate stage and collaborating with Klaus and a few kindred spirits in theatrical experiments at Hamburg. One such kindred spirit was Pamela Wedekind (daughter of the author of *Lulu*), whom Klaus became engaged to, but as a minor could not yet marry; another was the up-and-coming actor Gustav Gründgens, whom Erika soon married.

The theatrical début of the four prompted newspaper comments mocking their extreme youth and privileged *fils à papa* status; one headline read, 'Bardic bairns (*Dichterkinder*) play at theatre'. Though reviews were mixed, Gründgens' talents got him noticed and he subsequently gained rapid advancement. Appointed Intendant of the Hamburg Kammerspiele, he created a 'revolutionary theatre' for which he commissioned his brother-in-law to write a cabaret style revue. However, when Klaus submitted his script, Gründgens, scenting failure, wanted

---

1. Bruno Walter (1876–1962): German-Jewish conductor known primarily for his interpretations of the Viennese school.

to drop the project; whereupon Erika all but threatened divorce unless it went on. She got her way—with the result that the revue was panned by the critics and Gründgens vindicated. This was not Klaus's only setback at the time: when, on reaching the age of majority, he asked for Pamela Wedekind's hand, she said she considered their engagement void and intended to marry the middle-aged playwright Carl Sternheim.[2] As a distraction from such excursions and alarums, the siblings undertook an American trip in the course of which they spent Christmas 1927 as Emil Jannings' guests at his Hollywood home. Thereafter extended travel became a favourite pursuit of theirs. Although this was not simply self-indulgence, since it yielded material for a series of travel books, costs far exceeded any 'returns'; it was only Thomas Mann's receipt of the Nobel Prize (for *The Magic Mountain*) in 1929 that enabled him to pay off the debts that his two first-born, gifted, but wilful children had run up on a round-the-world trip.

In the year of her father's Nobel award Erika and Gründgens divorced; their marriage, which had never been consummated, since he was homosexual and she lesbian, finally came to grief when Erika suddenly withdrew from a scheduled production so that she could join Klaus on a car safari across Africa. The actress who replaced her at short notice, Marianne Hoppe, was to be even more useful to Gründgens in the long term: during the homophobe Third Reich her collusion in a *mariage blanc* provided him with an alibi similar to Elsa Lanchester's for Charles Laughton in contemporary Hollywood. Klaus was homosexual, too. He also shared another trait with Gründgens, serious drug dependence, but his most intractable problem throughout life was having to stand in his father's shadow.

As for the father, he could not but be censorious of the son on personal as well as artistic grounds. Mann, whose fiction often depicted the contrast between the values of the bourgeoisie and of the artist, was still enough of a bourgeois himself to deprecate Klaus's bohemian life-style (which had made a right-wing critic dub him 'the narcissus of the swamps'). As

2. Carl Sternheim (1878–1942): German-Jewish playwright and anti-bourgeois satirist (*A Pair of Drawers*, *The Snob*).

for literary creation the father, who was habituated to a pattern of work that aimed at solidity, not to say ponderousness, entertained grave doubts about the worth of the son's facile-seeming over-production (in one year, 1932, Klaus published five titles). This fraught relationship curiously did not affect Erika—now a rising actress—who remained both her father's trusted counsellor and her brother's soul-mate. ('Chum' might be a better term, since she was a chain-smoker, car rally driver and doughty combatant in the escalating fight against Hitler-Lucifer *ante portas.*)

Erika's unique closeness to Klaus contrasted markedly with sibling relationships in the previous generation: Thomas and Heinrich Mann had hardly been on speaking terms for years. This owed something to professional jealousy, but more to profound disagreements about culture and politics; regarding the latter the conservative-minded Thomas had pleaded the German cause in the First World War, while the radically-inclined Heinrich had decried it. Post-war, however, the painfully evident fragility of the Weimar Republic had gradually converted Thomas Mann into a staunch partisan of democracy. Even so, he wanted to defend the Republic from a moderated conservative standpoint miles removed from Heinrich's and Klaus's radicalism. Thus, although the whole family was anti-Nazi, their responses to the catastrophe threatening to overwhelm Germany in the winter of 1932–33 differed somewhat. In early January Erika inaugurated, together with the well-known actress Theresa Giehse, the political cabaret *The Pepper Mill,* which made an instant impact in Munich's supercharged political atmosphere. Thomas and Katja Mann happened to be on a lecture tour outside the country at the time. When the burning of the Reichstag in February provided the Nazis with the pretext to round up all political opponents, Heinrich fled to France and Erika and Klaus phoned their parents in Switzerland warning them that 'bad weather' in Germany made a return inadvisable. In early March, as Hitler's election victory rang down the final curtain on German freedom, Erika and Klaus escaped to Switzerland. However, in April Erika returned clandestinely to Munich, at grave personal risk, to rescue her father's incomplete

Joseph manuscript—the fruit of years of work—from the locked-up riverside villa and take it back to him. Back in Zurich she and fellow fugitive Theresa Giehse reconstituted the *Pepper Mill* cabaret; its sketches, mainly written by Erika, captivated local audiences. Later *The Pepper Mill* was to tour Switzerland, Czechoslovakia and Holland—havens adjacent to Germany, where anti-Nazi emigrés assembled to continue a fight, the first round of which they had so disastrously lost. Commuting frequently between Zürich and Amsterdam, seat of an emigré publishing-house, Klaus conducted his fight by the (to him) familiar means of the printed word. He founded, together with André Gide and Aldous Huxley, the anti-Nazi journal *Die Sammlung*, wrote political novels, and addressed indignation-charged open letters to ex-colleagues of his, like the poet Gottfried Benn and the actress Emmy Sonnemann, who were collaborating with the Nazis. The latter, who became Frau Goering, smoothed her friend Gründgens' path to the summit of the German theatrical profession. Goering, who as Minister President of Prussia had the directorship of the Prussian state theatres in his gift, appointed Gründgens to the post. Thus, while Klaus Mann subsisted on the bitter bread of exile, albeit materially somewhat sweetened by parental subsidies, Gründgens, his incriminating past (i.e. the revolutionary theatre at Hamburg) happily forgotten, enjoyed the patronage of the second most powerful man in Nazi Germany. In addition, he garnered a succession of triumphs as director, film-star and stage-actor—the latter particularly in the rôle of Mephisto in Goethe's *Faust*. That archetypal figure gave Klaus the title and central image for a novel in which he settled scores with his turncoat brother-in-law. In *Mephisto* he depicted Gründgens (disguised as the actor Hoefgens) as an opportunist ready to sell his soul to the devil for the sake of self-advancement; the novel's subsidiary characters, turncoats of various shades of villainy or vanity, were likewise based on people prominent in German cultural life. In only one respect did the author depart from verisimilitude: to avoid giving any sort of legitimacy to the current Nazi witch-hunt against gays ('the men with the pink triangles') he changed the despicable Hoefgens from a homosexual into a masochist. *Mephisto* came out in a limited edition in Amsterdam, the town that served Klaus as home (in so far as an exile can be described as having one at all). Another temporary resident of Amsterdam was Christopher Isherwood who lived there with his German lover, Heinz. Klaus knew Isherwood and introduced him to his sister. At the time the intrepid Erika had a number of reasons for acute worry. Gestapo agents were kidnapping anti-Nazi emigrés, she herself had had *Pepper Mill* performances disrupted by gunshots outside the theatre and, most threatening, she had heard that Berlin was about to deprive her of her German passport. She therefore seized the opportunity of her first encounter with Isherwood to ask him to marry her (and give her the protection of British citizenship). Isherwood refused. He feared any publicity that would endanger Heinz and was, moreover, ideologically opposed to marriage—but volunteered to pass on the request to his friend Auden. He told Erika he was certain Wystan would oblige. Auden, currently teaching at a boys' school near Malvern, proved as good as Isherwood's word. Immediately on receiving news of Erika's plight he telegraphed the one-word reply, 'Delighted'. The wedding ceremony duly took place at Ledbury Registry Office; as soon as it was over the groom returned to afternoon school and the bride drove back to London. (This did not betoken any strained relations; Auden was to remain on friendly terms with Erika, and her family, for several years.) Some time after the Ledbury ceremony Erika's *Pepper Mill* colleague Theresa Giehse got married in a like manner. On this occasion Auden, appealed to as a potential marriage broker, had commented 'That's what buggers are for', and instituted a search which eventually yielded a suitable paper husband in the shape of one of E. M. Forster's acquaintances.

Erika was meanwhile engaged in a crucial trial of strength with her father, who since settling in Switzerland three years earlier had refrained from making any public anti-Nazi gestures; he had even allowed *The Tales of Jacob* (first volume of his *Joseph* cycle) to be published in Germany in late 1933. The publishers involved, the Jewish-owned Bermann Fischer Verlag, were still in business in Nazi Germany in 1936—an arrangement which suited the firm for business reasons and the régime for propagandist ones. Because Bermann

Fischer helped drape a fig-leaf over the nakedness of Nazi culture, a Paris-based emigré paper dubbed them *'Goebbels' Schutzjuden'* (protected Jews). The attack on his publishers angered Thomas Mann, who sprang to their defence in the columns of the *Züricher Zeitung*. This in turn brought Erika into the fray. She addressed a letter to Mann, chiding him for his silence since 1933, and charging that the statement in the Swiss paper had been a stab-in-the-back for the emigration. In an emotional *envoi* she all but threatened to break off contact with him unless he abandoned his detachment from the other anti-Nazi emigrés. This appeal, strongly echoed by Klaus, had an effect on the writer, who within days published a ringing denunciation of the Nazi régime. Mann's change of stance coincided with the outbreak of fighting in Spain, which Erika covered as a war correspondent for several months. Meanwhile Klaus, whose Amsterdam-based journal had closed for lack of funds, contemplated emigration to the United States.

With the escalation of the international crisis the latter country was becoming preferable to Western Europe as a place of refuge, though few emigrés realized it at the time. Once again it was left to Erika, by then—1938—resident in New York, to pressure Thomas and Katja, vacillating in France, into taking the decisive step of emigrating to the United States. (Her farsightedness in this respect became clear after the Fall of France when 69-year-old Heinrich Mann—and he counted himself fortunate—had to scramble across the peaks of the Pyrenees to escape the clutches of the Gestapo.) By 1939 Klaus, too, as well as some other Mann children, had settled permanently in America. A few weeks later when Auden and Isherwood arrived in New York—a 'flight from danger' that earned them a bad press in Britain—Erika, accompanied as so often in her life, by Klaus, was at the quayside to meet her 'husband' and their erstwhile go-between. In autumn 1940 Heinrich Mann, his wife, and Erika's and Klaus's brother Golo arrived in the States after their nerve-wracking escape from France. Golo and Auden rented a house in Middagh Street, Brooklyn, which during 1940–41 accommodated a collection of diverse artistic personalities: Benjamin Britten, Peter Pears, Carson

McCullers,[3] Chester Kallman and others (Kallman, Auden's newly acquired lover, co-wrote the libretto of Stravinsky's *The Rake's Progress*). Erika also lived at the house for a while, and Carson McCullers, who had come to Brooklyn in the aftermath of a painful marital break-up, embarrassingly developed a passion for her which she did not reciprocate.

At the time other, weightier matters were claiming Erika's attention. She collaborated with Klaus on two books: one with the self-explanatory title *The Other Germany*: the second, *Escape to Life*, recounted the siblings' dangerous work in, and escape from, Nazi-infested Europe. But danger attracted rather than repelled Erika, prompting her to become a war correspondent again. In this capacity she toured Britain during the Blitz—making some Fleet Street headlines en route by revealing Auden's total lack of interest in the progress of the war—the Persian Gulf in 1943 and, after D-Day, France, Belgium and Germany. She alternated these tours of 'frontline' duty with periods back in the States which were largely given over to assisting her father in his work. She accompanied Mann (whose spoken English left much to be desired) on lecture tours, acting as his mouthpiece at question time. More importantly, she helped in the Herculean labours involved in the gestation of Mann's final masterwork, *Dr. Faustus*. (Erika's part in the correction and rewriting of the huge *Faustus* manuscript earned her the soubriquet 'the best publisher's reader ever'.)

However, this increasing devotion to her father's work could not but affect the intimacy that had previously existed between her and Klaus. This hit the latter, already unsettled by the problems of peace-time readjustment, quite hard. Founder-editor of the *Decision*, a politico-literary journal in pre-Pearl Harbour days, he had subsequently served in an U.S. army psychological warfare unit. A stay in Germany at the war's end had taught him, in his own words, that he was not 'wanted' there. Lacking roots in America, where Thomas and Katja were hardly welcoming, he perforce went back to the old haunts of his exile in Western Europe. Before

---

3. Carson McCullers (1917–67): American writer of stories focusing on the inner lives of lonely people (*The Heart is a Lonely Hunter, The Member of the Wedding*).

that happened, however, he had a bizarre encounter with Gustav Gründgens, who had survived the Third Reich and post-war tribunal hearings with his reputation unimpaired. (The actor's defence against the charge of Nazi collaboration had been that five people—including his aged parents and a Jewish friend—depended on his income and/or protection.) Duly de-nazified, he made his post-war début in 1946 at a Berlin theatre where Klaus, in the front seat, was deafened by the applause that greeted the stage idol's return. By malign coincidence the play he appeared in was by Carl Sternheim, whom Pamela Wedekind had preferred to Klaus twenty years earlier.

The late '40s were a period of deepening depression for Klaus. After a first suicide attempt in 1948 had miscarried, he was cheered by the news that a West German publisher was about to reissue *Mephisto*. Then, in May 1949, the publishers informed him that Gründgens had obtained a court order banning the book as defamatory. A few days later Klaus killed himself in a hotel room at Cannes. No member of the Mann family attended the funeral, not even Klaus's favourite sister, which, considering that the rage that had fuelled his writing of *Mephisto* had in part been motivated by Gründgens' divorce, did not reflect too creditably on her.

Erika's absence was probably due to a mixture of the impatience of the strong-willed with their weaker brethren and involvement in her father's work. Even more than in the case of the *Faust* novel, she had to encourage, chivvy and manipulate the septuagenarian, whose gestation of the *Confessions of Felix Krull* was impeded by recurrent depressions and writer's block. Although Thomas Mann could now look back on a nonpareil writing career in which he scaled peaks of creativity three times over—*The Magic Mountain*, the *Joseph* cycle and *Dr. Faustus*—the late '40s were a bad time for him. While near-Olympian detachment insulated him from various family disasters (the suicides of Klaus and of Heinrich's wife, and Heinrich's own lapse into terminal melancholy), he found it hard to deal with buffetings received in the public arena. In the course of a visit to Germany for the 1949 Goethe bicentenary he outraged West German opinion by delivering commemorative addresses at Weimar, in the Soviet Zone, as well as in Frankfurt. He was also drawn into an acrimonious debate with some writers who claimed a moral superiority for 'inner emigration' over exile (i.e. leaving one's country). Like Klaus, who had already realized at the end of the war that he could never go home again, Thomas—the universally acknowledged spokesman for 'the other Germany' during the Hitler years—now definitely decided against resettling in his native country. When Wilhelm Furtwängler, whose musicianship had helped conjure up a mirage of culture in the Nazi desert, wanted to renew their old acquaintance, Mann, influenced by Erika in this, as in so many other matters, snubbed him; the conductor countered with the quip, 'Unlike Thomas Mann I don't change nationalities like shirts.'

Unable to settle in post-war Germany on account of its unexorcized past, the Manns no longer felt welcome in their adopted American homeland either. In the late '40s the United States was gripped by an intensifying Cold War psychosis, which enabled Senator McCarthy and his minions to smear any individual with a prominent anti-Fascist record as a Communist agent. Feeling herself an imminent target of the anti-Red witch-hunt, Erika persuaded her parents, for the third time in their lives, to change their country of domicile. In 1952 the Manns left the U.S.A. for Switzerland, where they settled in a villa overlooking Lake Zürich. Here Erika assisted her father in the literary labours of his declining years. After his death in 1955, she occupied herself with the administration of his estate—overseeing the publication of his diaries and voluminous correspondence. She also acted as the literary legatee of Klaus, the brother to whom she had once been so close that she referred to both of them jointly as 'Erimaus' in her diary entries.

Debilitated by a bone disease, Erika struggled on gamely into the 1960s. 1963 brought news of the death of her ex-husband Gustav Gründgens of a drug overdose at a Manila hotel. Three years later a German film-producer approached her with a project for making a TV documentary about *The Pepper Mill*. She turned it down, arguing that the German public had no interest in the Nazi—and even less in the anti-Nazi(!)—past. In 1969 Erika Mann died.

In 1985 the American Motion Picture Academy awarded the

161

Oscar for best foreign film to *Mephisto*, a Hungarian-German co-production based on Klaus Mann's eponymous novel. If only Erika could have made her sibling bide his time for thirty-six years!

IX

Politicians

Golda Meir

THE 1960s witnessed a break with a host of traditional attitudes and usages. One innovation little remarked on at the time was the assumption of political power in some countries by women. Mrs. Bandaranaike became prime minister of Ceylon in 1960, Indira Gandhi followed suit in India in 1966, and Golda Meir in Israel in 1969. (Mrs. Thatcher's premiership, the next in the sequence, commenced in 1979.) Misogynists with a bent for history must have recalled the mid-sixteenth century when a conjunction of several female rulers prompted John Knox's *First Blast of the Trumpet against the Monstrous Regiment of Women*. The latter were, of course, all crowned heads. Although four centuries had elapsed, two of the afore-mentioned women prime ministers resembled the targets of Knox's trumpet blast in owing high office to inheritance rather than merit: Mrs. Bandaranaike was the widow of Solomon Bandaranaike, the previous premier of Ceylon, and Indira Gandhi the daughter of Pandit Nehru.

The only female prime minister of the '60s who owed her elevation entirely to merit was Golda Meir. Even Mrs. Thatcher, who entered politics as something of an outsider, enjoyed advantages of background, education and wealth through marriage that Golda Meir could not even dream of. Golda did however resemble Maggie in being a grocer's daughter—that is if a woman who peddles loaves of home-baked bread from door to door merits the appellation grocer. Mrs. Bluma Mabovitch was obliged to eke out a living in this manner because hers was, temporarily, a one-parent family. Her carpenter husband's skill had once earned them the right to reside in Kiev (where Golda was born). After a few years discrimination and fear of pogroms had driven the father to try his luck in America, and the rest of the family were obliged to return to Bluma's hometown, Pinsk. This was an agglomeration of drab dwellings inhabited by 50,000 souls, a third of them Jews; its main characteristics were muddy, unpaved roads and close proximity to the malarial Pripet Marshes. The conjunction of poverty and unhealthy environment had taken its toll of the Mabovitch progeny. Five of the eight children having failed to survive infancy, Golda had just two sisters: the eldest Chana, and Zipporah, the 'baby'.

One day when Golda and some of her little playmates were building mud castles in an alleyway, they froze as they heard the neighing of horses and thunder of hooves. Within seconds mounted Cossacks were upon them, slashing at the air with whips and sabres. By a miracle the horses jumped clear of the little huddled bodies; as the murderous cavalcade moved on, the alleyway echoed to cries of 'Death to the Jews'. At this time, the early 1900s, the Czarist authorities deployed Cossacks as readily against striking workers and left-wing demonstrators as against Jews. Not surprisingly, some young Jews espoused the left-wing cause; others subscribed to the Zionist vision of returning to Palestine. Revolution, Socialism, Jewish self-help, Zionism—all these ideas were debated by Chana's teenage friends and became part of little Golda's mental universe early on.

When Golda was 8 her father sent for the family. After a strenuous journey they arrived in Milwaukee, only to find no proper accommodation awaiting them. They took a couple of rooms at the back of a dingy store which Mrs. Mabovitch, reluctantly assisted by Chana and Golda, turned into a grocery catering for penurious customers in the neighbourhood. The father meanwhile worked as a railway carpenter.

In Milwaukee Golda went to school, but not regularly. Every so often, when Mrs. Mabovitch had to go to market or elsewhere, Golda was obliged to play truant and mind the store; the mother's stock reply to the girl's protests would be, 'So you'll be a learned lady a day later!' In other words, the Mabovitches hardly conformed to prevalent notions of all Jews being education-minded and most immigrants progressing from rags to riches. But for all that her father lacked ambition—a self-styled building contractor, he always remained a railway carpenter—and her mother's horizon hardly extended beyond the walls of the grocery, Golda showed a spark from early on. At the age of 10, finding that while schooling was free in America school books were not, she organized a fund-raising drive to purchase books for needy classmates. When she was 12, in addition to working hard at school, in the grocery and at home all week, she put in Saturday stints at a local department store.

The completion of her High School education brought on a crisis. She had set her heart on becoming a teacher, but Mrs. Mabovitch, who knew that women teachers had to be single, vehemently opposed the idea. 'You want to be an old maid?', she screamed, 'Is that what you're studying for?' Golda's father supported his wife and the 14-year-old was given the alternative of going to work or taking a secretarial course. A third possibility was also mooted: matrimony. A 28-year-old estate agent had become attracted to the pubescent girl and approached the parents. When Golda pointed to the suitor's age being twice her own, she received an assurance that he was willing to wait a couple of years.

The 'proposal' compounded her anger over the frustrated teaching ambition and Golda decided to leave home. Helped by a friend she ran away to her married sister Chana in Denver. Here she proved as headstrong as she had done in the parental home. Provoked by Chana's censure for staying out late, she moved into a furnished room and went to work in a laundry.

Around this time she met Morris Myerson, a sign-painter of Russian-Jewish origin, who took her to a concert on their first date. The bespectacled, outwardly unprepossessing Myerson impressed her with, as she put it, his 'beautiful soul'. When her father wrote agreeing that she undertake teacher training, Golda moved back to Milwaukee. She was now secretly engaged and the flood of Myerson's letters aroused her mother's suspicion. But, as it turned out, parental disapproval jeopardized the burgeoning love affair far less than Zionism, which in 1917—year of the Balfour Declaration adumbrating a Jewish National Home in Palestine—took on overwhelming importance for Golda. Myerson showed himself extremely reluctant to join her in the pioneering existence in Israel on which she had set her heart.

His objections were overcome, however, and three years after their marriage, in 1918, they found themselves in the Holy Land. Life was incredibly hard at Golda's chosen destination—a kibbutz where Myerson dug stones, she picked olives, and quinine tablets were handed out at every meal. Here he found the lack of privacy as little to his taste as the back-breaking work and the danger of malaria. 'I do not want to start a family', he told Golda, 'that will be brought up in a Childrens' House.' This time she relented. They went to Jerusalem and lived in a small flat lit by oil lamps, with a tin shack serving as kitchen, where their two children Menachem and Sarah were born. Soon after the move Golda became a full-time Zionist functionary, whose work increasingly took her abroad (mainly to the U.S.A.). This spelt the end of the marriage; thereafter Myerson lived in Haifa, and Golda—unless abroad—with the children in Tel Aviv.

Meanwhile her political career flourished. Elected to the *Histadrut* (Trade Union) executive she took charge of its Health Service. In 1938 she was Jewish representative at the Evian Conference on Refugees which President Roosevelt convened after Hitler's annexation of Austria. A year later, on the eve of hostilities, a British White Paper revoked the Balfour Declaration and shut the gates of Palestine on the Jews in their moment of greatest need. During the war, when the Royal Navy turned back refugee-laden coffin ships, like the *Struma*, which thereupon sank, Golda composed the text for English language leaflets and posters aimed at British personnel who, by denying the refugees entry, condemned them to certain death.

After the war, with the Palestine Question moving to the forefront of the world's political agenda, Golda's importance increased. She addressed the Anglo-American Committee of Inquiry and soon after, when the British interned the male members of the Jewish Agency for Palestine, she became its acting head. Just before the Israeli War of Independence, disguised in Arab robes, she visited King Abdullah of Trans-jordan in a forlorn attempt at soliciting his neutrality. On 14 May 1948, as the guns started firing, hers was one of the thirty-eight signatures on Israel's Declaration of Independence read out at the Tel Aviv Museum of Art.

In June, with the war, in which Israel received Soviet arms, still raging, she was appointed Ambassador to Russia—the country she had left forty-two years earlier. Phlebitis delayed her departure and, before she left, she attended her daughter Sarah's wedding, as did Myerson. He told reporters: 'I came to Palestine for one reason only: to be with Golda. But she was never there!'

Golda arrived in the Soviet capital in September. On the first Saturday after presenting her credentials she and an Embassy party attended service at Moscow Synagogue. There the rabbi, the only person apprised of the visit in advance, followed a prayer for Stalin with one for Golda Myerson, Ambassador of Israel. At this a wave of emotion rippled through the congregation of old men, who turned to stare up at her in the Womens' Gallery. When some weeks later, on the Jewish New Year, the Israelis attended divine service again, the streets around the synagogue were thronged with a crowd that brought the traffic to a halt. On the way back to the Embassy Golda had to ride in a taxi that inched its way through the heaving mass of humanity. She lowered the window and called out (in Yiddish), 'I thank you for having remained Jews!'

Soviet officialdom quickly learnt the lesson. At Golda's next visit, on the Day of Atonement, policemen were posted all round the synagogue to press the crowd back. Soon after, Stalin's wrath descended: Jewish theatres and newspapers were closed down, Yiddish writers liquidated and the 'Doctors Plot'—to poison Soviet leaders—discovered. However, by the time the so-called murderers in white coats stood in the dock, Stalin's death supervened and the trial was adjourned *sine die*. In the interim, Golda had long been recalled to Israel and joined the cabinet as Minister of Labour and Development. Her seven years' tenure of that office coincided with a period of mass immigration—mainly of Jews from Arab countries—which more than doubled the country's population. By the time she changed portfolios, thanks to a vast house-building programme, which was underpinned by the creation of the necessary infrastructure of roads, water works, sewage plant, etc. none of the immigrants lived in tents any more. During this period of change for the country in which she took a leading part, Golda's personal circumstances also changed. Myerson died, she became a grandmother and acquired a daughter-in-law. She, also, in line with other pioneers of the new state, hebraized her surname to Meir.

Appointed Foreign Minister in mid-1956 she was at first crucially involved in the preparation for the Suez Campaign. Then, after Israel's military achievements in the Sinai were set at nought by the superpowers, she master-minded a diplomatic 'charm offensive' in the Third World, especially Africa.

Eventually she retired from ministerial office in 1965. The Six Days' War two years later saw her address huge fund-raising rallies in the U.S.A. Back in Israel she re-emerged as a key player in the political game by launching a reunified Labour Party, and in 1969, aged 71 she was back in government—at its head!

As prime minister she guided Israel through the Suez Canal bombardments which were initiated by Colonel Nasser in retaliation for the Egyptian debacle in the Six Days' War. At the same time she scotched attempts undertaken by World Jewish Congress president Hahum Goldmann to mediate between Nasser and herself. She likewise adopted a hardline stance on the increasingly contentious Palestinian issue. 'There was', she told *The Times* in 1969, 'no such thing as Palestinians when the Jews came. It was not as though there was a Palestinian people and we threw them out; they did not exist.' In a literal sense she was right. The inhabitants encountered by the Zionist pioneers had little perception of themselves as Palestinians; their sense of identity derived either from membership of their clan or of the ill-defined Arab nation. On the other hand, there could be no gainsaying the fact that in the interim their sense of being Palestinians had intensified in response to the Jewish influx.

If her attitude towards the Palestinians was rigidly unimaginative, she showed herself flexible on another issue that deeply divided the Israeli public: Germany. Having earlier disagreed with Prime Minister Ben-Gurion's policy of

German-Jewish *rapprochement*, she warmly welcomed Chancellor Brandt to Jerusalem in 1973. That visit occurred during the penultimate year of her premiership, a year crowded with drama. Despite shock defeats in the opening rounds of the Yom Kippur War, Golda managed to get her party re-elected to power in 1974; shortly afterwards she retired, aged 74.

Six years later she died. At the funeral, Labour Party leader Shimon Peres eulogized her as a 'stalwart lioness'. The Labour Mayor of Jerusalem Teddy Kollek, by contrast, has described her as a 'dogmatic adherent of obsolete slogans' who 'saw everything in black and white'. Others have charged that as a self-declared secularist she showed unprincipled readiness to accommodate the rabbinical lobby over the 'who is a Jew' controversy. But such criticism notwithstanding, Golda Meir was a most remarkable woman. Probably no other woman had to overcome comparable drawbacks of gender, class, culture and, not least, race—and risen to such heights. The girl who built castles of mud at Pinsk had gone on to help build a nation out of pioneers, refugees and camp survivors on the history- and blood-encrusted strip of land between the desert and the sea.

Eva Perón

It is not given to many individuals to be widely known just by their first name—even Stalin was not simply Joe, but Uncle Joe—yet at 30 a one-time tango dancer enjoyed sufficient name recognition, both in her native Argentina and the wider world, to require neither patronymic nor married name. Earlier on in her life, though, things had been drastically different for the woman baptised Eva, but dubbed Evita; she had had quite a struggle to come both by her patronymic, Duarte, and by her married name, which was, of course, Perón.

The problem as regards Duarte was that Eva's father, an *estanciero* (landowner) had not, despite fathering five children, married her mother. He, in fact, had another family on the right side of the blanket. On his death—Eva was 6 at the time—the legitimate Duarte family barred her mother and siblings from attending the wake. They barged their way in, nonetheless, and in the ensuing brouhaha it required the intervention of the local mayor to grant the deceased's concubine and bastard brood a minor part in his *pompes funèbres*.

Although she had no claim to the name in law, Eva continued calling herself Duarte till her marriage. At 15, with the country in the trough of the Depression, she left her poverty-stricken provincial home for the capital. Buenos Aires, metropolis of Argentina and largest city of South America, had a widely ramified entertainments industry in which the gawky girl from the Pampas hoped to find employment. Unfortunately, the theatre was in crisis, too, with the cinema (especially since the advent of sound) making deep inroads into its traditional audience. After several years of semi-starvation as well as, according to her detractors, semi-prostitution, she finally got her foot on the lowest rung of the ladder in the third medium of mass entertainment: radio. Some time after that in 1943, when she was 25, Eva Duarte could be said to have arrived. She signed contracts for the title rôles of a new radio series broadcast weekly under the umbrella title 'Famous Women'. During the following months she assumed the persona, in turn, of Elizabeth of England, Catherine the Great, Carlotta of Mexico and other women of destiny, over the air-waves.

On the ground, meanwhile, two related developments began the process of turning Eva herself into Evita, woman of destiny. One was her encounter with Colonel Juan Perón, a politically ambitious soldier with considerable clout within the country's ruling Junta. Eva had the nous to realize how much a liaison with Perón, who, though twice her age, still cut a dash, could benefit her career. The other was that the deviser of the 'Famous Women' series, Munoz Azpiri, a right-wing sympathizer, put his skill as a manipulator of public opinion at their disposal: Perón, a minister in the Junta, had the script-writer appointed government Director of Information. As such Azpiri orchestrated a campaign projecting Eva as the harbinger of a new political force over the air-waves. In a thrice-weekly programme entitled 'Towards a better future' the announcer would intone, 'Here is the voice of the people—she herself of the anonymous masses—in whose voice has been revealed the nature . . . of this saving revolution day by day.' Eva would then be heard declaring, 'I am a woman like your mothers, wives, sweethearts, sisters. . . . From me came the son who is in the barracks . . . the worker who is creating a new Argentina. . . .' As 'Everywoman' she built up a faithful radio audience to whom she addressed an open letter:

> My greatest satisfaction as a woman and as an actress, would be to offer my hand to all those who carry inside them the flame of faith in something or someone and in those who harbour a hope. . . .

The 'faith in something or someone' she had in mind was *Peronismo*, a mish-mash of Fascist and Socialist ideas that held out the twin goals of achieving national greatness and social justice. It addressed its appeal to such disparate constituencies as the Army, the Church and the Trades Unions, but the main source of its support was among the urban poor, the *descamisados*, or shirtless ones. This became evident in autumn 1945 when Perón's enemies within the military stripped him of his government posts and sent him into internal exile. Eva, simultaneously dismissed from her influential position on the radio, tried to rally his middle-class supporters, but they melted away. Then she turned to the 'shirtless ones' who responded. Mobilized by their unions, they set out from the factories on the morning of 17 October to march in huge converging columns to the spacious square in front of the Casa Rosada, the Pink House of government. There the huge throng remained chanting Perón's name throughout a long hot day, until he was released and appeared on the balcony alongside the men who had tried to cut him down to size. In token of reconciliation he embraced them, whereupon the shirtsleeved workaday crowd in the square returned peaceably to the industrial suburbs.

Five days later Perón and Eva married. The nuptials over, they embarked on a presidential election campaign which, masterminded by Eva's Svengali-like mentor Azpiri, made them occupants of the Pink House early in 1946. (One of the extraordinary features of this contest was that the U.S.

State Department's revelations of Perón's war-time backing of Nazi Germany boosted, rather than diminished, his support. Over the next few years Argentina became a haven for fugitive Nazi criminals like Eichmann.)

With Perón installed at the Casa Rosada, 27-year-old Evita chafed at being simply the President's wife; she laid claim to the status of a power-sharing First Lady. In a still largely patriarchal society her claim was adjudged presumptuous twice over—in terms both of gender and of class. Women in Argentina did not have the vote (even France only introduced female suffrage in 1945), and Presidents' wives had hitherto discharged merely decorative functions. As to class, the notion that Eva, whom a detractor described as 'born in the ill-disguised brothel of her mother, linked at 15 to a tango singer, whom she probably seduced and thereafter, a partner in whirlwind affairs with theatrical, business and political figures', should claim First Lady status struck the top echelons of Argentinian society as a downright provocation. Presidents' wives had traditionally been offered the presidency of the exclusive charity *Sociedad de Beneficencia*, but this honour was signally refused Eva Perón. She retaliated by arranging for a state take-over of the charity and established her own office in its building. This office became the nucleus of her mushrooming social welfare organization, the multi-million dollar *Fundación Eva Perón*.

Her projection of the image of caring for the unsheltered and needy went hand in hand with another self-arrogated public rôle—that of apostle of women's rights. She founded a Women's Suffrage Association, and within a year of its formation Parliament granted female enfranchisement. In the interim, she had set out on a foreign tour designed to give her as high a profile world-wide as she had already (in a prodigiously brief span of time) assumed inside Argentina. Her trip was by no means a succession of triumphs, but it contained sufficient highlights to enable Azpiri's adroit propaganda to present it as such. Thwarted in her intention of undertaking a sea journey by the navy's refusal to co-operate, Eva had to take a plane—an inauspicious start which the convergence of 500,000 cheering Perónists upon the airport turned into a triumphal send-off. In her first port of call, the

Motherland Spain, then (under Franco) suffering European ostracism, the arrival of an emissary from the leading South American country naturally aroused great enthusiasm. Eva, resplendent in gold lamé, mantilla and tiara, was received by General Franco, who invested her with the Cross of Isabel the Catholic. Italy, on the second leg of her journey, proved a disappointment. Though Pope Pius XII granted her an audience, he withheld the hoped-for honour of Pontifical Marquise—a slight for which being received by ex-King Umberto hardly compensated; in addition there were hostile demonstrations in Rome. The next intended point on the itinerary was Great Britain, but when the Royal Family announced they would be in Scotland at the germane time—even as Argentine press reports spoke of their *Presidenta*'s upcoming stay at Buckingham Palace—Eva, pleading exhaustion, officially called off the visit. In France the focus was on ministerial dinners and commercial agreements, but in Switzerland the public took a hand. Hostile demonstrators pelted the visitor with vegetables—which prompted Argentine opposition newspapers to publish cartoons of Eva with tomatoes splotching her dress, whereupon the régime closed them down.

On the way home, though, the *Presidenta* was made guest of honour at a special session of the Brazilian Parliament, and her husband had ample cause for satisfaction when, cheered by thousands of Perónists, they embraced on a launch in the port of Buenos Aires. Eyewitnesses of their reunion noticed a significant change in Eva's appearance. Whereas prior to her journey she had worn a staggering array of dresses—with original models being flown in daily by official plane from Paris—she now essayed an austere image, as befitted the intercessor on behalf of the shirtless ones. Instead of letting her blonde hair cascade in elaborate curls, she combed it back austerely and affected sweaters and skirts, slacks or simple cotton dresses.

The projection of this new image heralded Eva's concentration on the activities that earned her such high-flown soubriquets as 'Lady of Hope', and 'Virgin of the Unsheltered'. These products of Azpiri's propaganda machine, incidentally, struck a chord in the hearts of many poorer Argentinians. The activities for which the shirtless ones gave thanks to the ill-named Virgin were, of course, the social programmes financed by the *Fundación Eva Perón*. These included housing projects, provision of hostels for migrant workers and students, installation of drinking water, care facilities for the young, vacation colonies for working-class children, old-age homes, clinics and schools. The huge amount of expenditure incurred—by the early '50s the *Fundación* handled a budget of 2,000,000,000 pesos—was met by the annual deduction of two days' pay from the entire national labour force, plus the receipt of (occasionally enforced) contributions from industry and commerce.

Eva also had a strongly developed charitable impulse *vis-à-vis* her own kith and kin. One of her sisters became Inspectress of Postal Savings, one brother-in-law a member of the Supreme Court, and another Head of Customs for the port of Buenos Aires. Most importantly, she got her brother Juan Duarte appointed Private Secretary to the President. This particular form of nepotism was motivated less by family feeling than by the compulsion to enlarge her own power base within the régime. The two spheres of most immediate interest to her were the media and the trades unions. She had already managed to established a considerable foothold in the state-controlled radio and sections of the press, before participating in a major coup of the Perónist dictatorship. This was the onslaught on *La Prensa*—South America's most prestigious newspaper—which, beginning with the news-vendors' union's claim to a share in its advertising revenue, led, via a work stoppage, to government-decreed confiscation. Eva, who during the stoppage paid the workers wages out of Foundation funds, benefited directly from the confiscation, because the paper's new owners, the C.G.T. (Trade Union Congress) leadership, included several of her henchmen.

The expansion of Eva's power and influence further antagonized the armed services, who had been hostile to her ever since, as an actress openly cohabiting with Perón at an army base, she had first brought the name of the military into disrepute. Aware of the general enmity towards herself, which she interpreted as threatening Perónism itself, Eva purchased arms out of Foundation funds so as to set up a C.G.T.-linked workers' militia. In the event, though, there was no bloody show-down between the C.G.T. militia and the army, which would have constituted an Argentinian version of Nazi Germany's Night of the Long Knives. Its avoidance resulted from the drama of renunciation which Eva acted out in the run-up to Perón's second presidential campaign in 1951.

In the early stages of the campaign she had come under enormous pressure from the C.G.T. rank and file to let herself be drafted as her husband's running-mate. At a huge 'Open Town' meeting called to propose the 'Perón-Perón' formula for the forthcoming election, Eva parried the clamour for her candidacy by stating:

> But I tell you, just as I have said for five years, that I prefer to be Evita rather than the President's wife, if 'Evita' is said in order to alleviate any pain of my country. Now I say that I continue to prefer to be Evita.

Dissatisfied with this sybilline utterance the crowd reiterated its demand for an affirmative commitment, even interrupting Perón's own address with shouts of 'Let the companero Eva speak.' When she spoke again, she persuaded the meeting to grant her a short breathing space in which to reflect. Before the week was out the secretariat of the C.G.T. officially proclaimed Eva's candidacy. Then, three days after that announcement, she broadcast the news that she had decided to withdraw from the contest:

> I have no more than one ambition: that it shall be said of me . . . that there was at the side of Perón a woman who dedicated herself to carrying the hopes of the people to the President and that the people affectionately called this woman 'Evita'.

Eva's extreme hesitation about initially accepting the joint candidacy with Perón, as well as her subsequent renunciation of it, resulted from the interaction of two constraints on her. One was the opposition of the army to any enlargement of her—and the C.G.T.'s—power. The other was the manifest inability of her diseased body to cope with the impossible demands her punishing work schedule placed upon it.

The first indications of Eva's indifferent health had appeared several years earlier during her European tour, when what cynics took to be 'diplomatic' indispositions were in fact genuine ones. Then, in 1950, she fainted at a public meeting. On examination she was found to have suffered pelvic pains and vaginal haemorrhaging for a considerable time. When the doctor recommended an instant hysterectomy, she demurred and it required Perón's intervention to make her submit to the operation. Surgery over, she convalesced briefly before returning to her former strenuous routine. It seemed as if she had a masochistic compulsion to undermine her health and to court martyrdom. Martyrdom and sacrifice were in fact threads that not only ran through Evita's speeches but which were woven into the elaborate mythology surrounding her. Not only was she—guardian angel to all Argentina's children—childless, but she also forwent the pleasures of sex. Earlier Perón, the soldierly early riser, and she, the bohemian 'nightbird', had rarely been in bed at the same time; thereafter her pelvic pains and deteriorating health ruled out sex for good. The *vox populi* responded to the situation with the catchphrase, 'She even gave up her happiness as a woman for us.' (This calls to mind the Nazi German image of Hitler as a man bereft of the solace of wife and family in self-sacrificial dedication to the good of his country. The resemblance does not end there. Analogously to Hitler, who watched—on film—the death agonies of the 20 July Plotters he himself had decreed, Eva Perón preserved the testicles of rebel leaders castrated at her behest in a glass receptacle at the *Fundación* office.)

It must be said in Eva's defence, however, that in her psyche, in contradistinction to Hitler's, Franco's and Perón's, the masochistic impulse was as powerful as the sadistic. Unless one assumes that she considered early death as inevitable and wanted to conform to the decree of Providence—an assumption totally at variance with what we know of her nature—the masochistic hypothesis is the only one that makes her deliberate physical self-impairment explicable. She absolutely wanted to drain herself of strength. When the arduous schedule after the hysterectomy prompted her doctor into a remonstrance, she cut him short with a slap across the face. 'I will give my all', she proclaimed in a later speech which continued:

I left my dreams by the wayside in order to watch over the dreams of others, I exhausted my physical forces in order to revive the forces of my vanquished brother. My soul knows it, my body has felt it. I now place my soul at the side of the soul of my people. I offer them all my energies so that my body may be a bridge erected toward the happiness of all. Pass over it . . . toward the supreme destiny of the new fatherland.

The obvious debility of the body she offered 'as a bridge' was officially ascribed to anaemia, but the truth of the matter was that she had cancer.

This alarming news, with its potentially drastic impact on national morale, and on Perón's chances of re-election, had to be kept from the public for as long as possible. Accordingly the régime obscured the fact with a flurry of publicity. Eva's inability to leave bed for weeks on end was explained away by reference to blood transfusions (to counteract her anaemia); the appearance of her autobiography *La Razón de mi Vida*, which lead to a rush on bookshops, provided another diversion. Then, on 17 October 1951, 'Loyalty Day' (which commemorated Perón's release from internal exile as a result of her efforts and those of the *descamisados*), Eva made a public appearance beside her husband—who, however, needed to hold her by the waist when she stood up. Immediately afterwards she had one operation followed by another. Although both were unsuccessful, she rallied sufficiently to make several brief token appearances. Her final public appearance was a macabre charade which was symbolic of the régime whose main buttress she had been. At the inaugural parade of Perón's second term of office, she stood—a semi-moribund corpse strapped into a wire-and-plaster contraption that held her upright—beside her husband in the open car that drove them through cheering crowds to the Pink House.

When the populace were at last taken into the régime's confidence concerning the state of Eva's health, they responded in a manner suggestive of the Middle Ages. Prayers for her recovery were offered up throughout the country. At a gigantic open-air mass which the trades unions held in Buenos Aires, her confessor described the dying First Lady as an example of self-sacrifice and faith that God had given the Argentinian nation. From different parts of the country people reported that they had seen her profile imprinted on the moon. Parliament spent days debating the construction of Santa Evita's tomb, which was intended to be the largest monument in the world.

The outpouring of mass grief following her death was, even after due allowance for orchestration, awesome to behold. The queues waiting to pass the corpse, as it lay in state at C.G.T. headquarters, stretched for thirty-five blocks—a vast slow-moving mass of humanity which necessitated the provision of hygiene and first aid facilities. An estimated 2,000,000 watched the procession that took the corpse to its intended last resting-place. However, in keeping with the violent tenor of her life Eva's mortal remains were to have no rest. In 1955, by which time Evita's resplendent tomb had still not been completed, an army coup deposed Perón—the husband who could not bear to go near her during her malodorous final agony. Simultaneously some officers stole her corpse and flew it to Milan. There they had it secretly buried under a false name. In 1970, when the military Junta was about to cede power to a civilian government, a key item in the hand-over negotiations concerned the secret location of Evita's cadaver. The Colonel who had master-minded the 'kidnap' said, 'We buried her standing up because she was a real *macho*.'

X

Free Spirits

Annie Besant

ANNE Wood, was born—or, as in middle-age she would put it, 'came out of the Everywhere into the Here'—in 1847, and died in 1933. 86 years was in her days, and still is in ours, an above average life span; she managed to pack so much activity and achievement, in so many diverse spheres, into it that the author of her definitive biography entitled it *The Nine Lives of Annie Besant*. Annie, the only girl among three children, grew up in London in middle-class circumstances, her father being something in the city. Mr. Wood, a former medical student, seems to have lacked fulfilment in his commercial career. He frequently visited ex-university friends at work in hospitals, sometimes assisting them in dissections. On one such occasion, he cut his finger on the breastbone of a patient who had died of consumption. Incomprehensibly he let the cut heal without treatment; when, soon after, he got soaked riding on the open top deck of a horse bus, he contracted galloping consumption, which carried him off in a matter of weeks. Annie, 6 years at the time, was to remember afterwards Mrs. Wood's hair turning white during the night of agony that followed her husband's death. She also remembered that on the day of his burial her mother sat at home with vacant eyes and fixed pallid face, re-enacting the funeral service in her mind stage by stage, then suddenly shouting out 'it is all over' and falling back in a faint.

But for all that Mrs. Wood may have been psychic—a point of some relevance, in view of Annie's later career—she also had her feet on the ground. When it transpired that Mr. Wood had failed to make adequate provision for his family, she devised a scheme that, at one and the same time, assured her of a modicum of middle-class comfort and her eldest son of a good public school education. Her scheme entailed moving to Harrow, where school fees were relatively low for pupils from the town, renting a suitable house and, with the headmaster's permission, taking in a number of boys as boarders.

Harrow thus became the Woods' home for the next ten years, but Annie spent little time there, save in the holiday months. That was because a wealthy spinster, the sister of Captain Marryat,[1] the novelist, 'adopted' her as study and travel companion for her niece. Thanks to this arrangement, Annie received as good an education as girls could aspire to at the time. The curriculum included foreign languages, learnt partly on the spot, but suffered from the typical Victorian suspicion of contemporary belles-lettres, to the extent that novel-reading was restricted to the works of Sir Walter Scott and Charles Kingsley. Miss Marryat being 'an Evangelical of the Evangelicals', there was a heavy emphasis on religious teaching, which was mediated in a clichéd and simplistic manner. At first Annie, whose adolescent psyche brimmed over with religiosity, drew sufficient sustenance from Evangelical Christianity, but after a while she turned to the more aesthetically and intellectually satisfying High Anglicanism associated with the Oxford theologians Keble and Pusey. She was even tempted by Rome, but let herself be swayed by Pusey's argument that the Anglican church, even though non-Roman, perpetuated the Catholic tradition in England.

One Easter after she had outgrown Miss Marryat's tutelage, Annie was helping to decorate a local church, where she chanced to meet a young clergyman recently down from Cambridge. The Reverend Frank Besant was so taken by her combination of Christian devotion and good looks that he speedily proposed marriage. She accepted with equal alacrity—less from affection for her suitor, whom she hardly knew, than out of consideration that marriage to a clergyman would enable her to serve God and help the needy, the two objects closest to her heart. (The second received an

---

1. Frederick Marryat (1792–1848): English naval officer and writer (*Mr. Midshipman Easy*).

additional stimulus when she spent her last holiday before the wedding with a lawyer friend of the family at Manchester, coming face to face with miners in their slum dwellings and Fenians in the courtroom.)

The marriage was a disaster from the outset. The 20-year-old bride who had hitherto had only the most superficial contact with members of the opposite sex, and had remained blissfully ignorant of the mechanics of reproduction, found her initiation into married life a shock. What was even worse was the revelation of the young husband's character as that of an unbending self-righteous patriarch. The Reverend Besant took it for his God-given right to dominate Annie and confine her entirely to the domestic sphere. In this he was only partly successful, for while bearing him two children (Arthur and Mabel) in fairly short succession and running the household, Annie still managed to find time for reading and eventually—and more crucially—writing. Being married to an insufferable husband, who was withal an ordained minister of the church, acted as a spur—in addition to her intrinsic interest in the subject—for the deeper examination of the Christian Gospels she now embarked on. The result of her researches was a profound disillusionment: not only did the accounts given in Matthew, Mark and Luke fail to conform, John would not fit in at all. The first seeds of doubt having been sewn in her mind, Annie went on to submit the Christian faith, which had hitherto been the mainstay of her life, to searching examination. Coincidentally it was borne in upon her, not through cerebral examination but by traumatizing experience, that the time-honoured Christian notion of a beneficent deity lacked foundation in fact. Little Mabel, who had been prematurely born, came close to dying of whooping cough; when she recovered, Annie collapsed—from exhaustion mingled with rage at a God who permitted the agony of a 'sinless babe'.

The crumbling of the cornerstone of her Christian faith, compounding as it did her marital unhappiness, nearly drove Annie to suicide; it was only by strenuous effort of the will that she resisted the temptation of making her quietus with the aid of the chloroform bottle left behind after Mabel's illness. When she recovered from her depression, she informed her husband she would henceforth withdraw from his services

181

before communion, since that rite was based on the premise of Christ's divinity which she now found unacceptable. He reluctantly accepted the arrangement which excited little comment; when she left the church before the communion service, the parishioners supposed that she was simply not well.

Soon after she published, anonymously, a pamphlet denying the divinity of Jesus. She then prepared a second pamphlet attacking the Fourth Gospel as unreliable and bigoted. At the time of its publication she suffered a breakdown in health and went (accompanied by Mabel) to stay with her mother in London, where a doctor diagnosed nervous exhaustion. The Reverend Besant, having meanwhile discovered his wife's authorship of the two pamphlets, now gave her an ultimatum: either to conform to the outward observances of the Church or not to return to him. (He was at the time vicar of Sibsey in Lincolnshire, a living worth £410 p.a. which had been obtained through Annie's intercession with her relative, Lord Chancellor Hatherley.) For her, there could be no doubt about how to respond to the ultimatum; despite her mother's tearful entreaties, she refused to return to her husband. In London, the 25-year-old 'separated' woman gravitated towards the Unitarians centred on South Place Chapel, Holborn. The impression she made was such that Monceur D. Conway, the minister of South Place, confessed himself astonished 'that a young man should be willing to part from this beautiful and accomplished wife for the sake of any creed'.

Such accomplishments as she possessed soon had to be pressed into service, for to her intense sorrow Mrs. Wood fell ill and died. After briefly working as a governess, Annie turned to freelance journalism (mainly pamphleteering) to pay for her own and Mabel's keep. The months after her mother's decease represented the absolute nadir of her life, but there was, ultimately, light at the end of the tunnel. Having passed beyond the Deism of South Place Chapel on her spiritual odyssey, she came upon the, to her hitherto unknown, National Secular Society. Within the ambit of the N.S.S., she encountered both a cause—Free Thought—to embrace with all the enthusiasm of the well-versed defector

from Christianity, and a spokesman—Charles Bradlaugh—
she could admire as a thinker as well as a man. Bradlaugh,
a self-taught radical journalist, was for some years' the most
controversial personality in English public life. He owed his
notoriety, in the main, to campaigning for the separation of
Church from State (which his detractors stigmatized as mili-
tant atheism), but was also active in a whole range of radical
causes from Irish Home Rule to Franchise reform.

Once enrolled in the N.S.S., Annie launched into multifari-
ous activity: lecturing at the Society's Hall of Science in City
Road, writing Free Thought pamphlets, doing journalistic
and editorial work on Bradlaugh's *National Reformer*—for
which she was paid £1 per week—and addressing public
meetings. After helping Bradlaugh contest Northampton in
the radical interest during the 1874 General Election, she
undertook a country-wide speaking tour the year after, focusing on Irish Home Rule, humane amendments to the penal
code and the grant of civic rights to women. (Despite advocacy of the last mentioned cause, the Womens' Movement
actually fought shy of associations too close with Annie,
because of the scandalous whiff of atheism that clung to her
name.) Ere long she aroused further scandal by propagating
ideas just as shocking to Victorian *bien pensant* as atheism.
Together with Bradlaugh she set up the Freethought Publishing Co. to disseminate an illustrated pamphlet popu-
larizing birth control. This led to them being arraigned on
an obscenity charge in the courts. They tried to subpoena
Charles Darwin as a defence witness, but he excused himself
on health grounds—adding characteristically that he deprecated checks on population increase because over-population
engendered the survival of the fittest. The trial nonetheless
resulted in their acquittal. Encouraged by this, and with the
publicity attendant on the court case boosting sales of the
pamphlet, Annie embarked on a full-length book entitled,
*The Law of Population: Its Consequences, and its Bearing upon
Human Conduct and Morals*. Within months of its publication,
she faced another and infinitely more upsetting lawsuit.

The Reverend Besant had, with funds subscribed to by
the Bishop of Lincoln and other diocesan clergy, applied to
the Court of Chancery for the custody of his daughter; his

petition alleged that because of Annie's association with an infidel lecturer named Charles Bradlaugh and her publication of an obscene and indecent pamphlet, she was not a fit person to bring up Mabel. At the trial Annie's conduct of her own case irritated the judge, but the outcome was virtually predetermined anyway. According to the Master of the Rolls, she acquired such a reputation by her propaganda of sentiments shocking to the community that the interest of the child would be more secure in the house of an English Clergyman (this despite the fact, revealed in the trial, that the Reverend Besant had subjected his wife to physical violence on several occasions—including just before her second premature delivery). The trial over, a court official removed the frantically shrieking Mabel from her mother's house and conveyed her to Lincolnshire.

Annie promptly succumbed to another bout of illness, rheumatic fever, through which Bradlaugh and his daughters devotedly nursed her. Recovered, she faced another blow: the Reverend Besant refused to let her see the children. She appealed to the court and was granted permission to see them alone once a month, and to have them stay with her, supervised by a clergyman guardian, for two weeks in the year. On a first visit to the seaside the guardian forbade her to bathe with Mabel; this interdict, with its nasty sexual innuendo, so revolted Annie that she decided to forgo seeing the children again until they were old enough to understand and judge the situation for themselves.

The self-control she exercised in this area of her emotions was almost paralleled in her relations with men. She and Charles Bradlaugh felt deep affection for one another, but since neither of them were 'free'—Annie still being legally married, while Bradlaugh had an alcohol-addicted wife living in the country—they maintained an extremely decorous relationship into which their detractors from among the clergy and the yellow press tried in vain to inject a whiff of scandal. Bradlaugh was the first man to whom Annie Besant felt drawn after the collapse of her disastrous marriage. The second was Dr. E. B. Aveling, a radical science lecturer and co-contributor to the *National Reformer*, under whose tutelage (London university examinations being open to women since 1878) she obtained qualifications in Physiology, Biology and Botany. This enabled her to take classes in the afore-mentioned subjects at the N.S.S.'s Hall of Science, but the association with Aveling also had less beneficial results. Aveling, a chronic womanizer, entangled in debt, conducted a convoluted affair with Eleanor Marx which aroused Annie's jealousy, and she used the columns of the *National Reformer* to denigrate Karl Marx's ill-starred daughter.

With Aveling and Eleanor we come to some of the dramatis personae in the Annie Besant story who have ever since lived a shadow life of their own on the British (and world) stage, because George Bernard Shaw used them as part models for characters in two of his plays. Aspects of Aveling and Eleanor Marx suffuse the personalities of Dubedat and Jenny in *The Doctor's Dilemma*, while Annie Besant herself is glimpsed in Raina, of the thrilling voice, the disingenuous heroine of *Arms and the Man*. Annie and G.B.S. first got to know each other when she serialized two early novels by the newly-arrived Irish-born author in *Our Corner*, the monthly magazine she owned and edited in the 1880s. Though Annie was nearly ten years Shaw's senior, they were bound together by common ancestry (three of her grandparents had been born in Ireland), love of music, and shared political convictions.

In the course of the 1880s, British politics became more heated than they had been at any time since Chartism had petered out as a force at the end of the hungry '40s. The decade's alarums and excursions began with Bradlaugh's election to Parliament, which then promptly excluded him for refusing, as an atheist, to take the oath on the Bible. Re-elected at two bitterly fought by-elections, he was finally, amid fears of riots, allowed to take his seat by simply 'affirm-ing'. By this time Annie Besant had already parted company with him because he clung to the individualistic creed of the radical Liberals, while she was gravitating towards Socialism, a newly emergent force in British public life. The Socialists, divided into quarrelling factions almost from the start, none-theless grew in strength throughout the '80s, a period of trade recession leading to mass lay-offs and hunger, particularly in the East End of London. Unemployment riots erupted periodically in the middle of the decade, and climaxed with a running battle between demonstrators and police in Trafalgar Square on what became known as 'Bloody Sunday'.

For Annie, that sanguinary event was an important turning-point. For all that a steadily increasing income from journalism had secured her a middle-class life-style exemplified by a comfortable house in St. John's Wood, she had reached a crisis in her life. In addition to the break-up of her family and long exposure to public vilification, she had been parted from her erstwhile comrade-in-arms, Bradlaugh, and disappointed by Dr. Aveling. Now Bernard Shaw was turning out to be no more than a flirtatious games-player, a platonic philanderer who took their friendship far less seriously than she did herself. Cumulatively the deep depression, which was brought on by this chain of disappointments and compounded by lack of a cause to energize her, had made Annie feel almost suicidal. 'Bloody Sunday' virtually proved the saving of her. It was not so much what she did on the day, when she tried to get a wagonette driver to place his vehicle athwart the route of the police advance into Trafalgar Square, as her subsequent activities. She acted as a sort of Florence Nightingale to the ultimate victims of 'Bloody Sunday': the 130 demonstrators that needed hospital treatment and, more especially, the 100 taken into police custody. Working round the clock, she raised funds for their defence and, pleading their case before the magistrate at the police court, got them released on bail. Her efforts did not end there. She helped organize subsequent meetings to uphold the freedom of assembly and founded, together with W. T. Stead, crusading editor of the *Pall Mall Gazette*, a weekly paper, the *Link*, to expose instances of police brutality and social injustice.

It was in the columns of the *Link* that Annie first highlighted the plight of the Bryant and May's match girls, with whose cause her name will remain forever linked. Under the headline 'White slavery in London', she described the girls as working at the unhealthy East End plant for 7s. a week (on average), while the firm's £5 shares were quoted at £18 on the Stock Exchange. Alluding to the fact that many Bryant and May's shareholders were clergymen, Annie's article continued:

Do you know that girls are used to carry boxes on their heads until the hair is rubbed off and the young heads are bald at 15 years of age? Country clergymen with shares in Bryant and May, draw down on your knee your fifteen year old daughter; pass your hand tenderly over the silky clustering curls, rejoice in the dainty beauty of the thick shiny stresses. . . .

The excerpt exemplified both Annie's full-blown polemical style and her sometimes shaky grasp of facts: girls in Africa and Asia have carried burdens on their heads since time immemorial without going bald. (Of course, in writing the above she may have been carried away by hurtful thoughts of the teenaged Mabel being brought up by the Reverend Frank Besant.) Be that as it may, in publishing 'White slavery in London' Annie had indited a new page in British social history. When Bryant and May tried to coerce the matchgirls into signing statements refuting the *Link* article, the latter, lacking any previous acquaintance with trade unionism, spontaneously came out on strike. They had no organization, no strike fund or cash reserves—nothing except a burning grievance. *Faut de mieux* Annie had to act as their strike organizer, negotiator, fund-raiser and publicity agent—and though good at all of these tasks, she excelled at the last. Within a fortnight of the outbreak of the strike, the shareholders, men of the cloth among them in particular, had had enough of the exposure of the tainted source of part of their income; Byrant and May, in turn, were ready to concede improved wages and conditions as well as to grant recognition to the newly formed Women's Matchmakers' Union, of which Annie remained secretary for several years.

The victory of the matchgirls was to be her last but one achievement—and, since the New Unionism helped along the birth of the Labour Party, probably her greatest in British public life. Her last was election, as a Social Democrat, to the London School Board, a post she held till 1891; by the time she resigned from the Board she had helped lay the foundations of the subsequent school meals and school health services for the Metropolis.

That resignation was only part of a larger transformation in Annie's life. Just as ten years earlier, she had been ready to sever her links with secularism, so now she prepared to

187

abjure trade union and Socialist activity, in fact politics as such. More, she stood ready to give up England and the West as a whole. What triggered Annie's decision to make a total break with her past was the fact that she had reached a mid-life crisis. Although the children had joined her of their own volition (as she had predicted) on attaining the age of majority, she did not feel fulfilled by motherhood. As a woman, she had lost the allure of her formerly fine features and near-fashionable appearance. She was now a stout, slightly stooped, figure with coarsened features and grey short-cropped hair, who dressed in heavy boots, short skirts and other items of unfashionable apparel.

Her way out of this manifold impasse—with the lack of fulfilment as a woman and mother compounded by alienation from all the causes she had once championed—lay, yet again, in religion, but the faith that transformed Annie's life in mature middle age could not have been more different from the one that had suffused her youthful psyche. It was esoteric and transcendental, a distillation of psychic phenomena, the transmigration of souls and Eastern philosophy. Her first acquaintance with it had stemmed from a chance reading, in the mid-'80s, of *The Occult World and Esoteric Buddhism* by A. P. Suinett, a theosophist and disciple of Madame Blavatsky.[2] When Blavatsky's own massive *Secret Doctrine* appeared in 1889, W. T. Stead asked Annie to review it—no one on the staff of the *Pall Mall Gazette* was prepared to—and the reviewing chore changed the direction of her life. She sat conscientiously at home ingesting Blatavsky's tome for days on end and, while doing so, experienced a revelation: the causation of phenomena and their interrelationship, the connection between matter and minds, the meaning of existence—all was revealed to her.

Later that year she went straight from the Labour Congress at Paris that set up the Second (Socialist) International to join Madame Blavatsky at Fontainebleau. Here, as she wrote later, she had her first psychic experience:

Sleeping in a small bedroom by myself one night, I waked

2. Helena Blavatsky (1831–91): Russian spiritualist, author and co-founder of the Theosophical Society.

suddenly and sat up in bed startled, to find the air of the room thrown into pulsating electrical waves, and there appeared the radiant astral Figure of the Master, visible to my physical eyes.

The vision recalled Saul's on the Road to Damascus. Annie's road finally took her to India in 1893. Between that date and her death in 1933, she concerned herself mainly with spreading the Theosophical gospel and preparing the advent of the World Teacher (whom she declared incarnate in the body of Jeddu Krishnamurti, a lad first glimpsed by her on an Indian beach).

Just as in England she had laboured mightily for a whole range of causes—Secularism, Birth Control, Women's Rights, Trade Unionism, Social Services, etc.—so in India theosophy alone could not absorb her abundant energies. She founded colleges and launched newspapers, all the while campaigning against child marriage, caste restrictions and sex discrimination. She also took a key part in the initial stages of what became the Indian Independence movement. During the Great War she, a white woman, even achieved election as President of the Indian National Congress, but after the Amritsar massacre her counsels of moderation were no longer listened to. As her star fell, Gandhi's rose—only to be eclipsed in turn by Nehru's twenty-five years later. Such is ever the way of an ever-changing world. Even so, one can confidently assert that Annie left her two homelands—her native Britain, and India, her country of adoption—better places than she had found them.

Nancy Cunard

'All happy families', wrote Tolstoy in *Anna Karenina*, 'resemble each other, each unhappy family is unhappy in its own way.' Anyone doubting the latter part of his postulate need only look at the Cunard shipping dynasty. That family's special form of unhappiness lay in the incompatibility of marriage partners along the generation chain. Matrimonial misery was passed on, under some law of the inheritance of acquired characteristics, from grandmother to mother and from mother to daughter, and would undoubtedly have affected granddaughters as well had Nancy Cunard not remained childless.

The clearest evidence that marital unhappiness dogged generation after generation of Cunards emerged outside of Nancy's
life story—from the fact that neither her grandfather nor her
father were the husbands of their respective wives.

The grandmother's lapse does not concern us here; the
mother's infidelity, though, does, since it helped shape
the environment in which Nancy grew up. Maud Cunard,
a spirited beauty who had married her wealthy estate-owner
husband on the rebound, subsequently found him philistine
and a clod-hopping bore. Her estrangement took various
cumulative forms: cuckoldry, living apart—she in Mayfair,
he in his manor house—and, ultimately, half a lifetime's
ill-requited devotion to the conductor Sir Thomas Beecham.
Nancy, a moodily pubescent 14-year-old when Maud started
her amour with Beecham, a married man, inferred from it
that she, too, could flout convention. When she saw her
mother conduct the affair with the discretion becoming a
member of the Edwardian *beau monde,* she charged her in the
callow tones of adolescence with hypocrisy. In consequence
of these and other contretemps, relations between mother
and daughter deteriorated to the point where Nancy, playing
the parlour game 'Who would you best like to see come into
the room?' in elevated company, said, 'Lady Cunard, dead!'
At the time of this incident which—with Lady Cunard being
a friend of the Prime Minister—actually occurred at Windsor
Castle, Nancy was 18 and had recently returned from finishing-school in France. Soon after her 'coming out', the First
World War started and she became a much photographed
participant at fund-raising events for soldiers' welfare. Unlike
some of her contemporaries, however, she did not take up
nursing but led a rather bohemian life, jointly renting a studio
with a student at the Slade, frequenting the Café Royal and
writing poetry.

In 1916, aged 20, she married an officer who had been
wounded at Gallipoli. It was a step, motivated mainly by the
desire to get away from her mother, which she soon came
to regret. The marriage lasted a mere twenty months, and
afterwards Nancy said it had made her so unhappy that she
stopped writing poetry.

By the end of the war, her marriage was factually (if

not legally) dissolved, and she was free to throw herself into the whirl of Café society with renewed abandon. She also resumed her poetic efforts, though she made less of a contribution to English literature by writing—*Parallax*, her *chef d'oeuvre* was derivative of Eliot's *The Waste Land*—than by simply being herself. An arresting-looking woman of independent means with a liberated attitude to sex and a consuming interest in the avant garde, she mingled with up-and-coming writers of the post-war period on both sides of the Channel. Some of them used her simply for copy—her hysterectomy, undergone in Paris in 1920, featured in Michael Arlen's *The Green Hat*—while others fell dramatically in love with Nancy and wrote about her as a form of exorcism. One of the latter was the newly prominent (and newly wed) novelist Aldous Huxley, who, in his lovelorn state, once spent an entire night pacing up and down outside her window. At the climax of Huxley's infatuation, his wife threatened to leave England the following morning, with or without him! She spent all night packing, and next morning both left together for Italy, where he wrote the novel *Antic Hay* at breakneck speed, thereby laying the ghost of the affair. Later in the 1920s the French writer Louis Aragon fell even more unrestrainedly in love with Nancy. When she failed to respond, he took an overdose in his hotel room at Venice, but was fortunately discovered in time. He, too, incorporated the quondam object of his affections into his next work, but just briefly; Huxley, by contrast, still deployed Nancy Cunard-inspired characters (i.e. beautiful, erratic and self-centred young upper-class women who play havoc with the emotions of their struggling unrequited lovers) in his later novels, *Those Barren Leaves* and *Point Counter Point*.

In Venice at around the same time that Aragon nearly succumbed to an overdose, Nancy encountered someone whom writer Richard Aldington dubbed 'a stronger sexual drug' for her. This was Henry Crowder, a black American pianist playing with a jazz quartet called 'Eddie South and the Alabamians'. Born to poor Southern Baptist parents, Crowder had made his way North, taken diverse jobs—among them postman, piano-player in a brothel, and war-time driver to an army general—and got married and fathered a son. The marriage collapsed, and the jazz boom of the '20s swept him first to Greenwich Village and thence to Europe, where he was based in France, with occasional forays into Italy. By the time Nancy met Crowder, she had focused her previously free-floating energy into the establishment of the Paris-based Hours Press, which published works by Ezra Pound, Richard Aldington[3] and Robert Graves in limited editions. Publishing had stimulated her interest in graphics and the visual arts. The '20s were a period when African art was coming into vogue, at least among the avant-garde, and Nancy, always in the van of fashion, had started a collection of amazing African jewellery and was in the habit of encasing her arms from the wrists practically up to the armpits in tribal bracelets and bangles. Having met Crowder, she invited him to her apartment, ostensibly to display African jewellery to his astonished gaze. That was simply a pretext for sexual entrapment—a pursuit in which she held the initiative all along. Crowder, although initially reluctant to cross the racial divide, went along with her out of calculation that this wealthy well-connected white woman could further his career. The latter hope was partly fulfilled when the Hours Press published some of Crowder's piano pieces. By then he had parted company with the Alabamians and was back in France with Nancy as her somewhat menial assistant in the publishing enterprise. He found his situation less than satisfactory in other respects, too, since Nancy, congenitally promiscuous, used him *inter alia* to engage in affairs with blacks of his acquaintance. In addition, her circle contained several homosexuals whose importunities he did not always feel it politic to resist.

Apart from involuntary pander and sex object, Crowder also had to act as Nancy's minder when she was drunk or otherwise incapacitated—a service she occasionally requited by striking him across the face with a bracelet-jangling forearm. Nancy's frequent irritability with Crowder had several reasons, one of them being his insufficiently 'liberated' attitude to sexual promiscuity and deviance. Another of Crowder's defects in

3. Richard Aldington (1892–1962): English biographer and novelist, exponent of post-war disillusionment (*Death of a Hero*).

her eyes was his lack of negritude. Thanks to a Red Indian admixture in his ancestry, he had a somewhat coppery skin that Nancy found fault with. She wanted him to have a darker pigmentation, or at least to compensate for his somewhat defective genetic make-up by behaving in a more primitive and exotic manner. Accordingly she took to admonishing him to be more African—to which he would reply, 'But I ain't African, I'm American.' In line with her increasing preoccupation with Africa, Nancy mooted a plan for them to visit the Dark Continent, but Crowder, foreseeing trouble for himself if he, a black man, turned up in a British African colony with a white woman who was given to making scenes, in a rare show of independence refused to go along with her. He was not all that wide off the mark in his estimate of the prevalence of colour prejudice among the British. Back in London, where, despite Nancy's prolonged sojourn in France, 'society' followed her unconventional progress through life with avid interest, Margot Asquith greeted Lady Cunard at a lunch party with the question, 'Hallo, Maud, what is it now—drink, drugs or niggers?' Understandably discomfited, Lady Cunard tried to forestall the worst eventuality—the arrival of the miscegenated couple in Britain—by getting a Home Office acquaintance to arrange for their deportation the instant they set on British soil. At the same time she had Sir Thomas Beecham send Nancy a letter instructing her not to come. Nancy reacted to the letter by immediately booking tickets for herself and Crowder on the next London-bound train. In the event, there were no deportation proceedings and the trip passed off uneventfully.

Nancy's feud with Lady Cunard reached a new pitch of acrimony when the latter, under the impact of the 1929 Stock Exchange crash, either drastically reduced or cut off—the available evidence in this matter is not very clear—her allowance. Soon after, Nancy privately printed *Black Man and White Ladyship*, a pamphlet that comprised a withering attack on her mother for prejudice and snobbery, as well as an account of black suffering down the ages, with special reference to the ongoing 'Scottsboro Boys' Case'. (This was a long drawn-out *cause célèbre* involving nine young Alabama blacks who, having been arrested and tried on dubious rape charges, languished in death row while the National Association for the Advancement of Coloured People, as well as the Communist Party, raised money and aroused public opinion in their defence.)

The Scottsboro case politicized Nancy. Perceiving the oppression of the blacks as part of a wider socio-economic framework, she began to gravitate towards the Communists—who were, coincidentally, proving more effective champions of the nine jailed men than the somewhat staid N.A.A.C.P. At around the same time she conceived the plan to publish a massive anthology entitled *Negro*, which would constitute an encyclopaedia both of the blacks' contribution to world culture and of their painful history. While she in consequence engaged in massive literary labours, another fictional portrait of her appeared, penned by Richard Aldington, a sometime friend and contributor of the Hours Press who had turned bitter critic. His short story, 'Now Lies She There', centred on a thinly disguised Nancy who was described in these words:

> Not a female Don Juan—one would applaud that legitimate *revanche* of her sex—but a kind of erotic boa constrictor. She swallowed men whole. You could almost see their feet sticking out of her mouth.

It was a harsh portrayal, cruelly drawn, but one which Crowder would not, in view of the current state of relations between himself and the perennially promiscuous Nancy, have substantially disagreed with. They were now living in London, in separate lodgings. Nancy was cohabiting with the Communist writer Edgell Rickword, while Crowder, whose rent she paid, lived elsewhere with a black girl-friend. The cash nexus, as well as the by then somewhat threadbare hope that Nancy would further his career, still kept Crowder tied to her, much as he deplored the change from her chic Parisian friends to the rather déclassé Communists and West Indians she gathered round herself in London.

During the three years Nancy expended on preparing the anthology *Negro*, she undertook extensive travels for research purposes, mainly to the West Indies and the United States. In Jamaica she met Marcus Garvey (the all-but-forgotten doyen of the black national revival) in an obscure setting, but her trip through the States proceeded in the glare of newspaper publicity. 'Disinherited by her mother for her unconventional conduct, the Heiress of the famous British Steamship Fortune Takes Up Residence in the Harlem Black Belt' read one headline; another mocked 'Lady Cunard's Search for Color in New York's Negro Quarter'.

Certain sections of the British press were not to be outdone in Nancy- and subliminal Negro-baiting. The *Manchester Empire News*, after quoting Sir Thomas Beecham to the effect that Nancy ought to be tarred-and-feathered under the sub-heading 'A Strong Beecham Pill', listed her hobbies as running the gamut from Interior Decorating to Communism and ended with the admonition that her efforts on behalf of the Scottsboro Boys constituted an unwarranted interference in the due judicial process of another country. 'How would we like it if Paul Robeson came over to sort out an unresolved murder in England?' In retaliation Nancy instituted libel proceedings against the *Empire News* and other papers involved in the smear campaign against her. She received £1,500 in compensation—a substantial sum in those days which she ploughed into the ever-escalating production costs of *Negro*.

Negro eventually appeared in 1934. It was a huge book of 855 pages of 12" × 10½" format that weighed nearly 8 lbs. It opened with a full-page portrait of a black worker captioned 'An American Beast of Burden'. On the facing page was a poem by Langston Hughes,[4] 'I, too':

> I too sing America
> I am the darker brother
> They send me to eat in the kitchen
> When company comes
> But I laugh
> And eat well
> And grow strong. . . .

There followed a vast and disparate array of material, including photographs, poetry and musical scores. Its very disparity made it difficult to review, which had a deleterious effect on sales. Politically it also fell between two stools: although it cleaved to the Communist party line, attacking the N.A.A.C.P. leader W. du Bois as reactionary, etc. other

---

4. Langston Hughes (1902–67): black American poet, writer, journalist and translator (*The Ways of White Folks*).

points of view were also represented, which meant that it pleased neither side. After the publication of, and disappointing response to *Negro*, Nancy had another dispiriting experience. In 1934–35 Communists switched globally from the class struggle and anti-imperialism to cementing a limited front against Nazi Germany and Fascist Italy. This involved the French Communists, for instance, in soft-pedalling the colonial question to smooth the path for the conclusion of a Franco-Soviet pact. A number of black activists, who had previously toed the Communist Party line, refused to comply with this new policy directive, which struck them as a subordination of the interests of their own people to the vagaries of European power politics. This split the ranks of the black radicals, previously Nancy's closest comrades-in-arms, and saddened and confused her.

1935 was not only the year when Communists and Black Nationalists parted company; Nancy's relationship with Crowder, which had in different ways precipitated drastic changes in both their lives, also came to a complete end.

1936 brought the Spanish Civil War and the English Abdication Crisis—the former event crucially involving Nancy and the latter her mother. Nancy, who visited Barcelona and Madrid soon after the fighting erupted, subsequently tried to mobilize public, particularly intellectual, opinion in France and Britain for the Republican cause through the output of her printing press. For Lady Cunard, indefatigable society hostess, the death of George V had brought an increment in influence via the elevation of her friends, the Prince of Wales and Mrs. Simpson, to the very pinnacle of British society. She used this influence to express views diametrically opposed to those of Nancy by, for instance, defending Italy's occupation of Abyssinia to her dinner guest Anthony Eden.

After the outbreak of hostilities in 1939, Nancy was able to use her expertise in French in the service of the Allied war effort. She worked as a translator for the Free French in London and subsequently at Supreme Allied headquarters in Europe. In between she turned out poems—one, entitled 'France' and dedicated to Louis Aragon, appeared in the *New Statesman and Nation*—and articles in favour of the Soviet Union and of post-war decolonization. In the last year of the war, she took a prominent part in agitating against the release of her mother's friends, the Mosleys, from prison. At around the same time she heard that her house-cum-studio in Normandy had been looted by local people—news which was particularly upsetting to her as a lifelong Francophile. Armed with commissions from several British magazines she, nonetheless, returned to France early in 1945. Her reports home, consistently over-stressing the resistance of the French against German occupation, were all of a piece with her other political pronouncements. Just as a month's stay in Moscow in 1935 had not given her much of an insight into the nature of Stalinism, so her own experience at the hands of the Norman villagers—and, more crucially, the evidence of the extent of French collaboration with the Nazi occupiers—could not dent her deep-seated Francophilia.

In consequence of her abiding sentimental attachment to France she, more or less, picked up her expatriate life where she had left off before the war, interspersing it with frequent trips back to England. In the early '50s she wrote reminiscences of two literary lions of her acquaintance, Norman Douglas and George Moore. Despite a favourable critical response, especially to the latter work, she felt increasingly dispirited and frustrated as the decade wore on. An entry in her diary for 1956 read:

> If you don't get what you want, nothing else counts. Sure it could count if you are male and could go into a career—but I am not a male and I have no career.

By the decade's end her sense of frustration had modulated to a pervasive consciousness of failure, which she abreacted in violent drinking bouts. Back in London she roamed the streets, insulting policemen and making sexual propositions to perfect strangers. Arrested and brought before a magistrate, she threw her shoe at him. Sent to Holloway for a medical report, she was diagnosed as insane. Institutionalized in Holloway sanitorium, she became the object of a political 'rescue' campaign abroad, particularly in France. Louis Aragon, her quondam suicidal lover turned chief literary adornment of the French Communist party, suggested in *Les Lettres Françaises* that the British Establishment had fabricated evidence of

Nancy's medical breakdown in order to silence her, possibly for good. Aragon's supposition was based on the double false premise that H.M. Government considered Nancy so effective an opponent as to warrant her incarceration on trumped-up evidence and that Britain operated psycho-prisons on the Soviet model. At any rate, Nancy gradually recovered, was released from Holloway, had a prolonged convalescence staying with friends in the English countryside, and returned to France.

She lingered on for a few more years, going inexorably downhill till she had dwindled to a chain-smoking, alcohol-sodden anorexic. In 1965 she died, aged 69, in the public ward of a hospital on the outskirts of Paris.

Maya Angelou

Marguerite Johnson worked as fry-cook, waitress, brothel-keeper, prostitute, and sales girl at a record shop—Maya Angelou as dancer, night-club singer, actress, black activist, journalist, writer and lecturer. Marguerite and Maya are in fact one and the same, a woman who has led a roller-coaster life in which she has changed rôles with such bewildering frequency as to leave the reader dizzy. That life began (to the best of Maya's recollection) in the Deep South of Depression America. Stamps was a dusty, out-of-the-way townlet in Arkansas with one paved road, a looming Ku-Klux-Klan presence and strictly segregated schools; some of the pupils at the black school were so poor that they went bald from malnutrition.

Maya and her adored older brother Bailey fared better than most of their classmates since the grandmother who brought them up owned a General Merchandise store. One day the parents turned up at Stamps, out of the blue, and took 7-year-old Maya and Bailey to live with them at St. Louis. A first glimpse of their mother filled the siblings with amazement: she not only looked beautiful but could almost have passed for white. At St. Louis another surprise awaited them: the mother's mother was friendly with certain white folks, mainly, it seemed policemen.

Soon after, the father faded from the scene, but the mother's business acumen kept the family comfortably off and her good looks attracted a succession of men. The first of these, Mr. Freeman, also lusted after Maya, who was 7-and-a-half at the time (though as a future six-footer she looked older). After a bungled first rape attempt, Mr. Freeman ensured her silence by threatening to kill Bailey. At the second attempt he succeeded. Maya, in shock and bleeding, kept a terrified silence, which lead the family to believe that she had an infectious disease, but she blurted the truth out to Bailey eventually. In consequence Mr. Freeman was arrested, tried and sent to jail. Though he came out soon enough, he did not survive the day of his release—having been, according to one of grandma's policemen friends, kicked to death on waste ground behind the town's slaughter-house. (The supposition was that the mother's gun-happy brothers had exacted vengeance.) Little Maya herself, convinced that in pronouncing Mr. Freeman's name she had killed him, by magic as it were, now abhorred her own voice as a 'killer'. So as not to kill anyone else she stopped speaking altogether for four years, during which she wrote whatever needed saying with chalk on a slate. By the time of her transfer to High School an acquaintance, who was a poetry enthusiast, coaxed Maya into speaking verse, thereby unlocking her tongue again. Thereafter life proceeded normally for a while. However, at 15, with school over, it occurred to Maya to meet the challenge of sex head on by propositioning the handsomest lad in their Californian neighbourhood. He obliged quite readily, and nature took its inevitable course. Maya announced news of her pregnancy on the morrow of VE (Victory in Europe) Day. Questioned by her mother she said she intended to bring up the baby by herself. Soon after the birth of a son, named Clyde, she left home with him to make her own way in the world. She was all of 16 years old at the time.

She obtained a job as a cook at a restaurant, where experience gained assisting her grandmother in the preparation of soul food stood her in good stead, and paid a minder out of her wages. Meeting a single man, she fell passionately in love with him. He responded to a degree, but made it clear that he intended to marry a woman currently living in another Californian town. Maya pushed the thought of the end of their affair out of her mind and lived for the day, till the inevitable dénouement. During her painful emotional convalescence she found diversion by joining in the jokey chatter of two young women customers at the restaurant. She discovered that they were lesbians living from hand to mouth on the proceeds of occasional prostitution. Though barely out of her middle teens, she was street-wise enough to devise a mutually acceptable scheme for transforming their amateurish operation into a steady venture run on sound business lines. This involved getting taxi-drivers to tout for potential customers among their fares and employing a bouncer who ensured the smooth handover of monies—including her own substantial cut. For a while business went swimmingly, enabling Maya to purchase a car, but all too soon a storm blew up that imperilled the partnership. Mindful of her own mother's ceaseless injunctions, Maya had admonished the girls never to cross the colour line. One day, checking up on business, she discovered them entertaining white customers. When she berated them for flouting her rules, they retaliated by accusing her of exploitation. A screaming contest ensued that spelt the end of Maya's career as a brothel-keeper. It was also, temporarily, the end of her stay in California. Panicky over the possible repercussions of her involvement in mixed-race prostitution, she packed Clyde and a few belongings into her newly acquired motor car and drove helter-skelter back to Stamps, Arkansas. There, in the sheltering presence of grandmother, she recovered from her fright—only to give the old lady a worse one in turn.

During her Californian sojourn, consciousness of black inferiority, which had been inculcated in Maya during childhood, became attenuated; consequently when a white store-proprietress treated her with Southern condescension ('What d'you want, Gal?'), she gave the flabbergasted woman a savage tongue-lashing before slamming the shop-door. News of the incident preceded her to her own home. The grandmother stood waiting in the doorway and asked her to leave Stamps at once—before the outrage caused by her uppity remarks brought a lynch mob to the house. Back in California again with her little son, Maya had a lucky break. She met a professional dancer keen for her to partner him in a dance routine he was in the process of choreographing.

The work-outs and rehearsals gave her a tremendous sense of release from the burden of past failures that she carried in her psychological baggage. Out of sheer gratitude for this liberation she fell in love with the dancer, but, disappointingly, his sexual needs appeared minimal. Eventually he told her that his former partner, who had been *hors de combat* on account of drug addiction, had returned to him and he intended to share both the dance floor and his bed with her again. There was nothing for it: Maya had to hang up her dancing shoes and go back to working as a cook in a restaurant. There, amid the steam and spicy odours, she dreamt of the real lover that would one day somehow emerge from somewhere. And as luck, or ill-luck, would have it, he emerged soon enough. He was mature (about Maya's father's age), well turned-out and suave. Above all, he showed great kindness, buying her and Clyde presents and taking them on car rides. He introduced Maya to his friends, a surprisingly large number of whom were madams. One day he confided to her that he had lost a large sum of money gambling and desperately needed her financial help. The best way in which she could render such help was to become a hooker in the establishment run by one of his friends. She readily obliged, and it took her some time to realize that he had been manipulating her with the aim of living off her immoral earnings in mind from their very first encounter.

The kindness of the next man in her life, by contrast, was genuine and not faked. He showed real concern for Maya and helped her find a job. Alas, he turned out to be a main-lining heroin addict, the sight of whose sore-encrusted body made her feel nauseous at the very thought of sex. What is more, he had entered the terminal stage of his addiction. By now she had nowhere to go but up. Working in a music show owned by a sympathetic white woman, a Christian Scientist, she began to shed some of her defensive racial reflexes. She got to know a white customer whose enthusiasm for black jazz musicians created a bond between them. He was Tosh, a Greek American about to finish his term in the U.S. navy. A romance developed, helped by the fact that Tosh hit it off with Clyde. Their wedding took place in the teeth of fierce opposition from her mother, who abhorred mixed marriages and looked upon working-class Tosh as white trash. Initially the marriage worked well, but tensions developed when Tosh revealed himself as a bigoted atheist, disabusing little Clyde of his belief in God and forcing Maya to resort to subterfuge when attending church. Gradually it dawned on her that Tosh was incapable of thinking himself inside the Negro mind. He, for his part, also felt disillusioned with the marriage. It consequently broke up with few regrets on either side, though Clyde mourned its passing.

A housewife no more, Maya graduated from dancing at one San Francisco night-club to singing at another, 'The Purple Onion'. Soon a real career in show-biz beckoned. When Eartha Kitt left the cast of *New Faces of 1953*, Maya auditioned successfully to replace her, but contractual obligations tied her to 'The Purple Onion'. She experienced the same frustration over the American run of *Porgy and Bess*, but when the original cast took the show on a European tour, she was in a position to join them as a featured dancer (while leaving Clyde behind to be looked after by her mother).

The European trip exposed her to varieties of colour consciousness. France seemed particularly free of it, and she briefly toyed with the idea of following in Josephine Baker's footsteps and settling there. Outside the strictly show-biz dimension of the tour, her greatest experience was the encounter with Africa. This took place in Egypt, a country which, though not black in the strict sense of the term, had many inhabitants with skins as dark as Maya's own. Her delight in this first 'homecoming' was far from unalloyed, however; the poverty disturbed her, as did the impression that in post-colonial Egypt skin pigmentation still determined social rank.

On returning to the States Maya's spirit plummeted. She found Clyde afflicted with an illness she blamed on her own neglect of him; in addition, she heard that her brother Bailey, by then a drug-addict, was in Sing-Sing. The shock of the news triggered a brainstorm in which she contemplated murdering both Clyde and herself. She was helped to pull back from the brink, however, and presently resumed her show-business career in Hawai (to which exotic location she took Clyde along).

There followed a twofold change in Maya's life. The first

was geographical: her place of domicile changed from the West to the East coast; the second professional: she moved from the entertainment sector of the performing arts towards a form of theatre that engaged with real issues. In New York she joined the Harlem Writers' Group and met representatives of the emergent black intelligentsia like Lorraine Hansbury and James Baldwin. She had a hand in briefly converting Harlem's Apollo Theatre from its customary rôle of providing diversion for black audiences to raising their consciousness. She cajoled black show-biz stars to participate in a 'Cabaret for Freedom' that helped fund the Civil Rights Movement. She met Dr. Martin Luther King, whose New York-based supporters approached her with the request that she replace Bayard Rustin as Northern co-ordinator of the Southern Christian Leadership Conference, an influential black rights organization. In accepting the post she finally left show business behind and became fully engaged in political activism. Such activism accorded ill with the feminine submissiveness which the latest man in Maya's life demanded of her. This was Thomas, a macho bail bondsman, through marriage to whom she hoped to provide a steady centre for her own and Clyde's life. Though Thomas showed himself increasingly insensitive to her needs as a woman, she did not finally jettison the marriage plans until another man, who actually became her second husband, thrust himself upon her attention. Vusumbi Make was a South African political deportee, who, having survived exposure in the Kalahari Desert, had made his way to the U.N. at New York where he acted as accredited 'petitioner' for the Pan-African Congress. Although several inches shorter than Maya, the portly Make, a member of the Xhosa tribe and a barrister by training, swept her off her feet. Their marriage coincided with a climacteric of the Black Liberation struggle: Wind of Change and Lumumba's[5] death in Africa, Malcolm X preaching black separatism in the United States. Make took her to London for a Third World Conference, whence he went on to Cairo for talks with President Nasser, a patron

---

5. Patrice Lumumba (1925–61): black African nationalist who became first Prime Minister of independent Zaire, was deposed and murdered.

of the Black Freedom Movement. Back in New York the first tensions within the marriage surfaced when Make told Maya, who had auditioned successfully for a part in Genet's *The Blacks*, that treading the boards was beneath the dignity of an African diplomat's wife—although, having read the play, he rescinded his veto. Also, while generally on good terms with Clyde, he raised the teenaged lad's hackles by portentous utterances like 'African youths never question an adult's statement'. Ethnic tradition was again invoked when Maya, having discovered tell-tale evidence of Make's womanizing, upbraided him for it—to which he made the curt rejoinder that an African husband expected submissiveness from his wife. For all that, the marriage held together—and was probably strengthened by anonymous callers who phoned to tell Maya that Make had met with a fatal accident and then rang off. These callers, she learnt, were South African Intelligence agents.

In due course the roller-coaster effect so characteristic of Maya's past life came into play again. One day the bailiffs turned up outside the matrimonial apartment to evict them for non-payment of rent. They moved to a dingy hotel where Make presently left Maya and Clyde behind in order to undertake another trip to Cairo. This time, he explained, he was simply acting as advance party that was going ahead to prepare accommodation for the three of them in what would soon be their permanent domicile.

Some time later the air tickets to Cairo arrived, enabling Maya to introduce the excited Clyde to his ancestral continent. The accommodation that awaited them appeared outlandishly luxurious. At first Maya felt trapped in the bijou refinement of their apartment and in the round of diplomatic cocktail parties where banalities were exchanged. Help was at hand, though, in the shape of a black American journalist, with whom she shared spasmodic pangs of homesickness for the United States and who helped her land a job at a newly established Middle Eastern news agency. As happened previously with her acting rôle, the acquisition of the journalistic job aroused Make's patriarchal ire: 'Are you a man', he demanded to know, 'that you make such a decision on your own?' Then he requested Maya to tell her would-be employer that she was not an American any more, but an African wife who had to obey her husband. Maya stood her ground, however, and reported for work at the agency, where she was introduced to the all-male staff as an African wife working only to help her husband out of financial difficulties. She settled into the job with what seemed to her to be astonishing ease and became a competent editor.

In contrast to the work situation, the domestic one left much to be desired. Not only was Make philandering again, but he and his inamorata showed so little circumspection that Maya and others too became fully cognisant of the *affaire*. When she remonstrated with Make, he told her *tout court* that as an African he was entitled to have more than one wife. Her objection that they had got married in the United States drew the retort that they were living in Africa now—which was, moreover, her ancestral homeland, too. For Maya it was the parting of the ways. However, when she announced her intention to leave Make, it was pointed out to her that the potential publicity arising out of the divorce of a black American activist from a prominent South African freedom-fighter might harm the cause of Black Liberation. The representatives of some of the newly independent African states which had been accredited to Cairo convened an informal colloquy designed to save the marriage. At the colloquy Make and Maya stated their respective cases, and a consensus emerged that she did have ample justification for a divorce.

Maya's next move, facilitated by contacts she had established at Cairo, took her and Clyde to Accra, the Ghanian capital. Ghana, newly independent under President Nkrumah,[6] was in the early 1960s the cynosure of all African eyes. On arrival at Accra airport, seeing smartly uniformed pilots and stewards walk across the tarmac, Maya experienced a *frisson* of pride; she felt as if, after a long wait in the Egyptian ante-chamber to Africa, she had come to the very heart of the Black Continent. A new chapter opened in her and her son's life. Clyde enrolled at the University of Accra, and she became editor of the influential *African Review* after a while.

6. Kwame Nkrumah (1909–72): West African nationalist politician, founder and first Prime Minister of Ghana, who was eventually deposed and exiled.

For all that, it was no true homecoming for Maya. Her American roots went too deep for her to achieve the sort of integration into the ancestral homeland demonstrated by Diaspora Jews in Israel. She consequently returned to the United States in due course. There, in middle-age, she engaged in the multiple activities her many-faceted personality and rich store of experience fitted her for. She acted in *Roots*, TV's ambitious reconstruction of the black experience since the inception of slavery, and herself produced a series about African traditions in America. She wrote a five-part autobiography—the opening section of which, *I Know Why the Caged Bird Sings*, became a TV movie—and published several volumes of poetry. Her final homecoming took place when Maya Angelou, who had started off as Marguerite Johnson, a gal in Stamps, Arkansas, returned to the South to teach American Studies at the University of Carolina.

Index